Southern Literary Studies

THE RATIONALE OF DECEPTION IN POE

David Ketterer

THE RATIONALE OF DECEPTION IN POE

Louisiana State University Press
Baton Rouge and London

Copyright © 1979 by Louisiana State University Press
All rights reserved
Manufactured in the United States of America

The author gratefully acknowledges permission to reprint, in slightly different
form, material that appeared in the following: "Protective Irony and the 'Full
Design' of Eureka," American Transcendental Quarterly: Journal of New England
Writers, no. 26 (Spring, 1975), 46–55, © 1975 by Kenneth W. Cameron; "Devious
Voyage: The Singular Narrative of A. Gordon Pym," American Transcendental
Quarterly: A Journal of New England Writers, no. 37 (Winter, 1978), 21–35, ©
1978 by the University of Rhode Island; "Poe's Usage of the Hoax and the Unity of
'Hans Pfaall,'" Criticism, XIII (1971), 377–85, by permission of the Wayne State
University Press.

Designer: Patricia Douglas Crowder
Type face: VIP Melior
Typesetter: Imperial Litho/Graphics, Phoenix, Arizona
Printer: Thomson-Shore, Inc.
Binder: John Dekker & Sons, Inc.

LIBRARY OF CONGRESS CATALOGING IN PUBLICATION DATA

Ketterer, David.
  The rationale of deception in Poe.

  (Southern literary studies)
  Includes index.
  1. Poe, Edgar Allan, 1809–1849—Criticism and interpretation.   2.
Deception in literature.   I. Title.   II. Series.
PS2638.K45   818'.3'09   79–1155
ISBN 0–8071–0561–9

For my students at Concordia University, 1967–1978

Contents

Preface

    Of all American writers, Poe is without doubt the most universally admired. In no way limited to the English-speaking world, his popularity continues unabated in lands as diverse as Russia, Hungary, the Scandinavian countries, Germany, France, Italy, Spain, and Central and South America. The literary cosmopolitanism that Poe so vigorously espoused has been spectacularly achieved. But in the English-speaking world, the ironic price that Poe has paid for popular success has been, and to some extent still is, a lack of serious literary recognition. On the other hand, the respect that Poe has been denied in America and England he has received abundantly in France. This has often been accounted for and discounted with the argument that the French have a tradition of according certain American citizens—the most familiar examples being film people such as Alfred Hitchcock and Jerry Lewis—a perverse reverence. At the same time, it has been argued that Baudelaire effected an alchemical rather than a verbal translation of Poe's text, transmuting vulgar lead or brass into pure gold.

    More telling, perhaps, is the sense that the mesmeric Poe personality clouds a just appreciation of his writings; certainly Poe's biographers and critics have long been compelled toward characterizing the human phantom. Baudelaire was drawn by what he felt to be a spiritual affinity between himself and Poe. Indeed, given the variety and allure of Poe's posthumous roles as an embittered, friendless alcoholic, an impotent neurotic, a sado-necrophiliac, or a masochistic homosexual, it was inevitable that Poe the writer would shrink from view.

Only in the past twelve or so years has criticism given any real sense of breaking through the barriers erected by Poe's popular appeal—misconceptions about both the man and the nature of his work. This has occurred largely as a result of the considerable resurgence of American academic interest in the actual words that Poe committed to paper. In fact, with the founding of the *Poe Newsletter* in 1968 (subsequently called *Poe Studies*), what might be called a Poe renaissance got truly underway. An orphan no more, Poe has returned home.

The Poe now recognized is a much more complicated, duplicitous, and conscious artist than was previously supposed. He can no longer be understood, as he has been popularly understood for so long, as merely a writer of horror stories. Those Hammer films, which relied upon Poe's name as a virtual synonym for horror, never did bear much relation to the tales themselves; and with our growing awareness of Poe's intent, the disjunction is increasingly apparent. It now seems probable that he used the horror format largely for market considerations. There is evidence in many of his tales of a burlesque irony at the expense of the gothic machinery and evidence also of very different concerns disguised, like the image of the Red Death, in the accouterments of horror. It is those very different concerns that are the subject of this book. For the sake of redressing a balance, I have deliberately avoided making much reference to the horrific aspect of Poe's work. Certainly, there is a genuinely horrific element to be accounted for, but it belongs as a corollary to an overall philosophical context. The pseudohorror, on the other hand, is explainable in its cultural and historical context. Poe *is* a master of the macabre and he *is* a tricky ironist; but above all else, the writer I recognize is a visionary.

In focusing on the matter of deception as theme and technique I hope to clarify what I understand to be the most consistent and dominant aspect of Poe's work. Operating on the belief that in relation to a sensed visionary reality everyday reality constitutes one gross deception, Poe finds himself in a better position to attack the false reality than to reveal the true. He hopes to destroy a deceptive reality by means of various technical and thematic deceptions of his own. This is what I mean by Poe's "rationale of deception."

The current confusion in Poe interpretation derives from a number of influential, but discordant, studies in recent years by such critics as Edward Davidson, Daniel Hoffman, Joseph J. Moldenhauer, Burton R. Pollin, Patrick Quinn, G. R. Thompson, and Richard Wilbur. Although the visionary Poe is well represented among this jumble of alternatives, the view offered by John F. Lynen in *The Design of the Present: Essays on Time and Form in American Literature* (New Haven, Conn.: Yale University Press, 1969) comes closest to my own. Therefore, it may be well to distinguish what I am doing from Lynen's chapter on Poe (pp. 205–71). First of all, Lynen's approach is nondevelopmental. Essentially, he interprets Poe in the light of the late work *Eureka*. Consequently, for Lynen, Poe's visionary reality is historically determined—it has occurred in the past; it will only occur again in the future when once more time will "end." I believe Lynen's view that Poe was unable to conceive how the "present moment is recognized as an epitome of all time" is mistaken (p. 213). I see a development from an immediately attainable supernal reality to a unified reality in the future with some attempt to reconcile these alternatives. Furthermore (and this is a second essential difference between Lynen's reading and mine), the developmental approach reveals an evolution in Poe's thought—from a position where reason (viewed as productive of deception) is opposed to imagination, to a position where a species of reason allied with imagination is valued in an ambiguous concept of *intuition*. Third, I make some attempt, admittedly speculative, to relate the assumptions underlying Poe's philosophical stance to what we know of his biography. Finally, unlike Lynen and all previous critics of Poe, I make considerable interpretive use of the terms *grotesque* and *arabesque*.

Poe strives to put matters in the widest possible context and, as far as possible, to see wholes rather than parts. It is remarkable, therefore, that so many Poe studies have contented themselves with a partial perspective. Books have appeared devoted, more or less exclusively, to the tales, the poetry, or the criticism. Even the more general studies have picked carefully over the ground, avoiding material that does not bear an immediate application to a particular approach. Whatever may be said about the limitations of the approach presented in this study, it does take detailed account of Poe's entire output and is, at this date, the only critical analysis to do so.

The truth is, of course, that Poe is a difficult writer to take whole. His work is very uneven in quality; much of it is fragmentary and occasional. Within the same period of time he wrote many different kinds of material, making it difficult to abstract an overall pattern of development. The very symmetrical pattern indicated by my chapter arrangement would seem to belie an actual chaos, although the structure emerged naturally out of an attempt to marry thematic and formal organizations with chronological development. After all, the difference between order and chaos is often, as Poe would say, merely a "perspective anomaly."

In working on this book I have benefited from the reactions and suggestions of several people. I am particularly grateful to John Whitley of the University of Sussex and John E. Becker of Fairleigh Dickinson University, both of whom read the entire manuscript at different stages of its development and commented helpfully. The suggestions of Richard P. Benton and Kenneth W. Cameron, both of Trinity College, led me to improve my discussion of Eureka. At Concordia University, I am indebted to my colleague Eyvind Ronquist, who assisted in the final revision, and to my research assistants, Wim van Voorst van Beest and James Wilson, whose talents as proofreaders have left their mark throughout the book. Although my dedication records a generalized debt to my students, I should single out Eleanor Speak, Trudy Stevenson, and Jack Todd. Their insights influenced my own thinking.

Three segments of this study have appeared, with minor alterations, as articles: "Poe's Usage of the Hoax and the Unity of 'Hans Pfaall,' " *Criticism*, XIII (1971); "Protective Irony and the 'Full

Design' of Eureka," *American Transcendental Quarterly*, no. 26 (Spring, 1975); and "Devious Voyage: The Singular *Narrative of A. Gordon Pym*," *American Transcendental Quarterly*, no. 37 (Winter, 1978). I am grateful to the editors of these journals for permission to republish this material.

For the most practical form of assistance, I wish to thank the Canada Council for awarding me a 1973–1974 leave fellowship to work on Poe. In the fullness of time, the result was efficiently converted into its final typed form by Gene Fryer and Joyce Granich and expertly edited by Linda Schexnaydre.

THE RATIONALE OF DECEPTION IN POE

1

The Half-Closed Eye

Fundamental to an understanding of Poe are those tales in which he seeks to undermine man's confidence in his perception of "reality," on the grounds that this "reality" is limited by man's position in space and time and by the mechanisms of his inner self. Space, time, and self are the three factors, or coordinates, that obstruct and mislead man's comprehension, consequently leaving him in a state of deception. In the nine tales examined below, Poe is concerned particularly with these three coordinates. The earliest and most nearly allegorical of these tales, "The Devil in the Belfry," first published in the Philadelphia Saturday Chronicle and Mirror of the Times on May 18, 1839, provides a clear illustration of the ways in which all these coordinates control human awareness. However, in terms of emphasis and metaphor, this tale may be viewed as exemplifying the coordinate of space.

Within "the Dutch borough of Vondervotteimittiss (wonderwhat-time-it-is), the regularity of life, dependent upon the great clock and the exclusion of external influences, has been maintained for as long as history records (M, II, 365).[1] Well off the beaten track,

1. Unless otherwise stated, all parenthetical references are to either James A. Harrison (ed.), The Complete Works of Edgar Allan Poe (17 vols.; 1902; rpr., New York: AMS Press, 1965); or Thomas Ollive Mabbott (ed.), Collected Works of Edgar Allan Poe (6 vols. projected; Cambridge, Mass.: Belknap Press of Harvard University Press, 1969–), I, Poems (1969); II, Tales and Sketches 1831–1842 (1978); III, Tales and Sketches 1843–1849 (1978). An H before the volume and page citation indicates that the source of a quotation is Harrison's Complete Works. An M before the volume and page citation indicates that the source of a quotation is Mabbott's Collected Works. The Mabbott edition is in the process of superceding Harrison. Consequently, wherever a choice is available, I always use the Mabbott text.

Vondervotteimittiss is set "in a perfectly circular valley . . . entirely surrounded by gentle hills, over whose summit the people have never yet ventured to pass. For this they assign the very good reason that they do not believe there is anything at all on the other side" (M, II, 366). Sixty houses skirt the circumference of the valley. Other aspects of the town express its inhabitants' obsession with time. Every garden has a sundial and twenty-four cabbages (there being twenty-four hours in a day). The great clock on the steeple of the House of the Town Council, upon which all attention is focused, has seven faces (seven being the number of days in a week). Experience is limited vertically as well as horizontally. To obscure skyward vision, "there are cornices, as big as all the rest of the house, over the eaves and over the main doors." The narrow windows, with "very tiny panes and a great deal of sash," blinker vision further (M, II, 367).

Everything is uniform, from the carving motifs (cabbages and timepieces) to the fat inhabitants themselves. Presiding over all, and fattest of all, is the belfryman. For "time out of mind" (this significantly ambiguous phrase occurs twice) nothing has changed (M, II, 367, 369). As in Poe's finest tales, every descriptive detail enhances the desired effect. In this case, he is suggesting that an exclusively rational and regulated life dulls the imagination and turns people into cabbages. A mental and physical diet of "sauer-kraut and pork" turns people to boredom and fat (M, II, 368). The natural propensity of the townspeople has been given the force of law, since the Council adopted "three important resolutions:"—

"That it is wrong to alter the good old course of things:"
"That there is nothing tolerable out of Vondervotteimittiss:" and—
"That we will stick by our clocks and our cabbages." (M, II, 369)

Clearly, the townspeople have succeeded in accepting the part for the whole, their portion of experience for the universal reality.

The narrator is struck in exactly the same restricted mould. He proposes, regarding Vondervotteimittiss, "to give a history of the calamitous events which have so lately occurred within its limits," but without being aware of the prophetic pun on "limits" (M, II, 365). Poe has here created a purblind persona, without Swift's subtlety but along the lines of his naïve commentators, with the irony depending upon the gap between Poe and his persona. The narrator displays the same narrow rigidity of mind that makes the village what it is: "No one who knows me will doubt that the duty thus self-imposed will be executed to the best of my ability, with all that rigid impartiality, all that cautious examination into facts, and diligent collation of authorities which should ever distinguish him who aspires to the title of historian" (M, II, 365). He consults "the united aid of medals, manuscripts and inscriptions" in order to determine the original date of the town's existence but "can only speak with that species of indefinite definiteness which mathematicians are, at times, forced to put up with in certain algebraic formulae. The date, I may thus say, in regard to the remoteness of its antiquity, cannot be less than any assignable quantity whatsoever" (M, II, 365–66). The "indefinite definiteness" of reason and insular scientific method paralyzes the village in a fixed system and represents the antagonist in Poe's conception of an alternative continuum reality. Wherever words like *distinct* or *definite* occur, the reader can be reasonably certain that what is being described is illusory or deceptive.

Everything in Vondervotteimittiss remains unchanged until the arrival of "a very diminutive foreign-looking young man" who is taken for the devil (M, II, 370). To judge from the *papillotes* in his hair and the *chapeau-de-bras* under his arm, he is a French devil and, thus, an embarrassing contrast to the phlegmatic Dutchmen. Poe is evidently making use of the stock type of the pedestrian Dutch to stand for what is wrong with humanity and the stock caricature of the irrepressible Frenchman to stand for what is lacking. But the most disturbing thing about the intruder is the way in which he cuts "all manner of fantastical steps" without "the remotest idea in the world of such a thing as keeping time in his steps" (M, II, 371). When the clock next strikes, instead of striking twelve times, the stranger (having incapacitated the belfryman) arranges that it strike thirteen, a time not represented on the clock. The village is thus confronted with a spatio-temporal reality beyond the norm—beyond the valley, off the face of the clock. The extra hour causes consternation and, in compensation, "the little old gentlemen" puff away at their pipes so furiously that an "impenetrable smoke" fills the entire valley. "Meantime the cabbages [the comparison is now plainly stated] all turned very red in the face, and it seemed as if old Nick himself had taken possession of everything in the shape of a time-piece," while "the scoundrel" in the belfry is scraping on his big fiddle "out of all time and tune" (M, II, 373–74).

Poe, in his creative and critical writing, *is* the devil in the belfry, campaigning against insular systems of reason that make the contours of life fixed and distinct. Constantly, Poe warns against taking the part for the whole. Dancing and playing out of tune, amidst a practically impenetrable and indistinct smoke, is preferable to an existence cramped by rigid distinctions and divisions.

Throughout his critical writings, Poe draws attention to the weakness of a position by pointing to its limited perspective and noninclusiveness. Among the "Marginalia" occurs this sentence: "An infinity of error makes its way into our Philosophy, through Man's habit of considering himself a citizen of a world solely—of an individual planet—instead of at least occasionally contemplating his position as cosmopolite proper—as a denizen of the universe" (H, XVI, 167). Macaulay's reputation, for example, is undeserved because he concentrates "force upon minutiae at the expense of a subject as a whole" (H, X, 158). With his penchant for logic, which appertains "rather to the trickery of thought's vehicle than to thought itself—rather to reason's shadow than to reason," Thomas Macaulay "attempts to deceive his readers, or has deceived himself, by confounding the nature of that proof from which we reason of the concerns of earth, considered as man's habitation, and the nature of that evidence from which we reason of the same earth regarded as a unit of that vast whole, the universe. In the former case the *data* being palpable, the proof is direct; in the later it is purely analogical" (H, X, 158–59). Poe doubts "whether he can distinctly state the difference between an epic and an epigram" (H, X, 166). This objection is repeated, in virtually the same words, five years later in "A Chapter of Suggestions," published in the *Opal for 1845,* where it is added: "Pleased at comprehending, we often are so excited as to take it for granted that we assent. Luminous writers may thus indulge, for a long time, in pure sophistry, without being detected. Macaulay is a remarkable instance of this species of mystification. We coincide with what he says, too frequently, because we so very *distinctly* understand what it is that he intends to say" (italics added; H, XIV, 191).

The desire to see the part in relation to the whole affects Poe's opinions on the question of a national literature. Sectional interests and even national interests, he reiterates in his reviews, should be subordinated to the composite glory of an international literature: "*the world* is the true theatre of the biblical histrio" (H, VIII, 277). He was particularly incensed by the attempts of cliques, particularly the *Knickerbocker* set led by Lewis Gaylord Clark, to promote a sectional literature at the expense of a national literature. In his projected *Penn Magazine*, he planned to incorporate literature from all sections.

Poe's constant quest—to see one thing in relation to another and everything as part of a whole—led him to view man's material existence as part of a larger purpose. In an important letter to James Russell Lowell, dated New York, July 2, 1844, Poe elaborates on this understanding. After denying a belief in spirituality except as "unparticled matter, permeating & impelling, all things," Poe says:

> Man, and other thinking beings, are individualizations of the unparticled matter. Man exists as a "person," by being clothed with matter (the particled matter) which individualizes him. Thus habited, his life is rudimental. What we call "death" is the painful metamorphosis. The stars are the habitations of rudimental beings. But for the necessity of the rudimental life, there would have been no worlds. At death, the worm is the butterfly—still material, but of a matter unrecognized by our organs—recognized, occasionally, perhaps, by the sleep-walker, directly—without organs—through the mesmeric medium. Thus a sleep-walker may see ghosts. Divested of the rudimental covering, the being inhabits *space*. (*Letters*, I, 257)[2]

This position is restated in "Mesmeric Revelation," published in August of the same year: "There are two bodies—the rudimental and the complete; corresponding with the two conditions of the worm and the butterfly. What we call 'death,' is but the painful metamorphosis. Our present incarnation is progressive, preparatory, tem-

2. Parenthetical references to Poe's letters may be located in John Ward Ostrom (ed.), *The Letters of Edgar Allan Poe* (2 vols.; rev. ed.; New York: Gordian Press, 1966).

porary. Our future is perfected, ultimate, immortal. The ultimate life is the full design" (M, III, 1037).

Let it be said at once that Poe's intention in his finest writing, some of the poetry and the arabesque tales, is to glimpse and describe that "full design." It is the purpose of this study to examine the strategy with which he attempts to accomplish such a vision. By positing the existence of "unparticled matter," Poe is dissolving the boundary that organ-oriented mankind assumes to exist between life and death. Thereby, he is justifying the reincarnation of Berenice, Morella, Ligeia, Madeline, and anyone else.

II

Phenomenology, the philosophy of Edmund Husserl and a basis for existentialism, posits the thesis that the experiences of the self constitute the only "reality," since "reality" necessarily has to be refracted through the individual psyche.[3] Poe fully recognized the inevitably phenomenological or, to use a less philosophically loaded word, idiopathic nature of man's appreciation and understanding and construed it as a further barrier to the perception of that truth which is ultimate and not relative. Thus, a second coordinate of deception is supplied by the internal limitations of the individual self. By the same token, the reasonable narrator in Poe's tales is not simply a means of securing verisimilitude; frequently he is also a satiric butt.

Man is limited then not only by the portion of space he inhabits but also by his attempts to comprehend even this restricted area because of his personal limitations, the configuration of his mentality, and his stance in relation to the external world. He necessarily fails even in perceiving the segment accurately—first, because he cannot see it in relation to the whole and, second, because he cannot help but see it in relation to himself. The coordinate of self is placed between the coordinates of space and time because, clearly, it involves the other two. The limitations of personal reason are, in part, the

---

3. Recently this philosophy has been applied to literary criticism. As one might expect, Poe provides an appropriate subject for such an approach. See David Halliburton, *Edgar Allan Poe: A Phenomenological View* (Princeton, N.J.: Princeton University Press, 1973).

consequence of man's fixed position in time and space, a crippling imprisonment from which Poe craves release. In fact, the locus of man's deception is always created by the interaction of the three coordinates. Although a number of Poe's tales are here arranged under three headings based on the coordinate that appears to predominate, this does not mean that the other two coordinates are nonexistent. Thus, as is evident in "The Devil in the Belfry," the time factor and the idiopathic factor contribute to the narrow spatial outlook of the villagers and the narrator.

Two rather trivial examples of idiopathic limitation are "Why the Little Frenchman Wears His Hand in a Sling," probably first published between 1837 and 1839 in a periodical as yet unlocated, and "The Spectacles," which first appeared in the Philadelphia *Dollar Newspaper* for March 27, 1844. Both tales concern the narrator's mistaken attitude toward a woman.

"Why the Little Frenchman Wears His Hand in a Sling" is narrated in the untutored Irish brogue of "Sir Pathrick O'Grandison, Barronitt."[4] His tone and the manner of his self-description stamp him as an insufferably arrogant and vain boor. He claims all the ladies fall for him because of "the iligant big figgur that I ave." "The little ould furrener Frinchman" across the road, his rival for the affections of "the purty widdy Misthress Tracle," is little more than "three fut and a bit" (M, II, 464). At Widow Tracle's, the three of them are seated on a sofa, the Frenchman on her right and O'Grandison on her left—with his right hand in what he assumes to be her hand, behind her back. During the ensuing conversation O'Grandison, projecting his own self-assurance, imagines the widow completely infatuated by him, winking at him and squeezing his hand. The Frenchman is out of the running. Eventually, O'Grandison and the Frenchman discover that they have been holding each other's hands and giving each other encouraging squeezes. Consequently, O'Grandison spitefully mashes the Frenchman's

---

4. Arthur Hobson Quinn points out that O'Grandison's address—39 Southampton Row, Russell Square—is the same as that of Poe's stepfather, John Allan, and family while living in London. See Quinn, *Edgar Allan Poe: A Critical Biography* (New York: Appleton-Century-Crofts, 1941), 77.

hand. He will not accept that the embarrassing mistake derives from the pompous, egocentric nature of his own personality.

"The Spectacles" is an overlong demonstration of much the same phenomenon. Its narrator, Napoleon Bonaparte Simpson, presents himself as a man whose vanity is exceeded only by his social snobbery, and his snobbery only by his greed for money. In the course of describing his situation he explains that, although he has weak eyesight, his vanity precludes his wearing glasses. He ironically dismisses "these merely personal details" as "of little importance," when in fact they are the *raison d'être* of the ensuing action (M, III, 888). At the theater with a friend (Mr. Talbot), Simpson, while perusing the audience to be confident that he is among "the very *élite* of the city," finds his glance "arrested and riveted by a figure in one of the private boxes which had escaped my observation" (M, III, 889). Variations of the word *rivet*, used five times in the course of the narrative, carry the same delimiting significance as Blake's "mindforg'd manacles" of man. Struck by her ideal beauty to be sure, what he especially admires is a diamond ring upon one of her "delicate fingers . . . which I at once saw was of extraordinary value" and a bracelet "clasped by a magnificent *aigrette* of jewels—telling, in words that could not be mistaken, at once of the wealth and fastidious taste of the wearer" (M, III, 890).

It is the "love at first sight" that Simpson is telling the story to illustrate, an inconsistency in retrospect, if he has learned anything from his experience (M, III, 886). First-sight impressions prove to be deceptive, particularly in view of Simpson's deficient character and vision. Actually, the "*magnetic* sympathy" is based on avarice (M, III, 890). To his amazement she regards him through "a double eyeglass" then turns to a male companion: "I saw distinctly, by the glances of both, that the conversation had reference to myself" (M, III, 894). She even consents to smile at him and makes "two distinct, pointed and unequivocal affirmative inclinations of the head" (M, III, 895). His love has been returned: "What other construction could I possibly put upon such conduct, on the part of a lady so beautiful—so wealthy—evidently so accomplished—of so high breeding—of so lofty a position in society—in every regard so entirely respectable as

I felt assured was Madame Lalande? Yes, she loved me . . . with an enthusiasm as *blind*—as uncompromising—as uncalculating . . . as my own" (italics added; M, III, 895–96). By a *tour de force* of projection, Simpson is almost saying that she is encouraging him because she feels herself to be sufficiently worthy of his attention. Talbot, who believes Simpson to be infatuated with another companion of the lady, a younger woman, identifies her as Madame Lalande.

Spurred by her apparent interest, Simpson later writes to the woman, having discovered her address: "I concealed nothing— nothing even of my weakness" (M, III, 899). The weakness referred to is his love. His more fundamental weakness, "hitherto carefully concealed," is only revealed later (M, III, 906). Poe's semantic ambiguity is of course deliberate since Simpson's love is connected so intimately with his weak eyesight. Included in the letter is "a frank declaration of my worldly circumstances—of my affluence" and a proposal (M, III, 899). After "what seemed the lapse of a century"— the passing of interior time is another aspect of the limitations imposed by the self—Madame Lalande sends an encouraging reply in imperfect English (M, III, 899). In the course of further misunderstandings and subterfuges, Simpson meets the lady, proposes marriage (although she mentions the discrepancy in their ages), and even tells her of his weak eyesight. Madame Lalande then agrees that Simpson may have her hand in marriage if he will consent, in return, to wear spectacles. He resolves to wear the spectacles on the day of his wedding, which is set immediately. The wedding is to be secret. Some form of deception characterizes every move in the tale.

After the wedding Simpson has his first opportunity to see his beloved in the light of day. True to his promise, he places the spectacles on his nose and discovers his wife to be an aged hag, eighty-two years old to be exact. Her female companion—the younger woman with her at the opera—is an "exceedingly lovely relative of her second husband's—a Madame Stéphanie Lalande" (M, III, 914). The hag is, in fact, Simpson's great-great-grandmother. He is horrified to see her as she is, toothless and wigless. To draw attention to the wider epistemological implications of the deception theme, the reader is informed that, as she jumped, she dropped "an entire universe of bustle" (M, III, 913). At the opera his great-great-grand-mother noticed him because "she was struck with a certain family resemblance to herself" (M, III, 914). Simpson recognizes himself "deceived by my weakness of vision, and the arts of the toilet" (M, III, 915).

But the layers of deception are thicker yet. The morning after the opera, Madame Lalande met Talbot, "an old Parisian acquaintance," who explained Simpson's "deficiencies of vision . . . and my good old relative discovered much to her chagrin, that she had been deceived in supposing me aware of her identity" (M, III, 915). To punish Simpson for his impudent advances, she concocts a plot with Talbot. To Simpson's relief, the wedding ceremony is part of the fabrication. Indeed, Simpson subsequently marries the beautiful Madame Stéphanie Lalande at the instigation of his old relative, who also makes him her sole heir when she dies. The tale has come full circle to Simpson's avarice—the shaping force of his perception—except that he is now never "met without SPECTACLES" (M, III, 916).

Although idiopathic deception is an element in almost all of Poe's tales, there are three more that are especially clear-cut examples. The first of these, "The Angel of the Odd," which appeared in the New York Columbian Magazine for October, 1844, is subtitled "an extravaganza"—a form that may be understood as wandering beyond bounds. During the course of the tale, the narrator is forced to discover that reality exceeds the bounds of his unimaginative mind. In a stupefied state, after a morning of heavy reading and "an unusually hearty dinner," he relaxes "with some miscellaneous bottles of wine, spirit and liqueur" and begins to survey the newspaper (M, III, 1100, 1101). He is about to throw the paper away in irritation at an incomprehensible editorial when he comes upon a paragraph that, noting "the avenues of death are numerous and strange," describes how a person playing "puff the dart . . . placed the needle at the wrong end of the tube" and sucked it into his throat, dying as a consequence.[5] The narrator angrily dismisses the account as "a con-

5. Thomas Ollive Mabbott located an almost identical account, entitled "Singular Death," in the Philadelphia Public Ledger of June 5, 1844. See Mabbott, "Origins of 'The Angel of the Odd,' " Notes and Queries, CLX (1931), 8.

temptible falsehood—a poor hoax" perpetrated for "the extravagant gullibility of the age," as opposed to his own "reflecting intellect" (M, III, 1101).

At this point, he is visited by a bizarre character who introduces himself in a German accent as the Angel of the Odd. Presumably the narrator is dreaming, but this is not totally verifiable within the story. Frequently, Poe leaves the reader poised between a fanciful and a realistic interpretation of a tale to underline one of his basic themes: the deceptive line between waking and sleeping reality, the mundane and the supernal world. The narrator throws a salt cellar at the Angel but succeeds only in breaking "the crystal which protected the dial of the clock upon the mantel piece" (M, III, 1104). Subsequently, one of the raisin stems, which the narrator takes to flicking about the room, catches in and prevents the movement of the minute hand. Time here, presumably, has the same symbolic equivalence as in "The Devil in the Belfry"; the stopped clock signals the intrusion of a realm beyond the temporal norm. The Angel, after explaining that it is his function to preside "over the contretemps" and "odd accidents which are continually astonishing the skeptic," arranges for the narrator a series of such experiences that result in the loss by fire of house and hair and a broken arm (M, III, 1104).

Thoroughly unhappy, the narrator decides to commit suicide. In order to die as he was born, he takes off his clothes and jumps into the nearest river, only to witness a drunken crow fly away with his breeches. He is now so committed to the odd that he performs his first unreasonable action and pursues the bird—over a precipice. Fortunately, he catches hold of the guide rope hanging from a passing balloon, manned by the Angel of the Odd. As his final act of disorientation, the Angel cuts the guide rope, and the narrator falls down the chimney of his house, "which, during my peregrinations, had been handsomely rebuilt," and comes to his senses at four o'clock in the morning "amid the fragments of a miscellaneous dessert, intermingled with a newspaper, some broken glasses and shattered bottles" (M, III, 1110). But he also awakens to a wider appreciation of the possibilities of existence, which the factual nature of his mind had hitherto precluded. Poe, as the devil in the belfry and the Angel of the Odd, fragments the orderly illusion of reality. The chaotic scene in which the narrator finds himself allows for new fluid possibilities.

An almost antithetical distortion of perceived reality to that exposed in "The Angel of the Odd" is presented in "The Sphinx," first published in *Arthur's Ladies' Magazine* (Philadelphia) for January, 1846. The function of the three otherwise unconnected introductory paragraphs is to suggest the basic prejudices of the narrator's mind. He is spending a fortnight by the Hudson River at the cottage of a relative, "during the dread reign of the Cholera in New York" (M, III, 1246). Typically, the tale begins with the arrival of the visitor. In spite of the summer diversions of country life, fear of bad news colors the outlook of both the narrator and his relative, but especially the narrator whose reading habits only serve to heighten his anxiety. He admits to reading "certain volumes . . . of a character to force into germination whatever seeds of hereditary superstition lay latent in my bosom" (M, III, 1246–47). Clearly the narrator, in his horrified state of mind, is in a state to see horrors.

It is in this frame of mind that the narrator, sitting at an open window, views a distant hill: "My thoughts had been long wandering from the volume before me to the gloom and desolation of the neighboring city. Uplifting my eyes from the page . . . I *distinctly* saw" what appears to be a monster (italics added; M, III, 1247). Poe's use of "distinctly" here hints at the deceptive nature of human perception, as does the sequence of the narrator's thoughts from the book to the plague to the hill. The narrator first conceives of the monster in terms of a "ship of the line" and therefore describes it with mechanical analogies (M, III, 1248). Like the insect in another tale, "The Gold-Bug," the creature displays a death's-head. Three or four evenings later, the narrator is sitting in the same seat: "I again had a *distinct* view of the monster" (italics added; M, III, 1249). His host proceeds to explain that he has been watching an insect, "about the sixteenth of an inch in its extreme length, and also about the sixteenth of an inch distant from" his eye, crawl along the thread left by a spider (M, III, 1251).

12

A. H. Quinn states somewhat vaguely that "the satiric purpose of the story is to call attention to the undue emphasis laid on Democracy by those who see it too near them."[6] Presumably, he is thinking of the following passage, describing the host's notion that

the principal source of error in all human investigations, lay in the liability of the understanding to under-rate or to over-value the importance of an object, through mere misadmeasurement of its propinquity. "To estimate properly, for example," he said, "the influence to be exercised on mankind at large by the thorough diffusion of Democracy, the distance of the epoch at which such diffusion may possibly be accomplished, should not fail to form an item in the estimate. Yet can you tell me one writer on the subject of government, who has ever thought this particular branch of the subject worthy of discussion at all?" (M, III, 1249–50)

Here the host is impinging on the third coordinate of deception imposed by the action of time. But Poe is talking about "all human investigations" and using democracy as an example. While the narrator magnifies an object out of all proportion, Quinn is unfairly diminishing the theme of the story: man's inevitable predilection to let his point of view determine what he sees. In demonstrating the theme in this story, however, Poe has somewhat violated verisimilitude. Even if the visual deception be granted, the sound that accompanies the "monster"—"a sound so loud and so expressive of wo, that it struck upon my nerves like a knell"—makes the whole business a little farfetched (M, III, 1248–49).

A final more or less direct example of idiopathic response is the otherwise uninteresting trifle, "X-ing a Paragrab," first published in the *Flag of Our Union* (Boston), May 12, 1849. The tale opens with a piece of specious logic, man's specious logic being the theme of the tale: "As it is well known that the 'wise men' came 'from the East,' and as Mr. Touch-and-go Bullet-head came from the East, it follows that Mr. Bullet-head was a wise man; and if collateral proof of the matter be needed, here we have it—Mr. B. was an editor" (M, III, 1368–69). His sole foible was irascibility, not his obstinacy, "since he justly considered it his *forte*" (M, III, 1369). His obstinacy is his strength simply because he regards it to be so. An external viewpoint

6. A. H. Quinn, *Edgar Allan Poe: A Critical Biography*, 499.

might lead to a totally different conclusion, although "it would have required all the logic of a Brownson to convince him that it was 'anything else' " (M, III, 1369). The tale performs the same function as "the logic of a Brownson."

On the only occasion Bullet-head "did not prove infallible," he left Frogpondium (Boston) in the East for Alexander-the-Great-o-nopolis in the West to establish what he believed to be the only newspaper, which he called the *Tea-Pot* (M, III, 1369). However, unknown to Bullet-head, there did exist an *Alexander-the-Great-o-nopolis Gazette*, edited by a John Smith. "It was solely, therefore, on account of having been misinformed, that Mr. Bullet-head found himself in Alex—suppose we call it Nopolis, 'for short'—but, as he *did* find himself there, he determined to keep up his character for obst—for firmness, and remain" (M, III, 1369). He will not even recognize his limitation under its proper name. By renaming it "firmness," it is converted into a virtue. Bullet-head's solution is to pan the editor of the *Gazette* in the first issue of the *Tea-Pot*. John Smith replies by pointing to the number of o's in the article and concludes that it reflects a certain limitation on the part of the writer. Mr. Bullet-head chooses to see his predilection for "the beautiful vowel" not as a deficiency but as a proper regard for "the emblem of Eternity" and composes a paragraph that contains as many o's as possible (M, III, 1371). The nonsense that results symbolizes in a wider sense the nonsensical projection that man's limitations impose upon reality.

Bob, the boy of twelve to whom the copy is entrusted, is a printer's devil, but he performs much the same role as the devil in "The Devil in the Belfry" and in other tales by Poe. Thus, he is the means by which Bullet-head is made to see his obstinacy as a crippling foible and not as a forte. When Bob begins to set the type, he finds the little-*o* box and the capital-*O* box empty and reflects that "one of them ere G'zette devils . . . gone and cabbaged em every one" (M, III, 1373). There is no alternative but "to x this ere paragrab"—x because, in such a circumstance, "he would have considered it heretical to employ any other character" and "paragrab" because such is Bob's idiosyncratic pronunciation of the word (M, III, 1374). With

14

this information, the sense of the tale's title is now clear. If the passage as originally penned was idiotic, as finally printed with an x in place of every o, it is unintelligible: "The uproar occasioned by this mystical and cabalistical article is not to be conceived. The first *definite* idea entertained by the populace was, that some diabolical treason lay concealed in the hieroglyphics" (italics added; M, III, 1374).

Bullet-head leaves town and is not heard of again. By the replacement of an x for each of his beloved o's, Bullet-head has been permitted an objective look at his own limitation. O can stand for obstinacy. The actual unreasonableness of his position is immediately apparent in the printed version of the paragraph. Poe's device is that of the debater who demonstrates the absurdity of his opponent's abstract position by expressing the same position with concrete examples. At the same time, the title and the printed paragraph "prove" once again the delicate edge on which our rational world is poised. Alter the angle of perspective just slightly, in this case transpose an x for an o, and the whole, apparently stable structure disintegrates. (Something of the same reasoning may underlie Poe's use of a peculiar, quasi-Germanic dialect in such tales as "The Angel of the Odd.") "Bob, the devil," explains the "unhappy affair" with a piece of specious logic, which is designed to balance that of the opening paragraph: "He said that, for his part, he had no doubt about the matter at all, that it was a clear case, that Mr. Bullet-head never *could* be 'persvaded fur to drink like other folks, but vas *continually* a-svigging o' that ere blessed XXX ale, and, as a naiteral consekvence, it just puffed him up savage, and made him X (cross) in the X-treme' " (M, III, 1374, 1375). A credible explanation is always preferable to a correct one.

Poe's review of Lowell's *A Fable for the Critics* contains the line, "Each person, in his own estimate, is the pivot on which all the rest of the world spins round" (H, XII, 166). As a result, each person must live in a slightly different world, and each such world is an illusion because it is dependent upon a subjective perspective. In a section of the "Marginalia," Poe details some of the contributive illusions to which men are subject. Because "we appreciate *time* by events alone," we are led to "the erroneous idea that events *are* time—that the more numerous the events, the longer the time; and the converse." The revolutions of the hands on a clock face and the movements of heavenly bodies, which we use to correct our impression, "we only *assume* to be regular" (H, XVI, 22). Similarly, "we might as rationally define . . . 'the succession of objects' " as space, which "tends to the false idea that objects *are* space" (H, XVI, 22). Our visual conception of distance varies according to whether or not there are objects between the points being estimated. As an example, Poe points to the fact that the sun, "in his meridian place," appears to be closer and smaller than "the same sun setting on the horizon of the ocean" or "in a mountainous region" (H, XVI, 24, 25).

"Man's chief idiosyncrasy being reason," it is man's reason which is chiefly to blame for perverting his idiopathic perception (H, XVI, 6). He is imprisoned within a fragmented universe that his reason, in structuring falsely, fragments further. Because reason divides man's experiences into distinct areas, he is condemned to the rack of polarity. Reason forces him to look at the world as if through a grid. While describing the nature of poetry, in an 1844 review of R. H. Horne's *Orion*, Poe deplores the activities of "men . . . who would trammel the soul in its flight to an ideal Helusion [Poe's spelling of the Greek for Elysium] by the quirks and quibbles of chopped logic" (H, XI, 256). "Truth," Poe goes on, "is, in its own essence sublime—but her loftiest sublimity, as derived from man's clouded and erratic reason, is valueless. . . . We regret to see any trivial or partial imperfection of detail; but we grieve deeply when we detect any radical error of conception" (H, XI, 257). In "The Mystery of Marie Rogêt," Poe, deducing a moral, speaks of "an infinite series of mistakes which arise in the path of Reason through her propensity for seeking truth *in detail*" (M, III, 773–74).

Among the "Marginalia" occurs the following criticism of a priori reasoning:

The *à priori* reasoners upon government are, of all plausible people, the most preposterous. They only argue too cleverly to permit my thinking them silly enough to be themselves deceived by their own arguments. Yet even this is possible; for there is something in the vanity of logic which addles a man's brains. Your true logician gets, in time, to be logicalized, and then, *so far as regards himself* [italics added], the universe is one *word*. A thing, for him, no longer exists. He deposits upon a sheet of paper a certain assemblage of syllables, and fancies that their meaning is *riveted* [italics added] by the act of deposition. (H, XVI, 37)

As an example, Poe notes, "In a single page of 'Mill,' I find the word 'force' employed four times; and each employment varies the idea. . . . By ringing small changes on the words 'leg-of-mutton' and 'turnip' (changes so *gradual* as to escape detection)," Poe claims, "I could *'demonstrate'* that a turnip was, is, and of right ought to be a leg-of-mutton" (H, XVI, 38). He is here anticipating the comparatively recent notion of semantic determinism, the notion that a person's perception of the external world is directed by his vocabulary. In a section of the "Marginalia" (which is of particular interest in view of the controversy concerning the relative excellence of Baudelaire's translations and the originals) Poe shows himself to be acutely aware of the idiomatic differences between English and French but asks whether or not, by "dexterity at paraphrase . . . *a translation may be made to convey to a foreigner a juster conception of an original than could the original itself?"* (H, XVI, 106).

A person sees only what he knows. In view of this fact, Poe in a later "Marginalia" entry states: "It is laughable to observe how easily any system of Philosophy can be proved false:—but then is it not mournful to perceive the impossibility of even fancying any particular system to be true?" (H, XVI, 164). This sentence is worth remembering in relation to Poe's belief that systematized "truth" has nothing to do with the "beauty" that justifies poetry. Also among the "Marginalia" Poe writes: "To me, it appears that, in all ages, the *most* preposterous falsities have been received as truths by at least the *mens* omnium hominum. As for the *sana* mens—how are we ever to determine what that is?" (H, XVI, 166).

III

Man's awareness is limited not only by his personal traits and spatial situation but also by his place in time—the third coordinate of deception. In "The Thousand-and-Second Tale of Scheherazade," first published in *Godey's Lady's Book*, February, 1845, Poe is concerned with demonstrating that the facts of a future age may be less credible than the fantasies of the present—that, in the words of the "Old Saying" used as an epigraph to the tale, "Truth is stranger than fiction."

Poe begins by retelling the familiar account, after pointing out that the true version is to be found not in the Arabian Nights but in something called the *Tellmenow Isitsoornot* (Tell me now, is it so or not?):

I was not a little astonished to discover that the literary world has hitherto been strangely in error respecting the fate of the vizier's daughter, Scheherazade, as that fate is depicted in the "Arabian Nights;" and that the *dénouement* there given, if not altogether inaccurate, *as far as it goes* [italics added], is at least to blame in not having gone very much farther. (M, III, 1152)

The phrase "as far as it goes" is important because of Poe's repeated insistence that the part not be mistaken for the whole and for its prefigurative value. Scheherazade's life depends upon her ability to keep the king in suspense about the endings of her stories. The king has lived a life of fixed, if unusual, routine, having made a vow "to espouse each night the most beautiful maiden in his dominions, and the next morning to deliver her up to the executioner" (M, III, 1152). Scheherazade decides to marry the king and keep him so interested in her stories that his curiosity will not allow him to have her executed. The plan succeeds, and after a thousand and one nights "the tariff upon beauty was repealed" (M, III, 1154). At least, so goes the Arabian Nights version.

In the true version the loquacious Scheherazade, on the thousand and second night, feels compelled to relate the further adventures of Sinbad. The next eighteen pages involve a Chinese-box technique. Poe is addressing to the reader Scheherazade's words to the king, and Scheherazade is repeating Sinbad's words to the caliph. Sinbad explains how he looked out to sea for a ship and sighted a monster. The monster in fact *is* a ship, a warship of the more advanced civilization of nineteenth-century England, but Sinbad (unlike the narrator in "The Sphinx" who thinks of an animal in terms of a ship) describes the ship as if it were a beast: "As the thing drew near we saw it very *distinctly*. . . . Its body, which was unlike that of ordinary fishes, was as solid as a rock, and of a jetty blackness throughout all that portion of it which floated above the water, with the exception of a narrow blood-red streak that completely begirdled it. The belly . . . was entirely covered with metallic scales" (italics added; M, III, 1156). Poe is utilizing the license of fantasy to bring the present and the future alongside in order to indicate how man's temporal perspective deceives him about the nature of reality. The men on board, because of their form-hugging garments, appear to Sinbad to be naked animals.

Where comprehension fails, myth is substituted; and so Sinbad's porter, when asked about the strange "monster" and its "creatures," replies

that he had once before heard of this sea-beast; that it was a cruel demon, with bowels of sulphur and blood of fire, created by evil genii as the means of inflicting misery upon mankind; that the things upon its back were vermin [shades of Jonathan Swift], such as sometimes infest cats and dogs, only a little larger and more savage; and that these vermin had their uses, however evil—for, through the torture they caused the beast by their nibblings and stingings, it was goaded into that degree of wrath which was requisite to make it roar and commit ill, and so fulfil the vengeful and malicious designs of the wicked genii. (M, III, 1158)

Both Sinbad and his porter flee, the porter with Sinbad's bundles, "of which I have no doubt he took excellent care—although this is a point I cannot determine, as I do not remember that I ever beheld him again" (M, III, 1158). Poe frequently uses this device of misplaced, inconsequential exactness, here in stark and ironic apposition to the incredible myth. Sinbad, however, is captured by the men-vermin, learns their language, and accepts the invitation to circumnavigate the globe with them.

During the first half of the voyage, Sinbad is confronted with various natural phenomena that seem incredible because they lie outside the sphere of his experience. The king makes incredulous and derisive exclamations throughout the account. Sinbad describes in a bewildered manner various strange sights, the "real" nature of which Poe identifies in footnotes. A myrmeleon or lion-ant is called a "monster," which leads the scrupulously perspective-minded Poe to comment in a footnote: "The term 'monster' is equally applicable to small abnormal things and to great, while such epithets as 'vast' are merely comparative. The cavern of the myrmeleon is *vast* in comparison with the hole of the common red ant. A gram of silex is, also, a 'rock' " (M, III, 1162). (In "The Sphinx" an insect is also a monster.) Poe's philosophy hinges on such questions of perceptual perspective. The second half of the voyage is mainly given over to the description of mechanical achievements of Poe's day, which the king's imagination refuses to encompass. They reach America where Sinbad confronts further marvels including a train, an incubating machine, Maelzel's Automaton Chess-Player, and a printing press, which all revolt the king's reason. The "Electrotype," the "Voltaic pile," the "Electro Telegraph," and "the Daguerreotype" are "absurd" and "preposterous" (M, III, 1167–69). But women's bustles are the last straw. The king tells Scheherazade, "You have already given me a dreadful headache with your lies," and has her throttled (M, III, 1169). Had she in fact continued spinning real lies—believable fictions—as before, she might have survived.

Time past can be almost as much a closed book as time future, at least such is the import of "Some Words with a Mummy," first published in the New York *American Review: A Whig Journal,* April, 1845. The narrator is aroused from deep sleep, as the mummy will be, by a message from his old friend, Doctor Ponnonner. "But when were the hopes of humanity fulfilled?" the narrator complains of his expectation of an undisturbed night's rest and with these words states the theme of the tale (M, III, 1178). Poe intends attacking man's misconception that the passing of time brings political, architectural, metaphysical, and scientific improvements by positing that historical knowledge of a bygone age is, if not totally inaccurate, at least severely limited. The revivification of an Egyptian mummy with the significant title, Count Allamistakeo, provides Poe with the dramatic vehicle. (Revivification occurs by means of the voltaic pile, a scientific marvel mentioned in "Scheherazade.")

Surprisingly, the company neither flees, has hysterics, nor swoons when the mummy sits up and speaks—a phenomenon that the narrator attributes to "the spirit of the age, which proceeds by the rule of contraries altogether, and is now usually admitted as the solution of everything in the way of paradox and impossibility," a sneer at Transcendentalism (M, III, 1183). During the subsequent conversation, conducted "in primitive Egyptian, through the medium ... of Messieurs Gliddon and Buckingham, as interpreters," various contemporary innovations are all discovered to have been anticipated by the ancient Egyptians (M, III, 1184).[7] Although Allamistakeo was embalmed in error, the Egyptians (whose average life span was about eight hundred years) had apparently discovered the secrets of suspended animation with the benefit "that a laudable curiosity might be gratified, and, at the same time, the interests of science much advanced, by living this natural term in instalments. A historian aged five hundred, having written a substantial book, would have himself embalmed to be revivified after perhaps another five hundred years in order to straighten out the interpretation of his work and thus help to prevent "our history from degenerating into absolute fable" (M, III, 1189). At the end of the tale, the narrator concludes that he is "heartily sick of this life and of the nineteenth century in general. I am convinced that everything is going wrong." Consequently, he resolves to "get embalmed for a couple of hundred years" (M, III, 1195). This victory for the mummy is balanced by the doctor's pyrrhic victory when he asks "if the Egyptians had comprehended, at any period, the manufacture of either Ponnonner's lozenges, or Brandreth's pills" (M, III, 1194–95). The Egyptian is overcome with shame, allowing the narrator to comment with punning sincerity, "Indeed I could not endure the spectacle of the poor Mummy's mortification." Thus, the narrator turns the tables on the mummy's opening remark: "I must say, gentlemen, that I am as much surprised as I am mortified, at your behavior" (M, III, 1183, 1195).

The three introductory paragraphs have not been dealt with because, at a first reading, it may be difficult to relate them to the rest of

---

7. For the influence of George Gliddon's *Ancient Egypt* (1843) on this tale and information about James Silk Buckingham, traveler, author, and lecturer, see Burton R. Pollin, "Poe's 'Some Words with a Mummy' Reconsidered," *Emerson Society Quarterly*, no. 60 (1970), 60–67.

the tale in accordance with Poe's insistence on unified plot structure. The narrator is spending the evening at home with a headache, stemming from a symposium the preceding evening. He decides to eat what he alternatively calls "a mouthful of supper," "a light supper," and a "frugal meal" and which consists of four pounds of Welsh rabbit: "My wife will have it five;—but, clearly, *she has confounded two very distinct affairs*. The abstract number, five, I am willing to admit; but, concretely, it has reference to bottles of Brown Stout, without which, in the way of condiment, Welsh rabbit is to be eschewed" (italics added; M, III, 1117–78). He then falls asleep to be awakened after three snores, has the experience with the mummy, returns to bed after four o'clock, and pens the account between seven and ten in the morning. It would seem likely from this chronology that the narrator, like the narrator in "The Angel of the Odd" (written just before "Some Words with a Mummy"), dreamt the entire episode—the dream being a product of strain, too much toasted cheese, and Brown Stout. He, not his wife, "has confounded two very distinct affairs." He has confused the deceptive line between illusion and reality, making the story an excellent exemplum of the razor-edge on which our awareness of the "real" both mentally and temporally rests.

In a future age, historical knowledge of the present is likely to be as mythical and distorted as contemporary understanding of the achievements of the ancient Egyptians. Such a situation arises in the tale first published in *Godey's Lady's Book* for February, 1849, and entitled "Mellonta Tauta" from the Greek for "these things are in the future."[8] One of the most poorly unified of Poe's tales, it is, for this reason, the most illuminating evidence of a dilemma in which he found himself toward the end of his philosophical life. Poe is attempting in "Mellonta Tauta" to fuse two themes that are mutually contradictory and exclusive. The first theme is the deceptive state of man's awareness, in this case primarily because of external temporal restrictions and internal idiopathic factors. A large part of the tale, consisting of material reworked for the opening burlesque section of

8. The same phrase, from Sophocles' *Antigone*, line 1333, is used as an epigraph to "The Colloquy of Monos and Una."

Eureka, constitutes a second theme: the justification of an intuitive process, rather than Aristotelian deduction or Baconian induction, as the only approach to truth. For the moment, the discussion focuses only on the first theme; the second theme and the revealing contradiction are taken up in Chapter 10.

Pundit the antiquarian and his wife Pundita are aboard the balloon "Skylark," which left the ground on April 1, 2848. With this hint of an April-Fools'-Day hoax, Poe delicately and characteristically undercuts the "reality" of the entire account, which consists of daily entries in "a long gossiping letter" of Pundita's to a friend—a letter that she finally corks up in a bottle and throws into the sea (M, III, 1291). Many of the various inconsistencies in "Mellonta Tauta" are understandable only by noting that Pundita shares the vacillating quality stereotypically attributed to women. For example, she is contradictory in her opinions concerning balloon travel. Her entry for April asks: "Are we forever to be doomed to the thousand inconveniences of the balloon?" (M, III, 1292). But on April 4 she exclaims: "How very safe, commodious, manageable, and in every respect convenient are our modern balloons" (M, III, 1298). Given the choice between traveling across "Kanadaw" (future English for Canada but the name appears to cover both the North and South American continents) at three hundred miles per hour or one hundred miles per hour, she prefers the latter because "something like a *distinct* view of the country was attainable," rather than one blurred mass (italics added; M, III, 1298, 1299).

Her opinion varies according to whether she is looking at a matter personally or generally. After noting that a balloon passing overhead "always seems to me like an immense bird of prey," she explains that "one went over us this morning about sunrise, and so nearly overhead that its drag-rope actually brushed the net-work suspending our car, and caused us very serious apprehension" (M, III, 1292). In just the next paragraph she notes: "Talking of drag-ropes—our own, it seems, has this moment knocked a man overboard from one of the small magnetic propellers that swarm in the ocean below us." She rejoices that the man "was not permitted to get on board again," seeing that "we live in an age so enlightened that no such thing as an individual is supposed to exist" (M, III, 1293). Living in a Malthusian, overpopulated world, she regards the civil war in Africa and the plague in "Yurope" and "Ayesher" as benefits. Pundita is both a creature of her time and a creature living in a world of her own creation.

What remains in "Mellonta Tauta" of the deception theme revolves around Pundita's inability to comprehend nineteenth-century man and nineteenth-century man's projected inability to comprehend Pundita's age. Time, the third coordinate of deception, is here at work. On April 8, a passing balloon "threw on board several late papers" that interest Pundit because "they contain some exceedingly curious information relative to . . . Amriccan antiquities" (M, III, 1302). It appears that Paradise (Manhattan Island) has been devastated by an earthquake with the result "that the most indefatigable of our antiquarians have never yet been able to obtain from the site any sufficient data . . . wherewith to build up even the ghost of a theory concerning the manners, customs, &c. &c. &c., of the aboriginal inhabitants" (M, III, 1303). Pundita is as incredulous as the king in "Scheherazade" to learn that women wore bustles. A further piece of data, Pundit reads, has just been unearthed in the shape of a monument with the following inscription:

> This Corner Stone of a Monument to the
> Memory of
> GEORGE WASHINGTON,
> was laid with appropriate ceremonies on the
> 19TH DAY OF OCTOBER, 1847,
> the anniversary of the surrender of
> Lord Cornwallis
> to General Washington at Yorktown,
> A.D. 1781,
> under the auspices of the
> Washington Monument Association of the
> city of New York.
> (M, III, 1304)

From this, it is ascertained "very distinctly" that Cornwallis was surrendered to be eaten (since the savages were cannibals) "under the auspices of . . . a charitable institution for the depositing of cornerstones," which laid cornerstones "as we do now," as an "indication of the design to erect a monument at some future time" (M, III, 1304, 1305). So much for the future understanding of mid-nineteenth-century America.

In these three tales exemplifying the coordinate of time, Poe impinges on the genres of fantasy and science fiction.[9] He uses these forms to illustrate the relativity of truth. As in *Eureka*: "It is clear, not only that what is obvious to one mind may not be obvious to another, but that what is obvious to one mind at one epoch may be anything but obvious, at another epoch, to the same mind" (H, XVI, 240–41). In the "Pinakidia," Poe offers this illustration of the uncertainty of ancient history: "Porphyry, than whom no one could be better acquainted with the theology of the ancients, acknowledged Vesta, Rhea, Ceres, Themis, Priapus, Proserpina, Bacchus, Attis, Adonis, Silenue, and the Satyrs to be one and the same" (H, XIV, 51). Elsewhere it is speculated that the quaintness of Old English poetry, in itself "a very powerful adjunct to ideality," may be merely historical (H, XII, 139). By the same token, speeches in ancient Greece were particularly effective because of the "circumstances of the audience" at that time: "The Greeks were a highly excitable and *unread* race" (H, X, 58). Consequently, "the idea of reproducing a Greek play before a modern audience, is the idea of a pedant and nothing beyond" (H, XII, 132).

In an interesting section of the "Marginalia," Poe counters the proposition that an old person would not choose to "relive his life, because he knows that its evil predominated over its good" with the assertion that he cannot know any such thing, it being impossible for man to gain a true conception of his past life; there is only "a *seeming*—a fictitious knowledge" that "leaves quite out of account that

9. For a full exploration of the science-fictional dimension of Poe's work including the relevant bibliography, see "Edgar Allan Poe and the Visionary Tradition of Science Fiction," in David Ketterer, *New Worlds for Old: The Apocalyptic Imagination, Science Fiction, and American Literature* (New York: Doubleday Anchor Press, and Bloomington: Indiana University Press, 1974), 50–75; David Ketterer, "The SF Element in the Work of Poe: A Chronological Survey," *Science-Fiction Studies*, I (1974), 197–213; Harold Beaver (ed.), *The Science Fiction of Edgar Allan Poe* (New York: Penguin Books, 1976).

elastic *Hope* which is the Harbinger and the Eos of all" (H, XVI, 32, 33). It is impossible to make correct "deductions" from an "ill-grounded" choice: "How out of error shall we fabricate truth?" (H, XVI, 34). Later in his "Marginalia" Poe exclaims: "Here is error on all sides" (H, XVI, 63). In this case, Poe is referring to the passage "in Isaiah respecting Idumea, that 'none shall pass through thee for ever and ever,' " which Dr. Keith misunderstands. By going back to the original meanings of the words, Poe argues that the sentence actually means no one shall live in the place. Apparently, Poe was especially proud of this interpretation because he repeats it in three different places (H, X, 12–19, 83, 180–81). In view of all this semantic, timebound misunderstanding and distortion, Poe concludes: "It is by no means an irrational fancy that, in a future existence, we shall look upon what we think our present existence, as a dream" (H, XVI, 161).

IV

Given the barriers of time, space, and self, the possibility of man's ever attaining any form of enlightenment seems remote indeed. Not only does he not see the whole of existence, but that portion which he does see he interprets out of all recognition. Conventional reality, apparently reliable, is in fact treacherous quicksand. Man lives in a constant state of externally and internally induced deception. Poe made it his life's work to destroy this fabric of deception, to reveal the quicksand, and if possible to see into that actuality beyond three-dimensional existence. According to Poe, the essential prerequisite for such insight is the acquisition of the correct point of view.

"The higher order of music," says Poe in the prefatory paragraphs to the 1841 "Island of the Fay," "is the most thoroughly estimated when we are exclusively alone." "The accessory sentiment of seclusion," an aspect of the point of view necessary to the contemplation of the "spiritual uses" of music, is also indispensable to "the happiness experienced in the contemplation of natural scenery. In truth the man who would behold aright the glory of God upon earth must in solitude behold that glory." This is "one pleasure still within the reach of fallen mortality" (M, II, 600). Equally important, however, is an analogical perspective enabling the viewer to regard valleys, waters, forests, and fountains as "the colossal members of one vast animate and sentient whole—a whole whose form (that of the sphere) is the most perfect and most inclusive of all; whose path is among associate planets; whose meek handmaiden is the moon; whose mediate sovereign is the sun; whose life is eternity; whose thought is that of a God; whose enjoyment is knowledge; whose destinies are lost in immensity; whose cognizance of ourselves is akin with our own cognizance of the *animalculae* which infest the brain —a being which we, in consequence, regard as purely inanimate and material, much in the same manner as these *animalculae* must thus regard us" (M, II, 600–601). The same elasticity of mind leads Poe to speak of the vitality of matter as "the *leading* principle in the operations of Deity. . . . As we find cycle within cycle without end—yet all revolving around one far distant centre which is the Godhead, may we not analogically suppose, in the same manner, life within life, the less within the greater, and all within the Spirit Divine?" (M, II, 601).

The clearest statement about the perspective to be adopted and the statement that more than any other explains Poe's artistic procedure is lodged in an early review of *The American in England* by Lieutenant Slidell, published in the *Southern Literary Messenger* (Richmond) for February, 1836:

As the touches of a painting which, to minute inspection, are "confusion worse confounded," will not fail to start boldly out to the cursory glance of a connoisseur—or as a star may be seen more distinctly in a sidelong survey than in any direct gaze however penetrating and intense—so there are, not unfrequently, times and methods, in which, and by means of which, a richer philosophy may be gathered on the surface of things than can be drawn up, even with great labor, e *profundis.* (H, VIII, 215)

The perspective suggested by "the cursory glance" and "the sidelong survey" is elsewhere referred to as "the half-closed eye." In the 1831 "Letter to B——" (probably Elam Bliss, Poe's publisher), Poe notes in a sentence cut from the 1836 revision (perhaps because he had recently appropriated virtually the same words in the Alexander Slidell review), that "Poetry, above all things, is a beautiful painting whose tints, to minute inspection, are confusion worse confounded, but start boldly out to the cursory glance of the connoisseur."[10] After this he speaks of "Coleridge's liability to err in his Biographia Literaria. . . . He goes wrong by reason of his very profundity, and of his error we have a natural type in the contemplation of a star. He who regards it directly and intensely sees, it is true, the star, but it is the star without a ray—while he who surveys it less inquisitively is conscious of all for which the star is useful to us below—its brilliance and its beauty" (H, VII, xxxix). In elaborating his definition of art in the "Marginalia" as "the reproduction of what the Senses perceive in Nature through the veil of the soul," Poe continues: "We can, at any time, double the true beauty of an actual landscape by half closing our eyes as we look at it. The naked Senses sometimes see too little—but then *always* they see too much" (H, XVI, 164). Three pages earlier, Poe refers to the same strategy in slightly different terms: "It is only the philosophical lynxeye that, through the indignity-mist of Man's life, can still discern the dignity of Man" (H, XVI, 161).

The effect of looking at the world through half-closed eyes is, of course, to blur the outlines and allow everything to fuse into everything else—in fact, to destroy the external universe as usually perceived and eradicate the barriers erected by time, space, and self. With the destruction of the reasoned world, the world of the imagination can take over. "The half-closed eye" is, then, a metaphor both for the imagination and for the situation essential to the fruitful operation of the imagination. In looking out through half-closed eyes, Poe confuses sight and sound, sight and smell, fire and water, life and death, and the various other elements which man's reason keeps apart or regards as polarities. Thus, in the "Marginalia" Poe is able to surmise that perhaps snow is black "if we could see the thing in the proper light" (H, XVI, 70). The manner in which Poe expresses his experience of a fused and fluid state is the subject of the three chapters grouped under the heading "Fusion." It is preeminently this aspect of Poe that drew Baudelaire and the French symbolists.

10. See the 1831 "Letter to B——" as reprinted in Sculley Bradley, Richmond Croom Beatty, E. Hudson Long, George Perkins (eds.), *The American Tradition in Literature* (4th ed.; 2 vols.; New York: Grosset & Dunlap, 1974), I, 869.

According to Edmund Wilson, to approximate the idefiniteness of music, to confuse the imaginary and the real worlds, and to confuse the senses were the principal aims of French symbolism.[11] Instances of Poe's use of synesthesia abound. For Monos, speaking in "The Colloquy of Monos and Una," the coming of night is both tangible and audible: "It oppressed my limbs with the oppression of some dull weight, and was palpable. There was also a moaning sound, not unlike the distant reverberation of surf, but more continuous, which, beginning with the first twilight, had grown in strength with the darkness" (M, II, 614). Poe notes in the "Marginalia" the assertion that "the right angle of light's incidence produces a sound upon one of the Egyptian pyramids" and in corroboration writes, "The orange ray of the spectrum and the buzz of the gnat (which never rises above the second A), affect me with nearly similar sensations. In hearing the gnat, I perceive the color. In perceiving the color, I seem to hear the gnat" (H, XVI, 17–18). Alfred, Lord Tennyson is valued because "he seems *to see with his ear*" (H, XVI, 30).

The fusion-imperative in Poe accounts for his predilection for median states, described in the "Marginalia" as "those mere points of time where the confines of the waking world blend with those of the world of dreams," points of time which produce "fancies" (H, XVI, 88). The narrator of "Eleonora" voices the suspicion "whether much that is glorious—whether all that is profound—does not spring from disease of thought—from *moods* of mind exalted at the expense of the general intellect." What is generally thought to be madness may be another median state, since "they who dream by day are cognizant of many things which escape those who dream only by night. In their grey visions they obtain glimpses of eternity, and thrill, in awaking, to find that they have been upon the verge of the great secret" (M, II, 638). As further examples of Poe's taste for median states, it should be observed that his favorite time of day seems to be twilight and his favorite time of year, autumn. In his

11. Edmund Wilson, *Axel's Castle* (New York: Scribners, 1931), 13–19. For firsthand evidence, see Charles Baudelaire, *Edgar Allan Poe: sa vie et ses ouvrages,* ed. W. T. Bandy (Toronto: University of Toronto Press, 1973); Lois Hyslop and Francis E. Hyslop, Jr. (eds.), *Baudelaire on Poe* (Philadelphia: Bald Eagle Press, 1952).

elaboration of the tripartite nature of the mind, "Taste," which "informs us of the Beautiful," is made to mediate between the "Pure Intellect" and the "Moral Sense": "It holds intimate relations with either extreme" (H, XIV, 272–73).

At the beginning of *Eureka* when Poe advocates "a mental gyration on the heel" on top of Mount Aetna, he is after the same inclusive, blurred, possibly dizzying view afforded by the half-closed eye: "We need so rapid a revolution of all things about a central point of sight that, while the minutiae vanish altogether, even the more conspicuous objects become blended into one" (H, XVI, 187). It will be recalled that the same experience explains Pundita's contrary preference for balloon travel instead of a swift train ride. It should be apparent by now why the words *distinct* or *definite* and *indistinct* or *indefinite* are of such loaded significance throughout Poe's work. What is distinct is usually deceptive and what is indistinct is usually not, because what is indistinct is usually seen as a blur through the half-closed eye or, alternatively, by means of a gyration on the heel.

V

If Poe's awareness of deception motivates the strategy of fusion, the strategy of fusion accounts in large measure for the bulk of his critical principles. These principles are too well known to need rehearsing in detail. Almost everything Poe has to say about prose writing is in the review of Nathaniel Hawthorne's *Twice-Told Tales*, published in *Graham's Magazine* (Philadelphia), May, 1842. His theories about the nature of poetry are presented in the "Letter to B——," introducing the 1831 edition of Poe's poems; "The Philosophy of Composition," published in *Graham's Magazine*, April, 1846; and "The Poetic Principle," published in *Sartain's Union Magazine* (Philadelphia), October, 1850. Many of these ideas appear elsewhere in Poe's criticism, but these four pieces provide the most convenient summary of Poe's theory. Poe's stress on unity and his prescriptions concerning the maximum length of a poem or a tale are obvious corollaries of his efforts to fuse experience. Once the divisions have been dissolved, out of a previous multiformity emerges a new unity. For Poe, the unity of a poem or tale depends upon the scrupulous adherence of all its component parts to a single preconceived effect. As for length, a poem or a tale should not exceed that amount which can be read at one sitting, or its unified effect will be lost.

In the case of poetry, the single effect intended must be "the Rhythmical Creation of Beauty" (H, XIV, 275). In the truest poetry that beauty is supernal: "It is the desire of the moth for the star. It is no mere appreciation of the Beauty before us—but a wild effort to reach the Beauty above" (H, XIV, 273). As a part of its character, this beauty will be allied with strangeness and melancholy. Francis Bacon's motto—"There is no exquisite beauty which has not some strangeness in its proportion" (H, XII, 33)—is seconded by Poe on several occasions (H, XI, 176; H, XII, 33; H, XVI, 85–86). In the 1836 review of Joseph Rodman Drake's *The Culprit Fay*, Poe notes "that a species of melancholy is inseparably connected with the higher manifestations of the beautiful" (H, VIII, 296). The nature of this melancholy is apparent in this statement from "The Poetic Principle": "We find ourselves melted into tears . . . at our inability to grasp now, wholly, here on earth, at once and for ever, those divine and rapturous joys, of which *through* the poem, or *through* the music, we attain to but brief and undeterminate glimpses" (H, XIV, 274).

Poetry should scrupulously avoid "the heresy of the didactic," or the communication of truth, which is the province of the intellect, and any call to duty, which is the province of the moral sense. Similarly, the homeliness of passion is anathema to beauty and therefore to poetry. Both truth and passion, however, are "attainable in prose" (H, XIV, 198). "If a thesis is to be demonstrated, we need *prose* for its demonstration" (H, XII, 11). But "he must be theory mad beyond redemption who . . . shall still persist in attempting to reconcile the obstinate oils and waters of Poetry and Truth" (H, XIV, 272). Poe's antagonism is to didactic truth and can be explained within the rationale that I have been proposing. Given man's inherent state of deception, *that* one fact is the only truth possible. For the same reason, Poe is opposed to imitation and verisimilitude and "those who, with true Flemish perception of truth, wish to copy her [Nature's] peculiarities in disarray" (H, X, 28). This applies to all the arts except

THE RATIONALE OF DECEPTION IN POE

drama (H, XII, 118; H, XIII, 52, 113). Poe's aversion to representational truth may have been further influenced by his knowledge of "the German terms *Dichtkunst*, the art of fiction, and *Dichten*, to feign, which are used for '*poetry*' and '*to make verses*,' " and his inability to comprehend "how any truth can be conveyed by that which is in itself confessedly a lie" (H, XI, 74; H, XIII, 113).

Poe's concern that the separate parts of a plot should be indistinguishable and his belief that the highest poetic quality involves the expression of the indefinite are further corollaries of the imperative toward fusion and the consequent elimination of contours and divisions. Plot, as "properly defined, is *that in which no part can be displaced without ruin to the whole*" (H, X, 117; H, XIII, 46). Thus, allegory is to be eschewed because of its tendency to separate itself from the story line and so disrupt the essential unity. Allegory is condemned as appealing only to "our faculties of comparison" or "the fancy" and as being incapable of enforcing a truth: "One thing is clear, that if allegory ever establishes a fact, it is by dint of overturning a fiction" (H, X, 130; H, XIII, 148). However, "where the suggested meaning runs through the obvious one in a *very* profound undercurrent so as never to show itself unless *called* to the surface, there only, for the proper uses of fictitious narrative, is it available at all" (H, XIII, 148; H, XI, 68, 79, 106). Poe's example of a successful creation, in this regard, is the *Undine* (1811) of Friedrich de la Motte Fouqué, successful because the literal and the allegorical levels are practically fused. The allegory is unobtrusive and "judiciously subdued" and appears only "as a shadow or by suggestive glimpses" (H, XIII, 149). It follows that metaphor, allegory's "softened image," should only be used sparingly and that the simile is a facile device that appertains "to the fancy alone" (H, X, 68, 130).

Poe evaluated a work of art according to its indefiniteness, that is, according to the degree to which it succeeded in doing what Poe attempted to do: destroy the material world by a process of fusion. In his first published attempt to define a poem, in the "Letter to B——," Poe introduces the notion of indefiniteness:

A poem, in my opinion, is opposed to a work of science by having for its *immediate* object, pleasure not truth; to romance, by having for its object an *indefinite* instead of a *definite* pleasure, being a poem only so far as this object is attained; romance presenting perceptible images with definite, poetry with indefinite sensations, to which end music is an *essential*, since the comprehension of sweet sound is our most indefinite conception. Music, when combined with a pleasureable idea, is poetry; music without the idea is simply music; the idea without the music is prose from its very definiteness. (H, VII, xliii)

So impressed is Poe by the indefiniteness of music that he says, "For my own part, I would much rather have written the best *song* of a nation than its noblest epic" (H, X, 44). Poe has been criticized on the grounds of vagueness and obscurity by Yvor Winters, but only because Winters makes the mistake that Poe does not make and confounds "obscurity of expression with the expression of obscurity" (H, XII, 6).[12] "What is worth thinking is distinctly thought: what is distinctly thought, can, and should be distinctly expressed or should not be expressed at all" (H, XII, 6). This distinction should be borne in mind in connection with those passages of prose and poetry that Poe claims particularly to admire as ideal. In each case, it is the quality of indefiniteness that Poe praises; and the indefiniteness, in each case, is the result of a merging or fusion of normally separate elements. There are many possible examples. Four have been selected.

Poe illustrates the distinction of degree between the fancy (or the faculty of comparison) and the imagination (the source of ideality) by comparing Drake's account of the "Sylphid Queen" in *The Culprit Fay* with Percy Bysshe Shelley's description of a fairy in *Queen Mab*. The "Sylphid Queen" is composed simply of a series of similes that might be easily substituted for another series. Shelley's fairy is inextricably bound up, fused with, and part and parcel of her description:

> The Fairy's frame was slight; yon fibrous cloud
> That catches but the faintest tinge of even,
> And which the straining eye can hardly seize
> When *melting* [italics added] into eastern twilight's shadow,
> Were scarce so thin, so slight; but the fair star
> That gems the glittering coronet of morn,

12. "Edgar Allan Poe: A Crisis in the History of American Obscurantism," in Yvor Winters, *In Defense of Reason* (Denver: University of Denver Press, 1947), 234–61.

> Sheds not a light so mild, so powerful,
> As that which, bursting from the Fairy's form,
> Spread a purpureal halo round the scene,
> Yet with an undulating motion
> Swayed to her outline gracefully.   (H, VIII, 300; H, X, 64)

Here are no edges, no sharp outlines. As Poe says, "Some physical elements are used collaterally as adjuncts" (H, VIII, 301; H, X, 65). Even in The Culprit Fay, Poe finds some lines which aspire to ideality:

> The moon looks down on old Cronest,
> She mellows [italics added] the shadow of his shaggy breast,
> And seems his huge grey form to throw
> In a silver cone on the wave below;
> His sides are broken by spots of shade,
> By the walnut bow and the cedar made,
> And through their clustering branches dark
> Glimmers and dies the fire-fly's spark—
> Like starry twinkles that momently break
> Through the rifts of the gathering tempest rack.   (H, VIII, 302)

The moon, old Cronest, the trees, and the water merge into one another and so Poe is impressed. The water and the shade have the effect of breaking down the outlines.

Poe applies the same criterion to prose. He singles out Undine (1811) "as the finest romance in existence" (H, X, 37–38) for the following reasons:[13]

We may call attention to the delicacy and grace of transition from subject to subject. . . . Again, we might dwell upon the exquisite management of imagination, which is so visible in the passages where the brooks are water-spirits, and the water-spirits brooks—neither distinctly either. What can be more ethereally ideal than the frequent indeterminate glimpses caught of Kühleborn—or than his singular and wild lapses into shower and foam?—or than the evanishing of the white wagoner and his white horses into the shrieking and devouring flood?—or than the gentle melting of the passionately weeping bride into the crystal waters of the Danube? What can be more divine than the character of the soulless Undine?—what more august than her transition into the soul-possessing wife? (H, X, 38–39; H, XVI, 50–51)

13. For a full treatment of Poe's interest, see Burton R. Pollin, "Undine in the Works of Poe," Studies in Romanticism, XIV (1975), 59–74.

Poe finds Dickens capable of similar subtlety. The relationship between the grandfather and the child in "The Old Curiosity Shop" is a "most beautiful" conception: "The decrepit imbecility of a doting and confining old age, whose stern knowledge of man, and of the world it leaves behind, is now merged in the sole consciousness of receiving love and protection from that weakness it has loved and protected" (italics added; H, X, 149). But, it is "the stealthy approach of Nell to her death—her gradual sinking away on the journey to the village, so skillfully indicated rather than described . . . this whole world of mournful yet peaceful idea merging, at length, into the decease of the child Nelly, and the uncomprehending despair of the grandfather," which evinces "most distinctly the ideality of the 'Curiosity Shop' " (H, X, 154). In this connection, Poe compares "The Old Curiosity Shop" with *Undine*.

All the passages quoted above (and others that are not quoted) substantiate the argument that the expression of fusion constitutes Poe's critical yardstick. These passages are ethereal in the sense that, having fused experience, they are free of the individuated earth and have perhaps dissolved it in the process. Almost all of them could, in fact, have been written by Poe himself.

VI

Now Poe's use of the term *arabesque* can be understood, as in the 1840 title, *Tales of the Grotesque and Arabesque*. In the preface to that volume he explains, "The epithets 'Grotesque' and 'Arabesque' will be found to indicate with sufficient precision the prevalent tenor of the tales here published" but neglects to define the terms, which A. H. Quinn suggests "were derived from an article by Walter Scott, 'On the Supernatural in Fictitious Composition.' " Quinn's distinction, that "the Arabesques are the product of powerful imagination and the Grotesques have a burlesque or satirical quality," is accurate as far as it goes.[14] L. Moffit Cecil has attempted to refine our understanding of Poe's use of *arabesque*. After pointing out that Poe thought of some of his tales as arabesques as early as May, 1833, and

14. A. H. Quinn, *Edgar Allan Poe: A Critical Biography*, 289.

quoting part of the New English Dictionary definition ("strangely mixed, fantastic"), he suggests that Poe's well-known direction in the 1840 Preface—that his thesis of terror "is not of Germany but of the soul"—implies that the reader look to Arabia.[15] To support his argument, Cecil reviews the Arabian elements in Poe's tales and concludes that, because "simoon" is an Arabian word, "MS. Found in a Bottle" is an arabesque.[16]

The term arabesque with all its associations is perfectly descriptive of Poe's purpose, and consequently, Cecil's elucidation of one such associative meaning is applicable. However, Cecil's understanding of the term was not primary in Poe's mind. The word can also refer to "a musical composition with analogous continuity." If this meaning be equated with Poe's belief that the vague suggestiveness of music is man's most practical avenue to ideality, then the word arabesque and the arabesque tapestries and fixtures that adorn the chambers in the tales may be interpreted as symbolic of reality as viewed through the half-closed eye. When man learns to view reality as a continuum, the lines that separate one thing from another blur and dissolve to reveal the shifting and fluid state, the quicksand, which may allow a perception of ideal reality.[17] The arabesque designs are active symbols of Poe's efforts to melt away the rigid pattern that is imposed by man's reason. The tales that emphasize this process might appropriately be designated arabesques. Opposed to the arabesque tales are the grotesques, a word that for Poe's purposes well describes the world created by man's divided perceptions.[18] A gargoyle is a grotesque and, like man's construct of

15. L. Moffit Cecil, "Poe's Arabesque," Comparative Literature, XVIII (1966), 55–70.

16. Ibid., 65–67.

17. This interpretation is close to that proposed by Patricia C. Smith, "Poe's Arabesque," Poe Studies, VII (1974), 42–45. She writes that "the word 'arabesque' and descriptions of art forms which, though unnamed, are clearly arabesques are never used casually. Inevitably, the word is inserted in a passage to evoke the sense of impending death and to suggest that the nature of that death is some sort of dissolution into Unity. . . . The arabesque [whether the word itself is present or not] is an attempt to suggest something kinetic—the motion towards unity—in a static medium, symbolically it is always moving in the direction of a form-obliterating spiral" (45).

18. For a survey of suggested possibilities, see Lewis A. Lawson, "Poe's Conception of the Grotesque," Mississippi Quarterly, XIX (1966), 220–25; Lewis A. Lawson, "Poe and the Grotesque: A Bibliography, 1695–1965," Poe Newsletter, I (1968), 9–10; Donald H. Ross, "The Grotesque: A Speculation," Poe Studies, IV (1971), 10–11.

material reality, is composed of fragments to become a production that does not actually exist.

It has been argued at length by G. R. Thompson that the terms *arabesque* and *grotesque* are used interchangeably as near synonyms.[19] However, this view is not irreconcilable with the premise being discussed. To see truly the deceptive nature of reality is to see simultaneously the actuality. In a sense, then, the arabesque concept subsumes the grotesque. To see human reality as grotesque is to intuit simultaneously intimations of an arabesque reality. An approximate analogy would be the kind of optical illusion that appears meaningless (an odd-angled photograph of some familiar object for example) until the moment of sudden recognition. There are here two apparently distinct experiences derived from a single object. It is not surprising, therefore, that similar themes receive both grotesque and arabesque treatments. Compare, for example, the decapitating minute hand in "A Predicament" with "The Pit and the Pendulum." The situations are similar, but the effects are very different.

Correspondingly, although the terms *grotesque* and *arabesque* may refer to much the same species of artistic or architectural design, the word *grotesque* has an additional cluster of meanings, either comic or negative (which in no way align with any meanings of the word *arabesque*), when it is used to refer to the unnatural, the incongruous, and the repellent.

At the same time, it should be emphasized that Poe's impression of a unified reality is necessarily contingent, vague, and incomplete —certainly in so far as it is translatable into language. The state that is frequently invoked in Poe's work and that might appropriately be called arabesque reality is a marginal one. It designates essentially what can be described, the ideal as perceived from mundane reality. And since the appreciation of one condition depends upon the appreciation of the other, the grotesque state is also marginal, the mundane as perceived from the projected ideal reality. One can see why the ambiguity of the concepts *grotesque* and *arabesque* suited Poe's requirements and why he pointedly avoided delimiting that indefi-

19. G. R. Thompson, *Poe's Fiction: Romantic Irony in the Gothic Tales* (Madison: University of Wisconsin Press, 1973), 105–38.

niteness by any attempt at definition. Although almost every example of Poe's creative work contains elements that might be identified as either grotesque or arabesque, most of the tales and all of the poems exhibit a perceptible tendency in one direction or the other. Thus the categorizing of tales that are not more directly categorized in different ways—such as the tales of ratiocination or the mesmeric tales—into grotesques and arabesques makes pragmatic sense. In fact, a separation of all Poe's creative writings—including such groupings as the ratiocinative and mesmeric tales—occurs quite naturally in terms of these two basic tendencies.

A review of Poe's descriptions of arabesque settings supports the above interpretation. What follows, published in the *Lady's Book* for January, 1834, describes the decor of the stranger's room in "The Visionary":

Rich draperies in every part of the room trembled to the vibrations of low, melancholy music, whose unseen origin undoubtedly lay in the recesses of the red coral trellice-work which tapestried the ceiling. The senses were oppressed by mingled and conflicting perfumes, reeking up from strange Arabesque censers, which seemed actually endued with a monstrous vitality as their particolored fires writhed up and down, and around about their extravagant proportions. The rays of the rising sun poured in upon the whole, through windows formed each of a single huge pane of crimson-tinted glass, and glancing to and fro, in a thousand reflections, from curtains which rolled from their cornices like streams of molten silver, mingled at length fitfully with the artificial light, and lay weltering and subdued upon a carpet of rich, liquid-looking cloth of gold.

Here then had the hand of genius been at work.—A wilderness—a chaos of beauty was before me; a sense of dreamy and incoherent grandeur took possession of my soul, and I remained speechless. (Reconstructed from the textual variants; M, II, 157–58)

In the revised and shortened version of this passage, printed in the *Broadway Journal* in 1845 under the new title "The Assignation," the adjective *convolute* is substituted for *Arabesque* (as in the earlier *Tales of the Grotesque and Arabesque* text), presumably as a partial synonym. In either case, all the characteristics of reality, as apparent to the half-closed eye, are present in this passage. The static, distinct world becomes fluid and indistinct—even animate. Drapery moves and perfumes mingle, as does the natural light with the artificial.

The arabesque censers seem to be alive. The effect is dizzying and kaleidoscopic. This is Poe's continuum reality, the new dimension, if man would only see it. In such a state, the bounding lines between fire and water, light and dark, sight and sound disappear. The line between life and death is similarly artificial, and thus the alchemy is complete.

The stranger, a one-time "decorist," explains the process as follows in the final version of the tale: "You behold around you, it is true, a medley of architectural embellishments. The chastity of Ionia is offended by antediluvian devices, and the sphynxes of Egypt are outstretched upon carpets of gold. Yet the effect is incongruous to the timid alone. *Proprieties of place, and especially of time, are the bugbears which terrify mankind from the contemplation of the magnificent*" (italics added; M, II, 165–66). By fusing what is normally kept apart, he conquers death. The transition is made specifically through the agency of the arabesque censers, with which he is in sympathy: "Like these arabesque censers my spirit is writhing in fire ["whirling" in the original version], and the delirium of this scene is fashioning me for the wilder visions of that land of real dreams whither I am now rapidly departing" (M, II, 166).

In "Metzengerstein," the section of the "faded tapestry" depicting a horse actually does come alive. The complete tapestry, which "represented the shadowy and majestic forms of a thousand illustrious ancestors," recalls the description of the frozen frieze on Keats's Grecian urn (M, II, 21). In the course of the tale, the animate and inanimate are inextricably confused. The Baron Metzengerstein gives identity to the palace that bears his name, much as Usher is identified with his house. The horse in the stable merges with the horse in the tapestry, and the Baron is finally merged with the ancestor who murdered a member of a rival family as depicted in the tapestry. Although the "quivering tapestry" is not called an arabesque, nor is it one, it does serve the same function as a medium between fixed, grotesque deception and arabesque reality where the distinction between life and death disappears (M, II, 23).

Perhaps the clearest account of the *active* role that Poe's arabesque interiors play is to be found in the description of the bridal chamber of the Lady Rowena in "Ligeia." The narrator minutely remembers every detail of the chamber, although "there was no system, no keeping, in the fantastic display, to take hold upon the memory," and what he remembers is similar, almost point for point, to the room described in "The Visionary." It is as if the sorcery depends upon a particular conformation of details. This room is pentagonal in shape (as required for the magic of conjuration), but again light is refracted weirdly through a single pane of tinted glass: "Occupying the whole southern face of the pentagon was the sole window—an immense sheet of unbroken glass from Venice—a single pane, and tinted of a leaden hue, so that the rays of either the sun or moon, passing through it, fell with a ghastly lustre on the objects within." From a central recess in the vaulted oak ceiling "depended, by a single chain of gold with long links, a huge censer of the same metal, Saracenic ["Arabesque" in the original version] in pattern, and with many perforations so contrived that there writhed in and out of them, as if endued with a serpent vitality, a continual succession of particolored fires" (M, II, 321). The censer in the stranger's room is also "endued" with "vitality" and emits "parti-colored flames." As Richard Wilbur observes, the supporting chain apparently goes through the ceiling.[20]

The room's special character of disorientation, however, is provided by the drapery. Once again, an extended quotation is necessary to illustrate the point:

But in the draping of the apartment lay, alas! the chief phantasy of all. The lofty walls, gigantic in height—even unproportionably so—were hung from summit to foot, in vast folds, with a heavy and massive-looking tapestry— tapestry of a material which was found alike as a carpet on the floor, as a covering for the ottomans and the ebony bed, as a canopy for the bed, and as the gorgeous volutes of the curtains which partially shaded the window. The material was the richest cloth of gold. It was spotted all over, at irregular intervals, with arabesque figures, about a foot in diameter, and wrought upon the cloth in patterns of the most jetty black. *But these figures partook of the true character of the arabesque only when regarded from a single point of view.* By a contrivance now common, and indeed traceable to a very remote

20. Richard Wilbur, "The House of Poe," in Robert Regan (ed.), *Poe: A Collection of Critical Essays* (Englewood Cliffs, N.J.: Prentice-Hall, 1967), 116. Wilbur also points out that Poe's rooms lack regular corners (112).

period of antiquity, they were made changeable in aspect. To one entering the room, they bore the appearance of simple monstrosities; but upon a farther advance, this appearance gradually departed; and step by step, as the visiter [sic] moved his station in the chamber, he saw himself surrounded by an endless succession of the ghastly forms which belong to the superstition of the Norman, or arise in the guilty slumbers of the monk. The phantasmagoric effect was vastly heightened by the artificial introduction of a strong continual current of wind behind the draperies—giving a hideous and uneasy animation to the whole. (Italics added; M, II, 322)

To enter such a room is to lose equilibrium. Once the arabesque room is viewed correctly, through the half-closed eye, the original impression is seen to be a deception. The dimensions of time and space give way to a new dimension that will allow Ligeia's return from the dead. The room itself, properly perceived, is the means of her resurrection.

"The Fall of the House of Usher" provides a further example. "Familiar" decor is present in the hall: "While the objects around me—while the carvings of the ceilings, the sombre tapestries of the walls, the ebon blackness of the floors, and the phantasmagoric armorial trophies which rattled as I strode, were but matters to which, or to such as which, I had been accustomed from my infancy—while I hesitated not to acknowledge how familiar was all this—I still wondered to find how unfamiliar were the fancies which ordinary images were stirring up" (M, II, 400–401). The "Arabesque expression" of Usher's "silken hair" the narrator is unable to connect "with any idea of simple humanity" (M, II, 402). The room, in which the narrator states "I found myself," is not described as fully as the apartment in "Ligeia," but it is clearly furnished along the same lines: "The windows were long, narrow, and pointed, and at so vast a distance from the black oaken floor as to be altogether inaccessible from within. Feeble gleams of encrimsoned light made their way through the trellised panes, and served to render sufficiently distinct the more prominent objects around: *the eye, however, struggled in vain to reach the remoter angles of the chamber, or the recesses of the vaulted and fretted ceiling. Dark draperies hung upon the walls"* (italics added; M, II, 401). Clearly, the dimensions of the room shade off into space. In this tale, not just the furnishings, but the whole house is animate, its "sentience" depending upon the arrangement of the parts.

The ideal room, which Poe describes in "The Philosophy of Furniture" in *Burton's Gentleman's Magazine* (Philadelphia) for May, 1840, is in accordance with the principles of decoration exhibited in the tales, the principles of surrealist art. Poe claims that "the soul of the apartment is the carpet," although not just any carpet (M, II, 497). Regarding its pattern, "distinct grounds, and vivid circular or cycloid figures, *of no meaning*, are here Median laws. . . . Indeed, whether on carpets, or curtains, or tapestry, or ottoman coverings, all upholstery of this nature should be rigidly Arabesque" (M, II, 498). The completed room, in Poe's "mind's eye," is a confusion of crimson, gold and silver "spotted with small Arabesque devices" (M, II, 500, 502). Glitter and the excessive use of mirrors must be avoided. The light should be cool and, if possible, derive from an Argand lamp. Add crimson-tinted glass windows and an octagonal table, and the effect—of repose according to Poe—is complete.

Poe's conception is very close to the notion of a warp in space-time, a favorite device of science-fiction writers who wish to transport their characters or material objects to other times or dimensions. Accidentally, in walking from one room to another, a person may pass through a dimensional intersection and find himself in an unfamiliar world. Alternatively, a machine may effect the same transposition. Likewise, Poe's rooms may be regarded as mechanical duplications of the appropriate conditions. For Poe the perception, accidental or otherwise, of the true arabesque design is enough, immediately, to effect a transcendence of mundane existence.

Wherever Poe seeks to fuse contraries or make fixed outlines fluctuate, he is invoking the fluid arabesque state. In "The Island of the Fay," the trees, their shadows, and the stream continually slide into each other. It may be suspected that life passed from the sitter to the oval portrait in the tale of that title because of the painting's "rich golden arabesque" frame (M, II, 662). The relationship between art and the mundane world is also the subject of "The Masque of the Red Death." Prince Prospero's variously tapestried construction, with its "arabesque figures," attempts to keep the outside world and death at bay and enable the masqueraders to step into immortality (M, II, 673). That the Red Death gains an entrance may represent either Poe's reluctant recognition that art can only approximate the arabesque or merely the imperfection of Prospero's art, his unstable mix of grotesque and arabesque elements. In "The Pit and the Pendulum" the victim's experience begins when he sees "for a few moments of delirious horror, the soft and nearly imperceptible waving of the sable draperies which enwrapped the walls of the apartment" (M, II, 681–82). The changing form of the chamber in which he next finds himself is, in actual fact, the agency of his survival.

As stated earlier, the effect of Poe's arabesque settings is dizzying. Their function is to disorient man's sense of reality. Poe conveys the same sense of spiraling vertigo, rather more frighteningly, in the conclusions to "MS. Found in a Bottle," "A Descent into the Maelström," and The Narrative of A. Gordon Pym. In each case, Poe describes a fall into an abyss. But such falls—and they include falling in love—are always fortunate. The causal relationship between the subjective experience of vertigo and the perception of objective arabesque reality is circular. The one may equally depend upon the other. Poe inevitably does a better job of destroying the outlines of conventional reality than in revealing a transcendent reality. Nevertheless, in so far as he fails, he fails in attempting the impossible.

VII

Notoriously, Poe has no place in F. O. Matthiessen's American Renaissance—and this, in spite of the fact that the Gothic imagination, as Leslie Fiedler and Harry Levin suggest, is somehow an American characteristic.[21] It was, at any rate, the first form to flower. It should be remembered that the first professional American writer, Charles Brockden Brown, wrote Gothic romances and in that sense was a precursor of Poe. However, in view of the approach to Poe outlined above, it is possible to place Poe in the rather different tradition dis-

21. F. O. Matthiessen, American Renaissance (New York: Oxford University Press, 1941); Harry Levin, The Power of Blackness (New York: Alfred A. Knopf, 1958); Leslie Fiedler, Love and Death in the American Novel (rev. ed.; New York: Stein & Day, 1966).

cussed by Tony Tanner in *The Reign of Wonder,* although Tanner does not do so himself.

According to Tanner, the basic theme in American literature is how man ought to view the world, as opposed to how he actually views it. Tanner argues that this particular concern makes Transcendentalism the dominant mode in American literature. Emerson preached either a doctrine of correspondences (the intuitive glimpse of the whole through the observed particular) or, alternatively, a gradual and cumulative analysis of the parts to understand the whole. In the course of his career, Poe adopted both strategies. Also like Poe, Ralph Waldo Emerson stressed "the angle of vision." Whereas Emerson concentrated on the whole, Henry David Thoreau focused on the accumulated facts. Walter Whitman, printer and journalist, similarly interested in a new response to the external universe and the "removal of previously erected barriers and filters," adopted the persona of "Walt Whitman, an American, one of the roughs, A Kosmos" in order to incorporate all America in his own being. Emerson, Thoreau, Whitman, and Poe all wrote in the first person and all aimed at "a new and unobstructed perspective on the world."[22]

It is highly ironic that Poe should find a home among the Transcendentalists when he appears to have viewed the word as an insult. A doctoral dissertation has been written on the subject,[23] but Poe himself deals succinctly with the central contradiction in a letter to Dr. Thomas H. Chivers, dated July 10, 1844: "You mistake me in supposing I dislike the transcendentalists—it is only the pretenders and sophists among them. My own faith is indeed my own" (*Letters,* I, 259). The details of that faith, Poe claims, can be found in "Mesmeric Revelation." Poe informs J. Hunt, Jr., the following year that

22. Tony Tanner, *The Reign of Wonder: Naivety and Reality in American Literature* (Cambridge: Cambridge University Press, 1965), 65, 67; Walt Whitman, *Leaves of Grass,* ed. Sculley Bradley and Harold W. Blodgett (New York: W. W. Norton, 1973), 52.

23. Ottavio M. Casale, "Edgar Allan Poe and Transcendentalism: Conflict and Affinity" (Ph.D. dissertation, University of Michigan, 1965); Ottavio M. Casale, "Poe on Transcendentalism," *Emerson Society Quarterly,* no. 50 (1968), 85–97; Killis Campbell, *The Mind of Poe and Other Studies* (1933; rpr., New York: Russell & Russell, 1962), 14–15; Arnold Smithline, "Eureka: Poe as Transcendentalist," *Emerson Society Quarterly,* no. 39 (1965), 28.

the Bostonians are in error in supposing their "burlesque philosophy . . . to be Transcendentalism" (*Letters*, I, 284). In the review of R. H. Horne's *Orion*, he writes of "the cant of the muddle-pates who dishonor a profound and ennobling philosophy by styling themselves transcendentalists. In fact, there are few highly sensitive or imaginative intellects for which the vortex of mysticism, in any shape, has not an almost irresistable influence, on account of the shadowy confines which separate the Unknown from the Sublime" (H, XI, 253–54). Possibly, Poe's antipathy derived from various transcendental pretenders, "those who degrade an ennobling philosophy by styling themselves such" (H, XII, 5). He would certainly not have approved of their calls for a relatively formless mode of composition. But more likely, his hatred of the Boston and New England literary cliques colored his judgment, since Transcendentalism was, basically, a New England movement. In becoming associated with the pressure for the abolition of slavery, Transcendentalism would further incur the disapproval of the southern-minded, indeed racist, Poe.

The phenomenon in American literature that the Transcendentalists epiphanize Tanner locates in "the shift from the minutely scrutinized particular to the large and often vague affirmative generalization, from the material to the metaphysical, from the concrete to the mystical." *Moby-Dick* is a paradigm of this shift. "The American writer tends to start from a closely perceived sub-social, or not social reality and attempts to move towards some sort of metaphysical or philosophical generalization."[24] Of this phenomenon, Poe is unquestionably a part. Aligned with the "transparent eye-ball" of Emerson and the "sauntering eye" of Thoreau is the "half-closed eye" of Edgar Allan Poe.

24. Tanner, *The Reign of Wonder*, 337.

Part One

DECEPTION

2

The Rudimental Life

"The portrait prepared, does not in the least resemble me," Poe wrote James R. Lowell on May 28, 1844 (*Letters*, I, 254). The portrait in question was to accompany a biographical notice, subsequently written by Lowell. This apparently was a continuing problem to judge from dissimilarities among the various portraits of Poe now extant. Scarcely any two of them look alike. A similar complaint may be directed at many of the typographical portraits. Evidently, Poe was painfully conscious of the violent distortions his flesh was heir to. On June 15, 1846, Poe wrote to Joseph M. Field asking him to condemn a personal attack in the New York *Mirror* editorial by Hiram Fuller and "to do away with the false impression of my personal appearance it *may* convey, in those parts of the country where I am not individually known" (*Letters*, II, 319).

Few studies of Poe have altogether avoided his tantalizing life story, and this one is no exception. This chapter isolates those elements in Poe's career that, in combination, may have encouraged him to formulate his philosophical rationale of deception. Poe's philosophy can be related to the fundamental condition of insecurity that characterized his entire life—from birth, into the theatrical world of his parents, to the melodramatic death in the "gutter." This insecurity may be attributed to: (1) the shifting nature of circumstance (for example, the deaths of Poe's parents and his wife, Virginia), (2) Poe's personal imp of the perverse (on a number of

49

occasions Poe's susceptibility to alcohol ruined opportunities for success), (3) the chicanery and dishonesty prevalent in the world, especially in the magazine business (plagiarism and puffing), and (4) Poe's own tendencies toward subterfuge (sometimes Poe used an alias and lied about his age; he also concocted a trip to Europe).

It is true that cases of fraud, subterfuge, trickery, and chicanery do not demonstrate the state of deception Poe attributes to man's perception of reality. An instance of plagiarism or an undeserved "puff" does not corroborate Poe's conviction that the fixed, everyday world is an illusion. (Poe would have been extremely hard put to find concrete evidence of such an extreme philosophical position in any case.) Both unconsciously and deliberately, Poe experienced dishonesty as analogous to man's larger condition of deception and, accordingly, utilized episodes of chicanery as basic subject matter for almost all of the grotesques. In addition, Poe's awareness of chicanery and "puffing" (extravagant advertising) would tend to heighten his sense of insecurity. The four categories above, in fact, add up to a full definition of deception. They could be used as headings under which the details of Poe's biography might be distributed. However, the rest of this chapter will present chronologically the elements of deception that account for the greater portion of his life.

II

The world of the theater, into which Edgar Poe was born in Boston on January 19, 1809, was a precarious one. Edgar's parents, David Poe of Irish extraction and Elizabeth Arnold Poe born in England, both made a career of the stage, his father somewhat less successfully than his mother. The quality of perverseness, an Irish trait according to A. H. Quinn, and a predilection for alcohol David Poe probably passed on to Edgar. Both traits may have contributed to the possible breakup of the marriage after the birth of Edgar's sister, Rosalie, in 1810. Poe's mother died of consumption on December 8, 1811, at the age of twenty-four. There is no documentary evidence, but David Poe seems to have died shortly thereafter. A few days later, on December 26, 1811, the Richmond Theatre went up in flames causing the death of seventy-two people.[1] It is a fitting emblem of the insecurity of theatrical life and of the general fate that orphaned Edgar, practically at birth.

Shortly after Mrs. Poe's death, Rosalie was taken in by Mrs. William Mackenzie and Edgar by John and Frances Keeling Allan. John Allan of Richmond was a partner in the firm of Ellis & Allan, general merchants and exporters of tobacco. In the early years John Allan seems to have been a considerate father, notwithstanding the fact that Mrs. Allan and her sister taught Edgar subterfuges to avoid punishment and his cousin Edward Valentine taught him a love of practical jokes—both accomplishments destined to play a part in his future. The period in England from June, 1815, to June, 1820, dictated by John Allan's business ambitions, may have been unsettling; but it widened Edgar's outlook. Back in Richmond, Edgar became secretly engaged to Sarah Elmira Royster in 1825, an engagement that —according to her nostalgic account in 1875—terminated with his move to the university when "my father intercepted the letters because we were too young." This is the first concrete instance in Poe's biography of the treachery that he was later to see on all sides. While Poe was at the University of Virginia from February to December, 1826, his relationship with John Allan underwent a reversal. It seems that Poe chalked up legitimate debts, which John Allan refused to pay. His friend John Preston supports his claim that he was forced into a dishonest life and gambled because of his financial embarrassment. It is possible that Allan's relation with Poe worsened because Poe learned of Allan's habitual infidelity to his wife. In his will, Allan allowed for three illegitimate children. Be that as it may, Poe was forced to leave the University of Virginia after only ten months—no doubt with an augmented sense of betrayal and alienation.[2]

1. Arthur Hobson Quinn, Edgar Allan Poe: A Critical Biography (New York: Appleton-Century-Crofts, 1941), 18, 46, 49. Throughout this biographical account I have checked the accuracy of my sources against the "Annals" in Thomas Ollive Mabbott (ed.), Collected Works of Edgar Allan Poe (6 vols. projected; Cambridge, Mass.: Belknap Press of Harvard University Press, 1969–), I, 529–72.
2. Hervey Allen, Israfel: The Life and Times of Edgar Allan Poe (rev. ed.; New York: Farrar & Rinehart, 1934), 47–48; A. H. Quinn, Edgar Allan Poe: A Critical Biography, 91, 168–69.

Poe's activities between returning to Richmond in December, 1826, and his enlistment in the United States Army in Boston on May 26, 1827, are uncertain. In a "Memorandum" prepared in 1841 for Dr. Rufus Wilmot Griswold, Poe accounted for the interval and his early army career as follows:

Mr. A. refused to pay some of the debts of honor and I ran away from home without a dollar on a quixotic expedition to join the Greeks, then struggling for liberty. Failed in reaching Greece, but made my way to St. Petersburg in Russia. Got into many difficulties, but was extricated by the kindness of Mr. H. Middleton, the American consul at St. P. Came home safe in 1829, found Mrs. A. dead, and immediately went to West Point as a Cadet. (H, I, 345)

The entire episode is now viewed as a fabrication, although William Bittner suggests that the reference to Mr. H. Middleton lends Poe credence.[3] However, the other falsifications in the "Memorandum" —Poe's claim that he was born in January, 1811, and that he spent three years at the university where he "took the first honors," together with the omission of his career as a regular soldier—discredit the European trip (H, I, 345).

After leaving the university and having experienced the unreliability of others, Poe was beginning to recognize the expediency, or inevitability, of dishonesty. Consequently, to enter the army he adopted an alias, Edgar A. Perry, and gave his age as twenty-two, although he was actually nineteen at the time. After serving two years of the five-year enlistment period and publishing *Tamerlane and Other Poems*—"the greater part of . . . which," according to the preface, had been written when "the author had not completed his fourteenth year (M, I, 21)—Poe decided he was wasting his life and resorted to further subterfuge to ensure his discharge. Following the death of Frances Allan on February 28, 1829, John Allan was sufficiently reconciled to Poe to formally request that Poe be discharged after providing a substitute. Accordingly, Sergeant Major "Edgar A. Perry" was discharged on April 15, 1829, and a Sergeant Samual Graves was reenlisted as Poe's substitute.

Normally, procuring a substitute (usually the first willing recruit) cost twelve dollars, and this was the amount Poe led Allan to believe

3. William Bittner, *Poe: A Biography* (Boston: Little, Brown, 1962), 287.

would be required. However, the absence of the commanding officers vitiated this procedure. Poe explained what actually happened in a letter to Allan dated July 15, 1829, and a further letter dated July 26, 1829: "As I told you it would only cost me $12 I did not wish to make you think me imposing upon you—so upon a substitute, offering for $75—I gave him $25 and gave him my note of hand for the balance—when you remitted me $100—thinking I had more than I should want, I thought it my best opportunity of taking up my note —which I did" (Letters, I, 25). The matter came to light when Poe, on July 15, 1829, asked for more money. His cousin Edward Mosher stole forty-six dollars (so Poe claimed), presumably all that remained of the hundred-dollar remittance:

I will explain the matter clearly—A cousin of my own (Edward Mosher) robbed me at Beltzhoover's Hotel while I was asleep in the same room with him of all the money I had with me (about 46 $) of which I recovered $10— by searching his pockets the ensuing night, when he acknowledged the theft —I have been endeavouring in vain to obtain the balance from him—he says he has not got it and begs me not to expose him—& for his wife's sake I will not. I have a letter from him referring to the subject, which I will show you on arriving in Richmond. (Letters, I, 22)

The letter from Edward Mosher, if it ever existed, is now lost. There is something decidedly curious about the whole episode. How did this obscure cousin of Poe's spend the money within so short a time? I would suggest that Poe concocted the story to cover some unknown transgression of his own. A forgetful, if not dishonest, trait in Poe is suggested by his letter to Allan of July 26, 1829, in which Poe mentioned the loss of forty-six dollars. If, as stated in the earlier letter, he recovered ten dollars, he only lost thirty-six dollars. It is worth stressing that Poe seems to have been perfectly capable of the double-dealing he was so eager to attribute to others.

Poe left the regular army with the intention of becoming an officer cadet at West Point, but not before publishing Al Aaraaf, Tamerlane and Minor Poems in December, 1829. In October or November, 1829, he wrote to John Neal about this volume of poems, repeating his customary lie: "the greater part written before I was fifteen" (Letters, I, 32). (On another occasion, he lied even more blatantly about the composition of Al Aaraaf.) Poe was beginning to create the legend of child prodigy and mistreated genius, which has bedeviled so many of his biographers. Geoffrey Rans notes of his persona of le poète maudit that "this deception by an expert literary practical joker, the perpetrator of 'The Balloon Hoax,' the inventor of 'Hop-Frog,' has defeated, in varying degrees, all his biographers."[4]

Having entered West Point in June, 1830, Poe decided almost immediately that he wanted to leave. But Allan, having remarried, was no longer on good terms with Poe and refused him both money and permission to leave West Point. Apparently, Allan had discovered that Poe still owed money to his substitute, Sergeant Graves. The case against Poe seems very black indeed. Unless he owed Graves money for other reasons, Poe's statements in the letters of June 25 and July 26, 1829, that he paid Graves the fifty dollars owing are further lies. Consequently, Allan resolved to sever all relations with Poe, who—ever resourceful—attempted to transfer the guilt and to obligate Allan by the following distortion of fact in a letter written on January 3, 1831:

> Did I, when an infant, sollicit [sic] your charity and protection, or was it of your own free will, that you volunteered your services on my behalf? It is well known to respectable individuals in Baltimore, and elsewhere, that my Grandfather (my natural protector at the time you interposed) was wealthy, and that I was his favourite child—But the promises of adoption, and liberal education which you held forth to him in a letter which is now in possession of my family, induced him to resign all care of me into your hands. (Letters, I, 39)

Much later, on July 14, 1839, Poe passed this bit of "information" to George W. Poe and attributed to Allan "offers of reconciliation" that he never made (Letters, II, 683). Subsequently, Poe secured a court-martial, in which he was charged with "Gross neglect of duty" and "Disobedience of Orders." He was found guilty on all charges, and his dismissal took effect after March 6, 1831.[5]

Perhaps beginning in the spring of 1831 until the middle of 1835,

4. Geoffrey Rans, Edgar Allan Poe (Edinburgh and London: Oliver & Boyd, 1965), 1.
5. A. H. Quinn, Edgar Allan Poe: A Critical Biography, 173. Poe's strategy in the Graves affair can perhaps be explained, if not exonerated, in terms analogous to Jean Paul Sartre's defense of Saint Genet (Paris: Gallimard, 1952). Poe acted dishonestly because, given the way of the world, he was expected to act accordingly.

Poe lodged in Baltimore with his aunt, Maria Clemm; her daughter, Virginia; his paternal grandmother (who died in 1835); and his brother by his father's first marriage, William Henry Poe (who died shortly after Poe's arrival). During this time Poe experimented with the short story, having won the Baltimore *Saturday Visitor* contest in October, 1833, with "MS. Found in a Bottle." John Allan died on March 27, 1834, leaving his second wife, Mrs. Louisa Allan, to testify of Poe, "All I heard of him from those who had lived with him was a tissue of ingratitude, fraud, and deceit." It must be admitted there is some truth in this judgment.[6]

III

For ten years, from July, 1835, to January, 1846, Poe was embroiled in the frenetic, cutthroat milieu of the literary magazine—first in Richmond, then in Philadelphia, and finally in New York. The chicanery that Poe saw operating on all sides has been documented by Perry Miller and Sidney P. Moss.[7] Moss presents Poe in the role of a literary reformer, forced upon occasion to adopt the dubious practices of his opponents. His principal antagonist was Lewis Gaylord Clark, the hub of the New York clique and the editor of the *Knickerbocker Magazine*. By puffing their own members' work and excluding or damning the writing of outsiders, the New York clique used the *Knickerbocker Magazine* to perpetuate its own influence. Consequently, there was a bias in Boston and New York against the South and the West. A further injustice, against which Poe fought, was the lack of an international copyright. Because publishers preferred to reprint English books without copyright costs, it was almost impossible for an American writer to make a living. On the other hand, the lack of an international copyright enabled a British magazine, *Bentley's Miscellany*, to pirate some of Poe's stories.

During this period, in terms of the possible categories of deception, Poe's own perversity, his masochistic tendency to act in his own worst interest, and—not surprisingly—the chicanery and dis-

6. A. H. Quinn, *Edgar Allan Poe: A Critical Biography*, 206.
7. Perry Miller, *The Raven and the Whale: The War of Words and Wit in the Era of Poe and Melville* (New York: Harcourt Brace, 1956); Sidney P. Moss, *Poe's Literary Battles* (Durham, N.C.: Duke University Press, 1963).

honesty prevalent in the world appear to predominate. In the early period of Poe's life, the shifting nature of circumstance and Poe's own tendencies toward subterfuge loomed large. However, at the end of the 1835–1846 period, Poe's personal dishonesty once again came to the fore.

Poe joined the Richmond *Southern Literary Messenger* in July or August, 1835, and in December the publisher, Thomas Willis White, made him editor. (On May 16, 1836, Poe, then aged twenty-seven, married his cousin Virginia, who was thirteen. The period of his marriage practically coincides with his period in the magazine business. Virginia died one year after the expiration of the *Broadway Journal.*) Poe had not been editor long before he informed his employer of the following instance of dishonesty, in a letter dated May 30, 1835:

I suppose you have heard about Wm Gwynn Jones of this place, late Editor of the Gazette. He was detected in purloining letters from the Office to which the Clerks were in the habit of admitting him familiarly. He acknowledged the theft of more than $2000 in this way at different times. He probably took even more than that, and I am quite sure that on the part of the Clerks themselves advantage was taken of his arrest to embezzle double that sum. I have been a loser myself to a small amount. (*Letters*, I, 59)

But Poe's real animus was directed at literary dishonesty. Before long, in November, 1835, the publication of the extravagantly puffed *Norman Leslie* by Theodore Sedgewick Fay, darling of the *Knickerbocker* fraternity, gave Poe an opportunity to expose the machinations behind the scenes and initiate his "literary battles." Undeserved reputation, chicanery, favoritism, and especially plagiarism never failed to provoke Poe's wrath and provided evidence for his belief in human gullibility. On the other hand, passages and books dealing with the theme of deception were invariably cited with approval.

On the subject of plagiarism, Poe believed that the "Moon-Hoax" article by Richard Adams Locke in the New York *Sun* newspaper (which Locke edited) was based on his own hoax, "Hans Pfaal—a Tale," which had appeared a few weeks earlier in the June, 1835, issue of the *Messenger*. But in the words of a contemporary, Lewis Clark (at Locke's request), concocted the story: "Clark was the real inventor of the incidents, the imaginative part, while to Locke was entrusted the ingenious task of unfolding the discoveries."[8] Was Clark, then, the plagiarist? In the "Literati" article on Locke, written in 1846, Poe rehearsed the incident and claimed that, after reading the "Moon Story," he "wrote an examination of its claims to credit, showing distinctly its fictitious character, but was astonished at finding that I could obtain few listeners, so really eager were all to be deceived" (H, XV, 129).

The remaining element of deception in the period of Poe's association with the Messenger concerns the circumstances of his resignation. Although never an alcoholic, on occasion he seems to have sought relief in liquor. This came to White's attention and caused him to dismiss Poe in September, 1835, and again in September, 1836, although he was reinstated almost immediately both times. The final rift came late in 1836. Poe ceased to be editor on January 3, 1837, and his "Valedictory" appeared in the issue of the Messenger for that month. Having raised "the circulation of the paper from about five hundred to thirty-five hundred copies," Poe found himself without a job.[9] Such reversals were characteristic of his career.

During this time Poe was also faced with money problems. Poe's claim against the United States on behalf of Maria Clemm, whose father, General David Poe, loaned forty thousand dollars to the state of Maryland, failed, as did his plan to help Maria Clemm open a boardinghouse. Poe moved to Philadelphia in 1838; and he collaborated in the publication of The Conchologist's First Book in 1839, "the only volume of Poe," Quinn notes, "that went into a second edition in the United States, during Poe's lifetime."[10] Unfortunately, it involved Poe in the charge of plagiarism because the work was compiled from material in The Conchologist's Text-Book by Captain Thomas Brown and Professor Thomas Wyatt's A Manual of Conchology. However, Wyatt, one of the collaborators in fact, had given his consent; and Poe, with some justice, stated that the accusation "is totally false" (Letters, II, 343).

Still in Philadelphia, Poe began his association with Burton's

8. Quoted in Moss, Poe's Literary Battles, 88.
9. A. H. Quinn, Edgar Allan Poe: A Critical Biography, 259.
10. Ibid., 277.

Gentleman's Magazine in May, 1839. The owner, William E. Burton, an English actor, accepted Poe as coeditor. At this time the first signs of Poe's paranoid tendencies made an appearance. In a letter to Joseph Evans Snodgrass dated October 7, 1839, Poe blamed his cousin Neilson Poe for inciting prejudicial feelings toward him and went on to tell Snodgrass that he valued his friendship, especially "in these days of double dealing" (*Letters*, I, 120). On the credit side, the *Tales of the Grotesque and Arabesque* appeared in December, 1839. Notwithstanding Rufus Griswold's account of the breakup between Poe and Burton (which Griswold supported by means of forgeries), their parting was not amicable. Charles W. Alexander, who published the journal, spoke of Poe as having "faults seriously detrimental to his own interests."[11] (This suggests that, once again, Poe's imp of the perverse manifested itself in the form of spirits.) Charging that Burton had shortchanged him, Poe, in a nonextant letter, resigned in June, 1840.

The deceptive nature of the material world frequently forced Poe into the compensatory world of his dreams. Virginia appears to have been part of that latter world, as does Poe's hope of founding an ideal literary magazine to be called the *Penn Magazine*. A prospectus for this journal appeared in the Philadelphia *Saturday Courier* on June 13, 1840.) As coeditor of *Burton's* and as one of the editors of *Graham's Magazine* after February, 1841 (George Rex Graham, owner of the *Casket*, having bought Burton's journal and merged his paper with it), Poe constantly sought means of turning the projected *Penn Magazine* into a reality. Indeed, he never abandoned the dream, although the magazine never materialized. The only development was the change of title in April, 1844, to the *Stylus*, since *Penn Magazine* "was a name somewhat too local in its suggestions."[12] Likewise, Poe's plans for a new collection of his work in 1842, called *Phantasy-Pieces*, never reached fruition. Then in January, 1842, Virginia Poe ruptured a blood vessel in her throat while singing. Repeatedly, Poe's dreamlife and his ambitions were undercut by the treacherous world of fact. In April, 1842, Poe resigned the editorship of *Gra-*

11. *Ibid.*, 297.
12. *Ibid.*, 375.

ham's and was succeeded by Rufus Wilmot Griswold. Apparently, Poe was dissatisfied with his salary and had expectations of securing a government position in the customs house at Philadelphia, expectations that turned out to be ill-founded. The failure of Poe's plans for the *Stylus* and his efforts to secure the government appointment (the latter to finance the former) provided experiences that confirmed his belief in the unreliable nature of mundane existence.

While editor of *Graham's Magazine,* Poe published assorted attacks on the malpractices of the magazine world; his fullest statement on the matter was in a review of the satire, *The Quacks of Helicon* by L. O. Wilmer. Poe tended to suspect dishonesty on insufficient evidence, almost as if deception were a universal principle. This may be illustrated by his efforts to discredit one Richard Bolton, who solved a cryptogram Poe believed only he could decipher. The cryptogram was submitted by Dr. Failey, in answer to Poe's challenge that he could decipher any cryptogram. Poe solved it and then published the cryptogram, offering a reward to anyone who shall read it *"with the key,* and I am pretty sure that no one will be found to do it" (H, I, 173). Bolton succeeded, and in a letter dated November 18, 1841, Poe grudgingly congratulated him. However, in a letter to Frederick W. Thomas dated November 26, 1841, Poe denied Bolton's claim by arguing that Bolton's letter was dated at a period "fully a month after the *preparation* of the number containing the answer by myself. He pretends not to have seen my solution— but his own contains internal evidence of the fact" (*Letters,* I, 190). Poe appears to be lying here. After studying the matter, William F. Friedman concludes: "Internal evidence in Bolton's solution . . . serves to indicate conclusively that his work was accomplished without the key."[13] There is something almost psychotic about Poe's inability to believe Bolton's claim.

Poe left Philadelphia for New York on April 6, 1844, and joined the staff of the New York *Evening Mirror* in October, 1844. (The pub-

13. William F. Friedman, "Edgar Allan Poe, Cryptographer," *American Literature,* VIII (1936), 276; W. T. Bandy, "Poe's Solution of the 'Frailey Land Office Cipher,' " *PMLA,* LXVIII (1935), 1240–41.

lication of "The Raven" by "Quarles"[14] in the *Evening Mirror* of January 29, 1845, was the major event of Poe's early struggles in New York.) Gradually, he transferred his allegiance from the *Mirror* to the *Broadway Journal* (founded in January, 1845) and joined its editorial department on February 22, 1845. Poe also transferred to the *Broadway Journal* a quarrel with Henry Wadsworth Longfellow (favorite of the cliquish *Knickerbocker* and *North American Review*) begun in the *Mirror* for January 13 and 14, 1845. Poe had reviewed Longfellow's *The Waif*, a collection of poems, including only one, the "Proem," by Longfellow. In Poe's opinion, the similarity between "The Death-Bed" by Thomas Hood, and a poem in Rufus Griswold's *Poets and Poetry of America* suggested that "somebody is a thief" and that the entire collection "is infected with a *moral taint*" in that "there *does* appear . . . a very careful avoidance of all American poets who may be supposed especially to interfere with the claims of Mr. Longfellow. These men Mr. Longfellow can continuously *imitate* (*is* that the word?) and yet never even incidentally commend" (H, XII, 42, 44). Nathaniel Parker Willis, editor of the *Mirror*, published a disclaimer of responsibility for Poe's review on January 20, 1845. This disclaimer prefaced the letter by a Mr. H. (George S. Hillard), a friend of Longfellow's, supporting him. Poe responded directly in a February 15, 1845, article entitled "Imitation—Plagiarism." He then continued his attack on Longfellow by openly accusing him of plagiarism in a lecture, "Poets and Poetry of America," delivered before the New York Society Library on February 28, 1845.[15]

On the following day, an article by "Outis" (Nobody) appeared in the *Mirror* in defense of Longfellow. Outis made an extremely cogent case, pointing out that "identities" between poems do not necessarily constitute evidence of plagiarism and, as an example, deduced

14. Poe's other aliases included Henri Le Rennet, Thaddeus Purley, and Littleton or Lyttleton Barry. He used the mailing name Le Rennet at one point to deceive his creditors. See Allen, *Israfel*, 161, and Bittner, *Poe: A Biography*, 48. For the circumstances of Purley's inception, see Allen, *Israfel*, 499–501. In reissuing some of his old stories, Poe adopted the pseudonym, Littleton Barry. See Bittner, *Poe: A Biography*, 209.

15. Moss, *Poe's Literary Battles*, 156; for the identification of Longfellow's friend, Mr. H., see R. Baird Shuman, "Longfellow, Poe and *The Waif*," *PMLA*, LXXVI (1961), 155–56.

eighteen similarities between "The Raven" and an anonymous poem, "The Bird of the Dream." Poe replied in a series of articles in the *Broadway Journal* for March 8, 15, 22, and 29, 1845. In spite of the lucidity and reasonableness of Outis' statements, Poe spoke of Outis' "desperation . . . to make out a case," repeatedly addressed himself to positions which Outis did not intend, and variously distorted his meaning (H, XII, 53). For example, Outis claimed to "have been disgusted with the wholesale mangling of victims without rhyme or reason." Poe chose to interpret the last phrase adjectivally, rather than as intended, adverbially: "The victims without rhyme or reason are precisely the victims that ought to be mangled" (H, XII, 83). Furthermore, Poe had the effrontery to complain of "the complacency with which Outis *supposes* me to make a certain charge and then vituperates me for his own absurd supposition" (H, XII, 87–88). The large amount of space that Poe devoted to his replies to Outis' single article suggests the desperation of Poe's position. Moreover, the replies employ a species of chicanery very much like that purportedly under attack. Of course, if "Outis" was Poe, as is not unlikely, a rather different kind of duplicity is at work.[16]

Longfellow, after Poe's death, said of him, "The harshness of his criticism I never attributed to anything but the irritation of a sensitive nature, chafed by an indefinite sense of wrong."[17] What we know of Poe confirms this verdict, as does Poe's statement in a letter to Sarah Helen Whitman dated November 14, 1848: "Is it any wonder that I was driven *mad* by the intolerable sense of wrong?" (*Letters*, II, 408). Accordingly, Poe continued uncovering plagiarisms, particularly in his "Marginalia," including a plagiarism from William Ellery Channing in the *New Monthly* and one by William W. Lord from Poe's "Haunted Palace" and "Lenore" (H, XVI, 143–44, 150–52).

By July 12, 1845, after complex machinations Poe became sole

16. Thomas Ollive Mabbott four times avers that "Outis" was Poe in Mabbott, *Collected Works*, I, 372, 557n5; III, 1378–79, 1387n17. As Mabbott points out, the unfinished satire entitled "A Reviewer Reviewed" by Walter G. Bowen (alias Poe), first published in its entirety in the *Collected Works*, III, 1378–86, tends to confirm this identification.
17. Quoted in Moss, *Poe's Literary Battles*, 189.

editor of the *Broadway Journal*. Other complications followed. In a letter dated August 15, 1845, addressed to Laughton Osborn, Poe denied having written an article adversely criticizing Osborn's "The Confessions of a Poet" and cited a similar "misconception" concerning an attack on Fitz-Greene Halleck's *Alnwick Castle* (H, I, 294). Apparently, James R. Lowell had written the review of *Alnwick Castle* and arranged to have it published anonymously, so "that the odium would inevitably fall upon myself" (H, I, 294). But internal evidence suggests that Poe *was* the author of the article Osborn complained of.[18] Once again, Poe was perfectly capable of falsifying the account.

The example par excellence of Poe's ability to lie blatantly concerns the Boston Lyceum "hoax," one of the three events that, in Moss's words, "combined to cause Poe's downfall as a critic."[19] (The other two were his relations with Mrs. Frances Sargent Osgood and the publication of "The Literati.") On October 16, 1845, Poe read "Al Aaraaf" before the bewildered and dwindling audience of the Boston Lyceum. In a statement published on November 1 in the *Broadway Journal*, retaliating the hostile criticisms of Miss Walter and others, Poe explained that, in view of the nature of "an audience of Transcendentalists . . . it could scarcely be supposed that we would put ourselves to the trouble of composing for the Bostonians anything in the shape of an *original* poem" but instead read a juvenile production, published "before we had fairly completed our tenth year" (H, XIII, 11–12). Poe was especially arrogant and rude toward Miss Walter, at the same time distorting her case:

Miss Walters (the Syren!) has seen cause, we find, to recant all the ill-natured little insinuations she has been making against us (mere white-lies —she need not take them so much to heart) and is now overwhelming us with apologies [untrue]—things which we have never yet been able to withstand. She defends our poem on the ground of its being "juvenile," and we think the more of her defence because she herself has been juvenile so long as to be a judge of juvenility. . . . You are a delightful creature and your heart is in the right place—would to Heaven that we could always say the same thing of your wig! (H, XIII, 8–9)

18. Ostrom cites the evidence (*Letters*, I, 294–95).
19. Moss, *Poe's Literary Battles*, 190.

Clearly, Poe is carrying his theoretical proposition—that truth is impossible—into practice: the external world can be distorted and continually reinterpreted to suit present needs.

Poe is hypocritical when he complains that others do the same reinterpreting of reality; for example, when he speaks of a foreigner's estimation of American literature: "He is not in condition to consider or to comprehend the innumerable petty arts by which, in America, a dexterous quack may force even the most contemptible work into notoriety and consequent circulation. The foreigner's opinions, and through him the opinions of his countrymen, are thus in danger of being based (at least for a time) upon a foundation, for which 'frothy' is far too solid—far too respectable a term" (H, XIII, 16). But it is the essential frothiness of the foundations of reality that makes one estimate of a work of literature every bit as fallacious as another. The double-bind nature of Poe's position is plain: while holding to an ideal, fluid, arabesque concept of reality, his operations in the everyday world and his own systematized and logical habits of thought compelled him to formulate ordered judgments. Torn between the two positions, a schizophrenic breakdown might have been a logical outcome, had not death intervened.

A decline in Poe's objectivity may be related to the extent of his now-frequent recourse to the easy alternative of name-calling. The inhabitants of Boston, or "Frogpondium," are dismissed as "transcendental vagabonds," and the North American Review (Boston) is referred to as the "Down East Review" (H, I, 254; H, XIII, 9, 15). Poe's reply to a Harbinger review of "The Raven" exemplifies his growing paranoid tendencies: " 'The Harbinger,' edited by 'the Brook-Farm Phalanx,' is, beyond doubt, the most reputable organ of the Crazyites" (H, XIII, 27). However, Miss Walter had the last word when she wrote of Poe on May 5, 1846: "This same individual is famous for indulging in gross falsehoods, and these have become so common with him that whenever seen in print they are ever met by the reader with the simple exclamation, Poh! Poe!"[20] Truly, Poe found himself in a double-bind situation. In exposing the "truth" about the "chicanery" of the publishing world, he was invalidating

20. Ibid., 207.

his conception of reality, whereas in falsifying or manipulating events, he was acting in accordance with his conception of reality.

IV

Poe's hopes of raising enough money to continue the publication of the Broadway Journal, like so many of his hopes, were ill-founded. The Journal expired on January 3, 1846. In May or June of that year Poe, Virginia, and Maria Clemm moved into a cottage at Fordham, thirteen miles from New York. It was at this retreat that a scandal, brewing throughout 1845, finally culminated.

Poe had met Mrs. Frances Sargent Locke Osgood in March, 1845, at a literary salon. They engaged in a poetic flirtation in the pages of the Broadway Journal, and Mrs. Osgood wrote him letters. During her absence Mrs. Elizabeth Frieze Lummis Ellet, another literary lady, addressed a flirtatious poem to Poe. He published amorous poetry by both women in the same issue of the Broadway Journal. Through Virginia, Mrs. Ellet discovered Mrs. Osgood's letters to Poe and proceeded to circulate malicious gossip. Mrs. Osgood denied the rumors and rebuked Mrs. Ellet in a poem published in the Broadway Journal, December 20, 1845. Mrs. Osgood's husband demanded that Mrs. Ellet apologize. Instead, Mrs. Ellet wrote a letter to Mrs. Osgood in which she blamed Poe for the whole matter: "The letter shown me by Mrs. Poe must have been a forgery." However, Mrs. Ellet continued slandering Mrs. Osgood (and Poe), "even as late as 1849, a year before her death."[21]

Friends of the two women asked for the return of Mrs. Osgood's letters. Aware that Mrs. Ellet was behind the affair and "stung to madness," Poe said that Mrs. Ellet should worry about her own compromising letters to him (Letters, II, 407). Whereupon, Mrs. Ellet demanded that her brother, William M. Lummis, make Poe produce the incriminating letters or declare himself a slanderer. Mr. Lummis, pistol in hand, searched for Poe. Poe asked Thomas Dunn English, editor of the New York Aristidean, for a pistol. English refused with the advice that Poe's "surest defence was a retraction of unfounded

21. Ibid., 217–18.

charges."[22] In the ensuing fistfight with English, Poe seems to have lost. And so the matter rested, but a letter written to Mrs. Whitman more than two years later on November 24, 1848, indicates that Poe continued to remember the experience: "No sooner will Mrs. E. hear of my proposals to yourself, than she will set in motion every conceivable chicanery to frustrate me. . . . You will be sure to receive anonymous letters so skillfully contrived as to deceive the most sagacious. . . . Mrs. Osgood . . . was for a long time completely blinded by the arts of this fiend. . . . My poor Virginia was continually tortured (although not deceived) by her anonymous letters, and on her death-bed declared that Mrs. E. had been her murderer" (*Letters*, II, 407–408).

In May, 1846, the first installment of "The Literati of New York City: Some honest Opinions at Random respecting their Authorial Merits, with occasional Words of Personality" appeared in *Godey's Lady's Book*. There were six monthly installments of "critical gossip," as Poe called them (H, I, 332). Each "Literati" portrait consists of a list of the writer's works with comments and a phrenological evaluation. Of the thirty-eight writers considered, only Charles Anthon, Freeman Hunt, Fitz-Greene Halleck, Evert A. Duyckinck, Christopher Pearse Cranch, Sarah Margaret Fuller, Catherine M. Sedgewick, and Richard Adams Locke have commendable foreheads. Poe's defense of Charles Anthon takes a characteristic turn: "These attacks upon the New York professor are to be attributed to a *clique* of pedants in and about Boston, gentlemen envious of his success, and whose own compilations are noticeable only for the singular patience and ingenuity with which their dovetailing chicanery is concealed from the *public* eye" (H, XV, 36). On the whole, however, these articles contain more attack than defense. Charles F. Briggs, for example, "has never composed in his life three consecutive sentences of grammatical English. He is grossly uneducated" (H, XV, 22). Lewis Gaylord Clark, "known principally as the twin brother of the late *Willis* Gaylord Clark . . . is noticeable for nothing. . . . His

22. See the account in the New York *Evening Mirror*, June 23, 1846, quoted in Moss, *Poe's Literary Battles*, 220.

forehead is, phrenologically, bad—round and what is termed 'bullety' " (H, XV, 114, 115, 116).

The most damaging "Literati" portrait was of Thomas Dunn English. English's role in the Ellet affair had not endeared him to Poe, who accused him of plagiarism and an ignorance that he absurdly tried to conceal: "No one of any generosity would think the worse of him for getting private instruction." In conclusion Poe wrote, "I do not personally know Mr. English" (H, XV, 66). In his scurrilous reply, which appeared in the New York *Morning Telegraph* and the New York *Evening Mirror*, English attributed this lie to the "severe treatment he received at my hands for brutal and dastardly conduct." A series of charges followed, most of them based on Poe's behavior under the influence of liquor; but two of them were more serious: (1) Poe had obtained a sum of money from him, under false pretenses, for the *Broadway Journal*, and (2) Poe, by his conduct, had virtually admitted the truth of an accusation of forgery, leveled against him by a "merchant of this city." Poe prepared a reply, denying the two principal charges, to be published in *Godey's Lady's Book*; but Louis A. Godey, fearing a libel suit, sent the reply to a paper of small circulation, the Philadelphia *Spirit of the Times*. Of that reply Poe later admitted, "The peevishness was all 'put on' as a part of my argument," without, apparently, realizing that a genuine argument is not in any way "put on" (*Letters*, II, 355). Poe initiated a libel suit against the editor and owner of the New York *Mirror* on July 23, 1846. A month earlier (June 27), Poe had written to Henry B. Hirst, asking him to furnish evidence against English and stating, "I gave E. a flogging which he will remember to the day of his death—and, luckily, in the presence of witnesses. He thinks to avenge himself by lies—by [sic] I shall be a match for him by means of simple truth" (*Letters*, II, 322). If Poe was referring to the fistfight, he was the one who was probably lying. Although rumors of Poe's insanity were steadily growing, he won his libel suit on February 17, 1847, and was awarded $225.06 in damages.[23]

23. For English's charges, see Moss, *Poe's Literary Battles*, 228. The entire matter is fully documented in Sidney P. Moss, *Poe's Major Crisis: His Libel Suit and New York's Literary World* (Durham, N.C.: Duke University Press, 1970).

Any pleasure he might have felt at the decision was nullified by Virginia's death eighteen days earlier on January 30, 1847. In a letter to George W. Eveleth dated January 4, 1847, Poe referred to the recurrent alternation of Virginia's illnesses and recoveries as "the horrible never-ending oscillation between hope & despair which I could not longer have endured without the total loss of reason" (Letters, II, 356). This "oscillation," or lack of stability, characterizes the movement of much of his fiction, particularly "The Pit and the Pendulum" and The Narrative of A. Gordon Pym.

For the rest of his life, Poe made vain attempts to reanchor his existence, mostly through attachments to Mrs. Sarah Helen Whitman, Mrs. Annie L. Richmond, and Mrs. Elmira Royster Shelton. In his last years, Poe seems to have fully experienced the arabesque reality that he had hitherto only sensed. "My whole existence has been the merest Romance," he told Jane E. Locke on May 19, 1848 (Letters, II, 366). From one point of view, Eureka, published by Putnam in June, 1848, may represent Poe's final inability to face arabesque reality, which he now replaces with a fixed construct of his own mind. Indeed, is it possible that Poe compensated for the death of Virginia, the only being who gave his life meaning, by claiming to solve the riddle of creation—a final, futile, paranoid gesture? There is no doubt that Poe saw Mrs. Whitman, a widow whom he hoped to marry, in extravagantly idealized terms. The theory of Poe's impotence might explain why he idealized women, why he married Virginia when she was thirteen, and why (if Marie Bonaparte is accurate) he sabotaged his hopes of marriage to Mrs. Whitman.[24] Poe certainly had no children by Virginia.

His first advances to Mrs. Whitman were made by letter, under the assumed name Edward S. J. Grey.[25] Mrs. Whitman, however, saw through the deceit. On October 1, 1848, Poe wrote Mrs. Whitman the longest extant letter of his career. He referred (conveniently for his

24. Joseph Wood Krutch, Edgar Allan Poe: A Study in Genius (New York: Alfred A. Knopf, 1926); Marie Bonaparte, The Life and Works of Edgar Allan Poe: A Psycho-Analytic Interpretation, trans. John Rodker (London: Imago Publishing Co., 1949). Bonaparte discusses Mrs. Whitman on p. 175.
25. Just before his death, Poe wrote to Maria Clemm, asking her to reply "to E. S. J. Grey Esqre" (Letters, II, 461).

biographers) to "our walk in the cemetery," "when I spoke to you of what I felt saying that I loved now for the *first* time" and affirmed that "if, throughout some long, dark summer night, I could but have held you close . . . then indeed you would have seen that I have been far from attempting to deceive you in this respect" (*Letters*, II, 383). In all probability, Poe's love for Virginia had been genuine and, thus, he was deceiving Mrs. Whitman. Poe, on the other hand, had thought that Mrs. Whitman was still married. Having been "undeceived in this respect," he elaborated on the nature of his feelings for her (*Letters*, II, 384). She elicited in him "a shuddering sixth sense, vaguely compounded of fear, ecstatic happiness and a wild inexplicable sentiment that resembled nothing so nearly as the consciousness of guilt," a sense akin to the extra sense of combination described in "MS. Found in a Bottle" and "The Conversation of Eiros and Charmion," which reveals arabesque reality. "I felt that nothing hereafter was to be doubted, and lost myself, for many weeks, in one continuous, delicious dream, where all was a vivid yet indistinct bliss" (*Letters*, II, 385). (This is the continuum reality.) "Undefinable sorrow," at Mrs. Whitman's silence, gave way to the consolation that "she will indistinctly feel who is her correspondent" (*Letters*, II, 386). "Tremulous ecstasy" gave way to a "praeternatural thrill." As she "moved to and fro . . . restlessly" about the room, very much like an animated arabesque tapestry, "it was with no merely human senses that I either saw or heard you" (*Letters*, II, 387). Poe's talk about their difference in age as being of no concern in view of the "soul love" that they shared is strikingly reminiscent of the narrator in "The Spectacles." He concluded by expressing his willingness to "go down *with* you into the night of the Grave," a sentiment rich in implications for the psychologically minded, as was his opening remark in his next letter to Helen: "Oh God! how I now curse the impotence of the pen" (*Letters*, II, 390, 391).

In that second letter of October 18, 1848, Poe recounted his life history, with some falsifications as usual. Through "a Quixotic sense of the honorable . . . in early youth, I deliberately threw away from me a large fortune, rather than endure a trivial wrong. It was for this that, at a later period, I did violence to my own heart, and married for another's happiness, where I knew that no possibility of my own existed" (Letters, II, 393). Poe had no hope of a large fortune from John Allan, and he clearly married Virginia for his own happiness. Visions of marriage to Helen in terms of regal splendor, on physical contact "melted sweetly away in the sunshine of a love ineffable" to reveal a dream cottage, "which no human being could ever pass without an ejaculation of wonder at its strange, weird, and incomprehensible yet most simple beauty" (Letters, II, 396). Unquestionably such description indicates that Helen Whitman, like the arabesque designs and vortices of Poe's fiction, provided the means by which Poe convinced himself of a supernal reality.

However, when Poe next referred to a dream cottage (November 16, 1848), it was to be located in Westford or Lowell, so he could be near Mrs. Annie Richmond. Apparently, Mrs. Whitman had consented to an engagement, conditional upon his abstaining from drink. Poe continued to drink, and the marriage did not take place. Nevertheless, it was Helen Whitman who wrote the first book in Poe's defense. After the broken engagement, Poe turned immediately to Mrs. Richmond. Quinn states: "That he loved 'Annie' as a man loves a woman, while he loved Helen Whitman as a poet loves a poetess, is clear."[26] But a man does not usually refer to the woman he loves as his sister: "my pure virtuous, generous, beautiful, beautiful sister Annie!" (Letters, II, 403). After Mrs. Whitman stopped the announcement of marriage banns, Poe wrote in January, 1849, "That you Mrs. W—— have uttered, promulgated or, in any way countenanced this pitiable falsehood, I do not & I cannot believe" (Letters, II, 420). Once again, he could not believe the truth of a situation. In a letter to Annie on February 8, 1848, he indicated that Helen had not replied because "her mother (who is an old devil) has intercepted the letter and will never give it to her" (Letters, II, 425). Poe had suffered similarly in his relationship with Sarah Elmira Royster, whom he was soon to visit.

26. A. H. Quinn, Edgar Allan Poe: A Critical Biography, 592; Helen Whitman's book is entitled Edgar Poe and His Critics (New York: Rudd & Carlton, 1859).

The circumstances of Poe's death are mysterious. The months preceding his death were marked by an increased desperation, increased feelings of persecution, and an almost total denial of any boundary between reality and illusion. Writing to Annie in April or May, 1849, Poe confessed, "My life seems wasted—the future looks a dreary blank" (*Letters*, II, 438). But a letter to Edward H. N. Patterson written in April, 1849, revealed he still had hopes for the *Stylus*. And a letter to Griswold the same year revealed Poe still lying about his age: "I was born Dec. 1813" (*Letters*, II, 445). On July 7, 1849, in a state of ill health, Poe wrote Maria Clemm, "I have no desire to live since I have done 'Eureka.' I could accomplish nothing more" (*Letters*, II, 452).

In the same letter, written from Philadelphia, where he stopped on his way from New York to a lecture appointment in Richmond, Poe spoke of being "taken to prison once since I came here for getting drunk" and attempting to pass a fifty-dollar counterfeit note (*Letters*, II, 452). There is no record of Poe's imprisonment. Writing to Maria Clemm on July 4, 1849, and still in ill health, Poe—after stating his period of absence as "more than three weeks" instead of two—reported: "My valise was lost for ten days. At last I found it at the depot in Philadelphia, but (you will scarcely credit it) they had opened it and stolen *both lectures*" (*Letters*, II, 453, 454). In the next letter to Maria Clemm (July 19, 1849) he explained, "All was hallucination, arising from an attack which I had never before experienced—an attack of *mania-à-potu* [delirium tremens]" (*Letters*, II, 455). While in Richmond Poe looked up Elmira Royster Shelton, now a widow, and proposed marriage.

On September 18, 1849, Poe wrote his last two extant letters—one to Maria Clemm telling that he expected to marry Elmira and that "the papers here are praising me to death," and one to Sarah Anne Lewis, "my dear sister Anne," confessing that he felt for her "the purest and profoundest affection—ah, *let* me say *love*" (*Letters*, II, 461, 462). On October 3, 1849, to appropriate words from the letter of Joseph W. Walker, a compositor, quoted in Harrison's Biography, "a gentleman, rather the worse for wear," was found in a

Baltimore street near a polling station; it was an election day (H, I, 328).[27]

Poe died on Sunday, October 7, at 3 A.M., after screaming for "Reynolds." Quinn's explanation is standard:

Perhaps to his dim and tortured brain, he seemed to be on the brink of a great descending circle sweeping down like the phantom ship in the "Manuscript Found in a Bottle" into "darkness and the distance."

It would have been natural enough for his favorite theme, the terror of the opening chasm, to lead his thoughts to that other story, *Arthur Gordon Pym*, and from that to Jeremiah Reynolds, projector of the voyages to the South Seas, whose very language he had used in that tale.[28]

Poe's entire career, in fact, may be viewed as a downward, accelerating spiral through layers of deception. Poe's own recourse to deceptive practices kept pace with his increased awareness of external deception; his personal imp of the perverse paralleled the perversity of circumstance, until nothing was distinguishable.

V

After Poe's death, his worst fears about the nature of reality were confirmed, notably in the forged correspondence Griswold used to support his deliberately distorted account of Poe's career.[29] The account begins: "Edgar Allan Poe is dead. He died in Baltimore the day before yesterday. This will startle many but *few will be grieved by it*. The poet was well-known personally or by reputation, in all this country; he has readers in England, and in several of the states of Continental Europe; *but he had few or no friends*. . . . He had made up his mind upon the numberless complexities of the social world,

27. There is no factual basis for the story that a sick and drunken Poe was dragged from one polling place to another and made to vote repeatedly. See Mabbott, "Annals," *Collected Works* I, 569n7. However, it is appropriate that the rumor, itself probably fraudulent, has long persisted that the circumstances preceding Poe's death were associated with fraud.

28. A. H. Quinn, *Edgar Allan Poe: A Critical Biography*, 640.

29. The infamous "Ludwig" article, first published in the New York *Tribune* (October 9, 1849) became, in expanded form, the "Memoir" in Griswold's collected edition, *The Works of the Late Edgar Allan Poe, With a Memoir by Rufus Wilmot Griswold and Notices of his Life and Genius by N. P. Willis and J. R. Lowell* (4 vols.; New York: J. S. Redfield, 1850–56).

and the whole system was with him an imposture" (H, I, 348–49, 356). (The latter part of this paragraph, the most powerfully written part, Griswold lifted from The Caxtons by Edward Bulwer, who later became Bulwer-Lytton.) Griswold also circulated the rumor that Poe had "criminal relations" with his mother-in-law. But, even in his own time, Griswold's dishonesty was notorious and found expression in the jibe, "Is that Griswold or a fact?"[30] Poe himself characterized Griswold with uncanny accuracy "as the unfaithful servant who abused his trust" (H, XI, 243). What perverse impulse, it may be wondered, led Poe to intimate that he wished Griswold to be his literary executor?

To a large extent, of course, Poe himself was responsible for the misrepresentations that characterized so many accounts of his life. Nathaniel Parker Willis, in defending Poe against Griswold's vicious attack, spoke of "To Helen" as "one of the shorter poems written when the author was only fourteen" (H, I, 373). George R. Graham also defended Poe and said many things that now appear true: "Could he have stepped down and chronicled small beer, made himself the shifting toady of the hour, and, with bow and cringe, hung upon the steps of greatness, sounding the glory of third-rate ability with a penny trumpet, he would have been fêted alive, and perhaps been praised when dead" (H, I, 441). However, since "literature with him was religion; and he its high priest," as a critic "his pen was regulated by the highest sense of duty. By a keen analysis, he separated and studied each piece which the skilful mechanist had put together. . . . The unfitted joint proves the bungler—the slightest blemish was a palpable fraud. . . . I do not believe that he wrote to give pain; but in combating what he conceived to be error, he used the strongest word that presented itself, even in conversation" (H, I, 404, 409). It may be remembered that Longfellow's estimate, quoted earlier, is similar.

Between the injustices of Poe's enemies and the forgiving enthusiasm of his friends, the pendulum of Poe's reputation has swung ever since. But a review of Poe's posthumous career would require a

30. A. H. Quinn, Edgar Allan Poe: A Critical Biography, 680; the jibe is quoted in P. Miller, The Raven and the Whale, 204.

volume to itself. It is sufficient for the moment to point out that, both before and after Poe's death, the deceptive element was constantly present. Fiction is a form of deception, and it is in no way surprising that Poe's career lends itself so readily to imaginative treatment.[31] The very names—the open sounds of Edgar Allan Poe, the leaden quality of Maria Clemm, and the obvious associations of Griswold— are suggestive. Furthermore, the character's names often have a representative significance beyond their immediate personalities, just as Virginia might suggest the person or the state, Mrs. Richmond, the person or the city, and Helen, "the glory that was Greece, / And the grandeur that was Rome" (M, I, 166).

---

31. Frances B. Dedmond, "Poe in Drama, Fiction and Poetry: A Bibliography," *Bulletin of Bibliography*, XXI (1954), 107–14. Some such pieces, but not the most interesting, are collected in Sam Moskowitz, *The Man Who Called Himself Poe* (New York: Doubleday, 1969).

3

Grotesques and *Politian*

The grotesques are defined in this work as those tales in which Poe expresses his reaction to conventional reality. Consequently, it is not surprising that the grotesques deal with the theme of deception, usually in the form of chicanery. Once again, although an account of malpractice does not demonstrate the deceptive nature of the everyday world, collectively such accounts add up to an analogical statement paralleling that made by the nine tales examined in Chapter 1. Concrete forms of deception lend themselves to fictionalization more readily than metaphysical proofs. The theme of deception is a major comic theme; accordingly, most of the grotesques are intended to be humorous, however unfunny they may actually appear.[1] Man is deceived because of his incongruous condition, and Poe designates "incongruity—the source of all mirth" or "the principle of all nonconvulsive laughter" (H, X, 153; H, XVI, 40). Furthermore, since Poe is describing the "real" world in

1. In Northrop Frye, *Anatomy of Criticism* (Princeton, N.J.: Princeton University Press, 1957), 169–70, Frye's delineation of the mythos of comedy allows for the importance of deception in these terms: "Thus the movement from *pistis to gnosis,* from a society controlled by habit, ritual bondage, arbitrary law and the older characters to a society controlled by youth and pragmatic freedom is fundamentally, as the Greek words suggest, a movement from illusion to reality. Illusion is whatever is fixed or definable, and reality is best understood as its negation: whatever reality is, it's not *that.* Hence the importance of the theme of creating and dispelling illusion in comedy: the illusions caused by disguise, obsession, hypocrisy, or unknown parentage." See also Stephen L. Mooney, "The Comic in Poe's Fiction," *American Literature,* XXXIII (1962), 433–44.

these tales and finding it an object for mirth, it is to be expected that many of the grotesques are satiric.[2] At the same time, in writing satires Poe might have been encouraged by the belief that he was making up for a deficiency in American literature (H, XII, 107–109; H, XIII, 105–107).

There is very little direct evidence concerning Poe's understanding of the term *grotesque,* but the tale entitled "Mystification" (published originally as "Von Jung, the Mystific" in the New York *American Monthly Magazine,* June, 1837) throws some light on the matter.[3] The Baron Ritzner Von Jung is shown to be adept at "that species of *grotesquerie"* called mystification, because he is aware of, and able to exploit, the illusory nature of appearances (M, II, 293). In this respect he is similar to Poe; and his appearance, although appropriately deceptive and inconclusive, hints at Poe's: "Of no particular age" and "by no means handsome—perhaps the reverse"—his "somewhat angular and harsh" features include a "lofty" forehead and "eyes large, heavy, glassy and meaningless" (M, II, 294). His disturbing influence over people, although widespread, is somehow "indefinitive and altogether unaccountable" because it is impossible to connect his sober countenance, especially the conformation of his lips, with the peculiar and comic incidents that occurred in his vicinity (M, II, 293). In his own person, he embodies the antithesis between appearance and reality. Particularly to be observed, apart from his "almost intuitive knowledge of human nature," is the adroitness "by which he contrived to shift the sense of the grotesque from the creator to the created—from his own person to the absurdities to which he had given rise" (M, II, 295).

This baron has an opportunity to demonstrate his talents at the expense of a silly gentleman named Hermann, whose admiration for the intricate etiquette of dueling constitutes his particular folly: "To

2. See, for example, the pioneering article by William Whipple, "Poe's Political Satire," *University of Texas Studies in English,* XXV (1956), 81–95.
3. The suggestion that "the tale seems almost an analysis of Poe's own psychology" is attributed to Harry Levin by G. R. Thompson, *Poe's Fiction: Romantic Irony in the Gothic Tales* (Madison: University of Wisconsin Press, 1973), 119. For a literary "key" see Burton R. Pollin, "Poe's 'Mystification': Its Source in Fay's *Norman Leslie," Mississippi Quarterly,* XXV (1972), 111–30.

Ritzner, ever upon the look-out for the grotesque, his peculiarities had for a long time past afforded food for mystification" (M, II, 298). The baron, after engineering a quarrel, reacts to an insult by hurling a "decanter of wine" at Hermann's reflection in a mirror, recognizing that their differences are apparent rather than real—a matter of injured images (M, II, 300). Hermann, of course, feels obligated to demand of the baron either an explanation or a duel, which he does via the narrator and a letter couched in the most delicately correct language. In reply, the baron refers Hermann to a passage in a dueling manual, which he had deliberately put in Hermann's way previously and for which Hermann professed respect. This passage appears to be an extremely involved description of some dueling propriety but, in actual fact, on "leaving out every second and third word alternately . . . proved to be a most horribly absurd account of a duel between two baboons" (M, II, 303). Rather than admit his inability to understand the passage, Hermann is compelled to accept it as a satisfactory explanation.

In other words, like Poe, the baron makes his point indirectly by drawing attention to the absurd and meaningless nature of conventional reality, which like any deceptive mystification imposes itself on the basis of human credulity. Not just a puerile satire on dueling, this tale approaches being Poe's artistic manifesto of the grotesque. Given that deception as theme and technique characterizes Poe's grotesque tales, the character of Hermann, who enjoys "a reputation for deep metaphysical thinking, and . . . some logical talent," requires further examination (M, II, 297). In his sketchy commentary on the tale, Edward H. Davidson points out that the finally excised description of Hermann is a near pen-portrait of Poe, which is to say that he resembles the baron.[4] It is his lips that are particularly remarkable, and as in the baron's case, his appearance is deceptive depending on whether or not the lower half of his face is covered. This suggestion of a doppelgänger relation between the baron and Hermann opens up previously unsuspected ironies. It provides an additional reason for the baron's decision to act against a reflection in a

4. Edward H. Davidson, *Poe: A Critical Study* (Cambridge, Mass.: Harvard University Press, 1957), 144.

mirror and casts doubt upon the statement regarding his ability always to avoid any rebound on himself of "the sense of the grotesque" (M, II, 295).

Chapter 2 has indicated that many of the facts in Poe's biography could be listed under the four possible meanings of the word *deception:* the trickery of others, the personal action of deceiving, the state of being deceived by the perverse nature of reality, and the state of being deceived by the perverse nature of the self. The grotesques may be grouped under corresponding headings: (1) the satires of chicanery (the trickery of others), (2) the hoaxes (the personal action of deceiving), (3) the tales that deal directly with the deceptive nature of reality (like those discussed in Chapter 1), and (4) the doppelgänger tales dealing with the imp of the perverse. This order is followed in the next four sections of this chapter. The fact that an identical ordering principle may be used in discussing Poe's life and his grotesques is, of course, mutually corroborative. And that "Mystification" impinges almost interchangeably on all four categories further justifies isolating that tale as an introduction to the grotesques.

II

When Poe first planned to publish a collection of eleven (in 1833), sixteen (in 1835), or seventeen (in 1836) of his tales under the title *Tales of the Folio Club,* he conceived a satirical framework (much like that devised by Chaucer for *The Canterbury Tales*) to justify dramatically the rendition of a series of tales.[5] Poe's tales will not be

5. For detailed, mind-spinning speculation concerning the names, number, and tellers of the tales intended for inclusion, as well as the satiric targets suggested by the tales in relationship to their tellers, see James A. Harrison (ed.), *The Complete Works of Edgar Allan Poe* (17 vols.; 1902; rpr., New York: AMS Press, 1965), III, xxxv–xxxvi; Thomas Ollive Mabbott, "On Poe's 'Tales of the Folio Club,'" *Sewanee Review,* XXXVI (1926), 171–76; James Southall Wilson, "The Devil Was in It," *American Mercury,* XXIV (1934), 215–20; Arthur Hobson Quinn, *Edgar Allan Poe: A Critical Biography* (New York: Appleton-Century-Crofts, 1941), 745–46; William Bittner, *Poe: A Biography* (Boston: Little, Brown, 1962), 288–92; Thompson, *Poe's Fiction,* 39–44; and four articles by Alexander Hammond: "Poe's 'Lionizing' and the Design of *Tales of the Folio Club,*" *Emerson Society Quarterly,* XVIII (1972), 154–65; "A Reconstruction of Poe's 1833 *Tales of the Folio Club,*" *Poe Studies,* V (1972), 25–32; "Further Notes on Poe's Folio Club Tales," *Poe Studies,* VIII (1975), 38–42; and

discussed in terms of this aborted project, but the introduction describing the setup relates to the first category—the satires of chicanery. Each of the club's eleven members is to compete in telling a tale, supposedly for the intellectual edification of the group. However, the club's expressed purpose is a mere pretext to cover up gluttony. The members are actually more interested in eating. Consequently, a tale is referred to as a "morceau" and, appropriately, the company "assembled in the dining-room" (M, II, 204, 205). The number of members is limited to eleven, not because "in the year three hundred and fifty before the Deluge, there are said to have been just eleven spots upon the sun"—the pretext the narrator ironically suggests—but probably because eleven people would fit conveniently around a dining table (M, II, 204). Poe acknowledges, in a letter to J. P. Kennedy dated February 11, 1836, that most of the Folio Club tales themselves are semisatirical but that " 'Lionizing' and 'Loss of Breath' were satires properly speaking—at least so meant— the one of the rage for Lions and the facility of becoming one—the other of the extravagances of Blackwood" (Letters, I, 84).

"Lionizing," first published in the Southern Literary Messenger for May, 1835, is, as Poe states, a satire on the vagaries of fashion and literary reputation. Poe may have been indebted to Jonathan Swift's account of windy greatness in A Tale of a Tub since his protagonist, Robert Jones, feels himself equipped with "the divine afflatus" (M, II, 179). Moreover, the source of his reputation, his extraordinary

---

"Edgar Allan Poe's Tales of the Folio Club: The Evolution of a Lost Book," University of Pennsylvania Library Chronicle, XLI (1976), 13–43. Hammond believes that Poe originally intended to gather the following eleven tales and tellers (M, I, 205) in the following order: "Diddling" (by Mr. Snap, the President), "The Visionary" (by M. Convolvulus Gondola), "Bon-Bon" (by De Rerun Natura, Esqr., the devil), "Siope—A Fable" (by "a very little man in a black coat," possibly Poe himself since his name is anagrammatically contained in Siope, the Greek for silence), "MS. Found in a Bottle" (by Mr. Solomon Seadrift), "Metzengerstein" (by Mr. Horribile Dictu), "Loss of Breath" (by Mr. Blackwood Blackwood), "The Duc De L'Omelette" (by Mr. Rouge-et-Noir), "King Pest the First" (by the "stout gentleman who admired Sir Walter Scott"), "Four Beasts in One" (by Chronologos Chronology), and "Lionizing" (by the narrator). It should be observed, however, that this list of attributions differs somewhat from Mabbott's last thoughts on the subject (M, I, 206–207). Mabbott assigns "Lionizing" to Mr. Snap, "Shadow" to the little man in black, "Four Beasts in One" to the stout gentleman, "A Tale of Jerusalem" to Chronologos Chronology, and "Siope" to the narrator.

nose, may, as Bonaparte and Davidson suggest, refer to his penis.[6] He is contantly "turning it up," causing an "ejaculated" expression of admiration by an artist "thrown quite off his guard by the beauty of the manoeuvre" (M, II, 180). "Bon-Bon," a similarly trivial piece first published in the Philadelphia *Saturday Courier* for December 1, 1832, satirizes metaphysical systematizers. In this tale, as in the Folio Club introduction, ideas are equated with food. Consequently, Bon-Bon's reputation as a philosopher depends upon the immensity of his stomach, in much the same fashion that Robert Jones benefits from his extraordinary nose. There is, then, some logic in the tale's proposition that the souls of great thinkers ultimately become food for the devil. Well supplied, the devil refuses the soul of Bon-Bon, who is struck by a divine thunderbolt in the form of a falling arabesque lamp that is twice associated with God.

In "How to Write a Blackwood Article," originally published as "The Psyche Zenobia" in the Baltimore *American Museum* for November, 1838, the Signora Psyche Zenobia—as she styles herself—is taught by Mr. Blackwood himself that literary success is all a matter of gimmickery and deceit.[7] In the field of the bizarre tale, a cultivation of the sensational and the recherché makes for success. Anything that is too absurd should be accompanied by a footnote reference to a profound-sounding work: "And yet above all things it is necessary that your article have an air of erudition, or at least afford evidence of extensive general reading" (M, II, 343). Poe himself is guilty of such sharp practice, but usually in the interests of

6. Marie Bonaparte, *The Life and Works of Edgar Allan Poe: A Psycho-Analytic Interpretation*, trans. John Rodker (London: Imago Publishing Co., 1949), 397; Davidson, *Poe: A Critical Study*, 146. For elucidation of the specific satiric targets in the tale—N. P. Willis, Edward Bulwer-Lytton, and Benjamin Disraeli's *Vivian Grey*—see Richard P. Benton, "Poe's 'Lionizing': A Quiz on Willis and Lady Blessington," *Studies in Short Fiction*, V (1968), 239–44; G. R. Thompson, "On the Nose—Further Speculation on the Sources and Meaning of Poe's 'Lionizing,' " *Studies in Short Fiction*, VI (1968), 94–96; Hammond, "Poe's 'Lionizing,' " 154–65.

7. For an explication of the satire, see Burton R. Pollin, "Poe's Tale of Psyche Zenobia: A Reading for Humor and Ingeneous Construction," in Richard Veler (ed.), *Papers on Poe: Essays in Honor of John Ward Ostrom* (Springfield, Ohio: Chantry Music Press at Witenberg University, 1972), 92–103. For a detailed account of Poe's own overall debt to *Blackwood's Edinburgh Magazine*, see Michael Allen, *Poe and the British Magazine Tradition* (New York: Oxford University Press, 1969).

hoaxing his readers for a philosophical purpose. The literary lady in this satire is simply interested in becoming a successful charlatan. The tale that Zenobia writes, in accordance with Mr. Blackwood's instructions, is entitled "A Predicament." Wherever possible, she introduces the learned allusions mentioned by Mr. Blackwood but with some inaccuracies. The three Muses become the "three Furies —Melty, Nimmy and Hetty—Meditation, Memory, and Fiddling," the last being particularly relevant (M, II, 349). However, this tale is more than an illustration of Mr. Blackwood's precepts. In fact, to interpret it simply in terms of "How to Write a Blackwood Article" is to fall victim to a Poe hoax. Consequently, the analysis of this tale will be included later among the third grouping of grotesques— those dealing with the perverse and deceptive nature of reality.

Pompey, Zenobia's Negro companion, flees in Zenobia's tale but reappears as an old Negro valet to General John A. B. C. Smith in "The Man That Was Used Up," which was originally published in *Burton's Gentleman's Magazine* for August, 1839.[8] The subtitle, "A Tale of the Late Bugaboo and Kickapoo Campaign," suggests a political reference, but undoubtedly the tale is also about the efficacy of deception.[9] In a tone that would now be called black humor, the narrator tells of his discovery that an impressive-looking general achieves his dignity by means of artificial limbs and other false mechanical apparatus, like Lemuel Pitkin in Nathanael West's *A Cool Million*. Hence the repeated pun on the words *invention* and *inventive*. The age is "inventive" because it makes possible the equipment that allows the general to look like a human being. But "inventive" may also mean fabricative. The impression that the narrator has of the general depends upon fabrication. Similarly, the anomalous reference to the general's "bust," followed as it is by a full-length description, serves as a pun to anticipate the tale's conclusion, when the narrator is faced with a broken, "used up" man (M, II, 379, 389). There are other perverse misunderstandings. The

8. In addition, the opening paragraphs of "Ligeia," written less than a year earlier, reappear in burlesque form as the opening paragraphs of this tale. See Thompson, *Poe's Fiction*, 83–85.

9. An attack on Vice-President Richard M. Johnson is intended according to Whipple, "Poe's Political Satire," 91–94.

general calls the narrator "Mr.—Thompson," although that is not his name (M, II, 382). Talk about "the man" is misconstrued as referring to "Captain Mann" or "Man-Fred" (M, II, 384, 385). The narrator decides to question the general at his home on the grounds that "here, at least, there should be no chance of equivocation," only to discover that the general's state is totally equivocal (M, II, 386).

Pompey, this time the name of a dog, makes a further appearance in "The Business Man," first published in *Burton's Gentleman's Magazine* for February, 1840. The orderly narrator of this piece realizes that sharp practice is the avenue to success; and after a succession of increasingly profitable fiddles, he considers himself "a made man" (M, II, 491). Likewise, "Diddling"—which originally appeared in the October 14, 1843, Philadelphia *Saturday Courier*—begins by defining man "as an animal that diddles" and consists of a series of increasingly elaborate confidence tricks (M, III, 869).[10] At the conclusion of the story, Plato's definition of man, perversely understood as a plucked chicken (alluded to at the beginning of the piece), is replaced by a "hen knee high," which is misunderstood as the letters *n. e. i.* standing for the phrase "*non est inventus*" (M, III, 880). Just as language and meaning can be subverted by the disjunction of sound and sense, so can reality itself. The "Literary Life of Thingum Bob, Esq.," which first appeared in the December, 1844, *Southern Literary Messenger*, offers more of the same. Success is shown to be based on chicanery and deceit.[11]

10. Although 1843 is the date of first publication, this tale's mediocre quality and the fact that the sentiment "Were he not Alexander he would be Diogenes" (V, 212) occurs at the end of "The Duc De L'Omelette" (published in 1832) argue for a much earlier initial composition date. See in this regard, Claude Richard, "Poe and the Yankee Hero: An Interpretation of 'Diddling Considered as One of the Exact Sciences,' " *Mississippi Quarterly*, XXI (1968), 93–109; Hammond, "Further Notes on Poe's Folio Club Tales," 39; Burton R. Pollin, "Poe's 'Diddling': More on the Dating and the Aim," *Poe Studies*, IX (1976), 11–13. Pollin attacks the arguments for an early dating to allow inclusion among the Folio Club tales and Richard's view that "Diddling" satirizes the literary career of John Neal, editor of the *Yankee*. It is Pollin's view that the tale derives from James Kenney's 1803 farce, *Raising the Wind*; see Burton R. Pollin, "Poe's 'Diddling': The Source of Title and Tale," *Southern Literary Journal*, II (1969), 106–11.

11. For the suggestion that Thingum Bob is both Lewis and Willis Gaylord Clark, see William Whipple, "Poe, Clark and Thingum Bob," *American Literature*, XXIX (1957), 312–16. Theodore Fay, author of *Norman Leslie*, a book that Poe pilloried, also appears to be a target of the satire. See Pollin, "Poe's 'Mystification,' " 118–21.

III

To turn from the trickery of others to personal trickery is to confront Poe's hoaxes. His predilection for the hoax, a form of satire and a constituent element in American folk humor, is in perfect accord with his philosophical framework.[12] People are deceived largely because of their gullibility. By perpetrating a successful hoax, Poe is demonstrating human gullibility, the equation of "Credulity" with "Insanity" (H, XIV, 179). The allegorical implication, then, is that the supposed human condition is also a hoax. Perhaps the purest example of this negative usage among the grotesques is "The Balloon Hoax," which appeared as an extra by the New York Sun on April 13, 1844 (The Extra Sun). More often, however, the hoax does not serve merely to indicate man's ability for and vulnerability to deception but becomes an aspect of Poe's methodology for suggesting the experience of that reality which is camouflaged by the illusive phenomenal universe. The hoax has a role to play among those fusing techniques that undermine accepted truth or muddy the distinction between appearance and reality. Stories like "The Premature Burial," "The System of Doctor Tarr and Professor Fether," and "Von Kempelen and His Discovery" benefit from the equivocation provided by the possibility that they are hoaxes. Thus Poe's experiments in hoaxing his readers contribute indirectly to his technique of what might be called dissolving, or fluid, form in The Narrative of A. Gordon Pym and certain of the arabesques, in which the reader is required to maintain in suspension various contradictory interpretations, including the possibility that all may be a dream or a hallucination. Finally, after this positive usage, it is but a short step (via the mesmeric tales) from the supposedly specious reasoning and pseudoscience, designed to help the hoax along, to the tales of ratiocination, which seem "more ingenious than they are" owing to "their air of method," and Eureka (Letters, II, 328). It would appear, then, that the hoax form may be regarded as a seedbed of common ground for aspects of the grotesques, the arabesques, and the tales of ratiocination.

12. Gilbert Highet treats the hoax as a form of satire in The Anatomy of Satire (Princeton, N.J.: Princeton University Press, 1962), 92–103. See also Constance Rourke, American Humor (New York: Harcourt Brace, 1931), 179–86.

The varied potential, implicit in Poe's use of the hoax, may give an unexpected basic unity to "The Unparalleled Adventure of One Hans Pfaal," a tale that exhibits an extreme heterogeneity of tone and other elements—grotesque, arabesque, and ratiocinative. Originally published in the June, 1835, *Southern Literary Messenger*, it is among the longest and least critically commented upon of Poe's tales. Largely because of the piece's highly problematical tone, critics have tended to dismiss it as somehow abortive. What appears to begin as a humorous satire of idiopathic perception (in the manner of "The Devil in the Belfry") slides into the factual ballast characteristic of a hoax; yet the hoax gradually assumes the force of a genuine scientific treatise. J. O. Bailey presumes that Poe was unsure of his material or changed his mind. However, this was the tale that Poe was exceptionally enthusiastic about, according to Mr. Latrobe. It therefore merits detailed attention before being dismissed as a botch.[13]

In actual fact, Poe defines the total structure of the tale in one sentence in the third paragraph: "From behind the huge bulk of one of those sharply defined masses of cloud already mentioned, was seen slowly to emerge into an open area of blue space, a queer, heterogeneous, but apparently solid substance, so oddly shaped, so whimsically put together, as not to be in any manner comprehended, and never to be sufficiently admired, by the host of sturdy burghers who stood open-mouthed below" (H, II, 43). For the "sharply defined masses of cloud" substitute the narrow-minded, pipe-smoking Dutchmen of Rotterdam, to be described in more detail as the in-

13. The nature of the attention that "Hans Pfaal" attracts may be gauged by the following studies: M. N. Posey, "Notes on Poe's 'Hans Pfaall,' " *Modern Language Notes*, XLV (1930), 501–507; R. S. Wilkinson, "Poe's 'Hans Pfaall' Reconsidered," *Notes and Queries*, XIII (1966), 333–37; William H. Gravely, Jr., "A Note on the Composition of Poe's 'Hans Pfaal,' " *Poe Newsletter*, III (1970), 2–5. The tale "passes from the grotesque into the arabesque group" according to A. H. Quinn, *Edgar Allan Poe: A Critical Biography*, 215. The possibility of Poe's change of mind is raised by J. O. Bailey, "Sources for Poe's *Arthur Gordon Pym*, 'Hans Pfaal' and Other Pieces," *PMLA*, LVII (1942), 531–33; and Edmund Reiss, "The Comic Setting of 'Hans Phaall,' " *American Literature*, XXIX (1957), 306–309. Latrobe's statement is quoted in Hervey Allen, *Israfel: The Life and Times of Edgar Allan Poe* (rev. ed.; New York: Farrar & Rinehart, 1934), 283. (The four different spellings that Poe used for Hans's surname—only "Phaal" is not represented in the above article titles—reflect his own indecision or forgetfulness.)

habitants of Vondervotteimittiss in "The Devil in the Belfry." In this connection, it is significant that Hans Pfaal's family lived "time out of mind" in the same place, a phrase which recurs in the later tale (H, II, 48). The burghers' "sharply defined" attitudes fail to account for the unexpected phenomena that have all Europe "in an uproar, all physics in a ferment, all reason and astronomy together by the ears" (H, II, 42). The expression "by the ears" is not accidental. The tale is, in part, a satire on political hot air.[14] Hans Pfaal, "a mender of bellows," is out of work because wind is being misapplied in support of democracy: "We soon began to feel the effects of liberty, and long speeches, and radicalism, and all that sort of thing. People who were formerly the very best customers in the world, had now not a moment of time to think of us at all. They had as much as they could do to read about the revolutions, and keep up with the march of intellect and the spirit of the age. If a fire wanted fanning, it could readily be fanned with a newspaper" (H, II, 48). Thus it is symbolically significant that the balloon seen by the fat citizens of Rotterdam is "manufactured entirely of dirty newspapers," "printed in Rotterdam" (H, II, 44, 102). It would appear that the opening clause of the sentence quoted above accurately describes the opening and closing phases of the narrative, which satirize the limitations of much-bruited human knowledge.

The "heterogeneous . . . whimsically put together," apparently solid substance may be equated with the central bulk of the narrative: the account of Pfaal's trip to the moon, which is suspected to be a hoax. But if it is a hoax, Poe's satiric intent is subverted. The description of the insular Dutchmen is designed to express Poe's conviction that there is more to reality than meets the average human eye. The account of Pfaal's trip to the moon is part of the reality that man is normally unaware of. If the entire trip is a fabrication, the bigotry of the Dutch is justified; and Poe's tale is incoherent. If the tale is to be consistent, Hans Pfaal's account cannot be a hoax. The hoax involves Poe deviously making the reader believe the account a hoax

14. The satirical aspects of the tale may be directed at President Andrew Jackson. See Allan H. Greer, "Poe's 'Hans Pfaall' and the Political Scene," *Emerson Society Quarterly*, no. 60 (1970), 67–73.

and thus ally himself with the Dutchmen: "Some of the over-wise even made themselves ridiculous by decrying the whole business as nothing better than a hoax. But hoax, with these sort of people, is, I believe, a general term for all matters above their comprehension" (H, II, 102). In comparing his tale with Richard Adams Locke's "Moon-Story" in the extended note appended to the tale, Poe is careful not to commit himself: "Both have the character of *hoaxes*, (although the one is in a tone of banter, the other downright earnest)" (H, II, 103).

Much of the information that Pfaal divulges, concerning the infinite rarefaction of air for instance, anticipates aspects of *Eureka* and would surely have been endorsed by Poe, although ostensibly he is opposed to, or uneasy with, reasoned logic. Later, however, Poe appears to have reconciled his love-hate relationship with reason by distinguishing between two types of reason—an inferior and untrustworthy type and a higher, valid reason that is linked with imagination. This solution Poe illustrates fully in the tales of ratiocination by means of the contrast between the plodding prefect of police and the brilliantly analytical Dupin. It is, therefore, extremely interesting to find Poe approaching a similar solution in "Hans Pfaal" in 1835, in words very close to those used in "The Murders in the Rue Morgue" in 1841. After leafing through an astronomical treatise, Phaal reflects:

There are some particular passages which affected my imagination in an extraordinary manner. . . . The limited nature of my education in general, and more especially my ignorance on subjects connected with natural philosophy, so far from rendering me diffident of my own ability to comprehend what I had read, or inducing me to mistrust the many vague notions which had arisen in consequence, merely served as a further stimulus to imagination; and I was vain enough, or perhaps reasonable enough, to doubt whether those crude ideas which, arising in ill-regulated minds, have all the appearance, may not often in effect possess all the force, the reality, and other inherent properties of instinct or intuition. (H, II, 50)

Dupin's results have "the whole air of intuition" (M, II, 528). And, immediately following the quoted passage in a section excised from the 1840 printing of "Hans Pfaal" and incorporated with slight variation in "The Murders in the Rue Morgue," the narrator speaks of the "superficial" nature of truth and the need "only to glance" at a star—in other words, the need to adopt the perspective of the half-closed eye (H, II, 332–33). Quite possibly, Poe transferred the passage from the 1835 tale because he saw the inconsistency between the use of this revealing image in "Hans Pfaal" and his earlier use of it, as illustrative of pure imagination, in the 1831 "Letter to B———." But in the tales of ratiocination, as will be demonstrated, Poe justifies his synthesis of reason and imagination; and there the reapplication of the image is explicable. In "Hans Pfaal," Poe is moving toward a position that he had not at the time consciously integrated into his philosophical framework.

So the reader is hoaxed if he believes the astronomical information to be a hoax. On the other hand, there is evidence within the tale to suggest that Hans Pfaal did not reach the moon in quite the manner he describes. The truth seems to be that he died in the unexpectedly powerful explosion at takeoff which killed the three creditors: "Scarcely, however, had I attained the height of fifty yards, when, roaring and rumbling up after me in the most tumultuous and terrible manner, came so dense a hurricane of fire, and gravel, and burning wood, and blazing metal, and mangled limbs, that my very heart sunk within me, and I fell down in the bottom of the car, trembling with terror" (H, II, 56). The unexpected force of this eruption is to be linked with the "radicalism" and "revolutions" that the narrator connects with the misuse of hot air. In the cause of his radical solution, Hans Pfaal—"good for nothing but building castles in the air"—involves himself in the web of human deception: "I contrived . . . with the greatest secrecy and caution, to dispose of what property I had remaining, and to borrow, in small sums, under various pretences . . . no inconsiderable quantity of ready money" (H, II, 51, 54). When a reckoning threatened, "I contrived . . . to pacify them [his three creditors] by promises of payment." In order to disguise his takeoff intentions, "dropping a lighted cigar on the ground, as if by accident . . . I took the opportunity, in stooping to pick it up, of igniting privately the piece of slow match," an act that leads to murder (H, II, 55). To further implicate Hans Pfaal's misfortune with newspaper radicalism, he compares his water alarm system, rather unexpectedly, to "the steam-engine" or "the art of printing itself" (H, II, 84).

The citizens are correct who believe that the human bones, "mixed up with a quantity of odd-looking rubbish . . . in a retired situation to the east of the city," belonged to "Hans Pfaal and his associates," who had disappeared five years earlier (H, II, 45). Pfaal's account of his voyage to the moon actually disguises the fact that he is making the transference from earth to some kind of purgatory or hell. The moment of *"bouleversement,"* as the gravity pull of the earth is exchanged for that of the moon, refers to the overturning of earthly perception and is preceded by three loud crackling noises (H, II, 94). This is the same explosion that accompanied the balloon's ascension, now segmented and stretched in time, to remind Pfaal of the three separate deaths for which he is responsible. The third sound is particularly reminiscent of the explosion as initially described: "It now, however, continued for some moments, and gathered intensity as it continued. At length, while, stupefied and terror-stricken, I stood in expectation of I know not what hideous destruction, the car vibrated with excessive violence, and a gigantic and flaming mass of some material which I could not distinguish, came with a voice of a thousand thunders, roaring and booming by the balloon" (H, II, 92).[15] These noises, an attenuated version of the initial explosion, mark the moment of Pfaal's death and his transference to the afterlife, or the moon, which (being in a state of constant volcanic eruption) provides a fitting purgatory for the sin of volcanic radicalism—the sin that the inhabitants of Rotterdam have committed and that Poe is satirizing. The initial explosion is, then, prefigurative of the eruptive activity on the moon. For purposes of literal detail, it is implied that the three crackling sounds, like subsequent similar disturbances, are attributable to meteoric eruptions from the moon. Moreover, the reader may surmise that the death of the cat and her three kittens is analogous to the death of Hans Pfaal and the three creditors. There is a tonal similarity between the two episodes.

15. This echo from Revelation 14:2 anticipates the collapse of the House of Usher, accompanied by the "voice of a thousand waters," into an arabesque dimension (M, II, 417).

As the basket containing the animals disappears, Pfaal, in a line remarkable for its mixed feelings, says, "My good wishes followed it to the earth, but, of course, I had no hope that either cat or kittens would ever live to tell the tale of their misfortune" (H, II, 82). In a similarly lighthearted manner, Pfaal speaks of the "trick" he played upon the creditors (H, II, 71).

Further evidence of Pfaal's death is the arabesque vision—amid "masses of cloud which floated to and fro"—that he experiences during the voyage (H, II, 79):

Fancy revelled in the wild and dreamy regions of the moon. Imagination, feeling herself for once unshackled, roamed at will among the ever-changing wonders of a shadowy and unstable land. Now there were hoary and time-honored forests, and craggy precipices, and waterfalls tumbling with a loud noise into abysses without a bottom. . . . Then again I journeyed far down away into another country where it was all one dim and vague lake, with a boundary-line of clouds. (H, II, 80)

Where the ellipses occur Poe originally included a description of trees and their shadows interfusing, but he cut this from the 1840 version and incorporated it in the 1841 "Island of the Fay," which details an arabesque landscape. But Pfaal also experiences "horrors of a nature most stern and most appalling," and it is toward such an existence that he is headed (H, II, 80). Perhaps, as for some time it appears, the North Pole is the object of Pfaal's voyage, not the moon. In *The Narrative of A. Gordon Pym* the South Pole represents death and arabesque reality.

At the beginning of his voyage, Pfaal is given a foretaste of his destination:

In a few seconds after my leaving the cloud, a flash of vivid lightning shot from one end of it to the other, and caused it to kindle up, throughout its vast extent, like a mass of ignited charcoal. . . . Hell itself might then have found a fitting image. Even as it was, my hair stood on end, while I gazed afar down within the yawning abysses, letting imagination descend, and stalk about in the strange vaulted halls, and ruddy gulfs, and red ghastly chasms of the hideous and unfathomable fire. (H, II, 69–70)

The moon is a place of punishment. In a section of what Harrison designates "Notes apparently to *Eureka*," but which are actually "Notes to 'Hans Pfaal,' " Poe writes, "Make the invisible half of the moon our hell" (H, XVI, 349–50).[16] Ears and voice boxes, so misused on earth, are denied the lunar beings. This fate possibly threatens most human beings, since Pfaal speaks "of the incomprehensible connection between each particular individual in the moon, with some particular individual on the earth" (H, II, 100). Hans Pfaal finds a double there because of the crimes he committed in connection with his radicalism. The double theme in Poe is one manifestation of the schizophrenic human condition.

After five years, Pfaal—it may be hypothesized—has made a deal with his diminutive double who is to return to earth, the land of the "living," and secure a pardon from the dignitaries of Rotterdam. The character who looks like Pfaal but is only "two feet in height," seen at the tale's opening, is actually his lunar double (H, II, 45). His feet cannot be seen, but a sentence, excised in 1840, notes "a horny substance of suspicious nature was occasionally protruded through a rent in the bottom of the car"—clearly a devil's tail (H, II, 331). The pardon is assured theoretically but is assumed to "be of little use, as no one but a man of the moon would undertake a voyage to so vast a distance" (H, II, 102). Consequently, it was not sent. However, Pfaal "and the three very idle gentlemen styled his creditors" are recently seen, "having just returned, with money in their pockets, from a trip beyond the sea" (H, II, 102). In other words, the pardon has been granted, and Pfaal, back from hell, is back from the dead, as are the creditors. And the "odd little dwarf . . . both of whose ears, for some misdemeanor, have been cut off close to his head," recently reported missing, is Pfaal's lunar double who has returned to the moon (H, II, 102). His balloon was covered with Rotterdam newspapers because that is where it was constructed.

If "Hans Pfaal" is read in the terms suggested above, all the otherwise incongruous details form a coherent design. To recapitulate: the voyage cannot be a total hoax because, if Poe is establishing that the account of dimensions of reality beyond mortal ken is untrue anyway, he is undercutting the satire of human idiopathic percep-

16. Margaret Alterton points out that the notes are actually for "Hans Pfaal." See Alterton, *Origins of Poe's Critical Theory* (Iowa City: University of Iowa Press, 1925), 133–38.

tion, the starting point of the tale. On the other hand, the reader is most definitely hoaxed if he believes the story to be about a journey to the moon, and so it is appropriate that Pfaal leaves the earth on "the first of April" and that the balloon, which the people of Rotterdam see, resembles "a huge fool's-cap turned upside down" (H, II, 44, 54). The balance on which the hoax rests is a very delicate one. Not so the "Moon-Hoax" of Richard Adams Locke, according to Poe's somewhat peevish illustration as to "why no one should have been deceived" (H, II, 103).

Commentators who complain about the tale's disunity have simply failed to perceive the cutting edge of the hoax and the logic on which it rests. Furthermore, given that Poe was able to exploit the potential of the hoax not just in his grotesque tales but also in the arabesques and the tales of ratiocination, the hoax may be said to provide a unifying matrix for these species of tales; and it is to be expected that a complex and fully developed hoax like "Hans Pfaal" should, by turns, appear to fall into the grotesque, arabesque, and ratiocinative categories. Consequently, it may be concluded that the discordance of tone and seeming intention in "Hans Pfaal" are actually paradoxical evidence for its fundamental unity in the context of Poe's exploitation of the hoax form.

"The Premature Burial," which first appeared in the Philadelphia *Dollar Newspaper*, July 31, 1844, is also an inverted hoax. After describing four supposedly genuine tales of premature burial, the narrator recounts his own experience, which is bogus. The enclosed area turns out to be the berth of a sloop, and the reader is as much deceived as the idiopathic narrator. In a letter to Evert A. Duyckinck dated March 8, 1849, Poe points out that "Von Kempelen and His Discovery," which first appeared in the April 14, 1849, Boston *Flag of Our Union*, was intended as a hoax to counteract what Poe saw as a much larger and more dangerous hoax, the California gold rush.[17] Three times in the tale, Poe links Von Kempelen's discovery of the philosopher's stone with recent events in California. But, in addi-

17. There also appear to be satirical elements in this tale, which the indefatigable Burton R. Pollin has teased out. See "Poe in 'Von Kempelen and His Discovery,' " in Pollin, *Discoveries in Poe* (Notre Dame, Ind.: University of Notre Dame Press, 1970), 166–89.

tion, the tale explores one of Poe's favorite themes—the variability and the relativity of truth—thus providing a convenient bridge between the hoaxes and those tales in the next section dealing with deceptive reality. Much space is taken up by the narrator "correcting ... misimpressions." The description of two crucibles, one "full of *lead* in a state of fusion," suggests that, in transmuting lead into gold, Von Kempelen is performing an action analogous to Poe's conversion of deceptive, everyday reality into arabesque reality (M, III, 1362). However, the disturbing consequence of Von Kempelen's discovery is that gold becomes no more valuable than lead.

IV

The tales to be considered in this section, like the nine tales analyzed in Chapter 1, deal with man's condition of material deception as it depends upon the factors of space, time, and idiopathic eccentricity—particularly the latter. In a number of these tales, which are much less straightforward than the nine excerpted previously, Poe seeks a widening of experience by exploding or releasing the potentialities of language and goading the reader into seeing the literal import of title phrases like "Loss of Breath," "The Scythe of Time," and "Never Bet the Devil Your Head," or by overturning the reader's faith in the commonsensical and making him acknowledge the truth of contradiction in, for example, "Three Sundays in a Week." The first five tales to be considered, whatever their eventual date of publication, all figure in Alexander Hammond's and Thomas Ollive Mabbott's attempts to reconstruct the Folio Club collection.

In "Loss of Breath"—which was originally entitled "A Decided Loss" in the November 10, 1832, Philadelphia *Saturday Courier*— Mr. Lackobreath, while searching for his missing respiration (like Peter Pan looking for his shadow), reflects:

Most philosophers, upon many points of philosophy, are still very unphilosophical. William Godwin, however, says in his "Mandeville," that "invisible things are the only realities," and this all will allow, is a case in point. I would have the judicious reader pause before accusing such asseverations of an undue quantum of absurdity. Anaxagoras, it will be remembered, maintained that snow is black, and this I have since found to be the case. (M, II, 64).

By the same token, breath may be tangible and as easily lost as a glove. The tale's whole function is to make ambiguous exactly what is meant by the expression "loss of breath" and to demonstrate that "it is a trait in the perversity of human nature to reject the obvious and the ready, for the far-distant and equivocal" (M, II, 63). Three possible ramifications of meaning for the expression are offered. First of all, loss of breath is treated as a physical accident.

Second, since loss of breath is usually accompanied by death, Poe explores the possibility that death does not involve loss of consciousness. After attempting to "conceal" his "unhappy calamity," Lackobreath puts his "affairs in order" and takes a carriage ride (M, II, 65). He is apparently in a horizontal position, "at full length"; so the carriage may be the hearse on the way to the cemetery (M, II, 66). He certainly ends up in a cemetery; and the hanging, with the escape of his double who lay "at full length" in the cart, suggests the precise moment of death and the release from mortality (M, II, 68). This aspect of the tale was considerably de-emphasized in the *Broadway Journal* version of January 3, 1846, by the excision of a long and more serious passage detailing Lackobreath's death on the gallows and his subsequent burial, possibly because, in describing the sensations accompanying death, Poe was tipping the tale toward the arabesque type. Furthermore, the two colloquies—that of Eiros and Charmion and that of Monos and Una—present an extended treatment of this subject. In dying, Lackobreath experiences an extension in dimension and merges into a primal unity, with the recognition that "reason is folly, and Philosophy a lie. . . . Yet will men still persist in reasoning, and philosophizing, and making themselves fools." He is thinking particularly of the "bugbear speculations of transcendentalism" (M, II, 80). In screwing down the coffin lid, the undertaker carelessly imbeds one of the screws in Lackobreath's shoulder, a detail that William Faulkner may have appropriated in *As I Lay Dying*. But arabesque relief is at hand, heralded by "the rapid variations in light and shade which the flapping to and fro of the sable hangings occasioned within the body of the vehicle" (M, II, 81).

Third, by a further linguistic extension, Poe equates breath with potency and its loss with impotence. Whether or not Poe himself was impotent, Marie Bonaparte is surely correct in seeing the tale, at least partially, in such terms.[18] It is the morning after the wedding night, and things presumably have not gone well. The opening paragraph about sieges would seem to be explicable only if it relates to Lackobreath's failure to gain sexual entrance. Thus, the subtitle, "A tale neither in nor out of 'Blackwood,' " acquires the force of innuendo, as does the following sentence: "I was preparing to launch forth a new and more decided epithet of opprobrium, which should not fail, if ejaculated, to convince her of her insignificance, when . . . I discovered that *I had lost my breath*" (M, II, 62). And of course, the presence of a rival in the potent form of Mr. Windenough underlines the agony of Lackobreath's situation. The hanging rectifies the neck dislocation caused by the fat man in the coach, but it would also effect an erection. Perhaps the two infirmities are synonymous. Perhaps, since Lackobreath is also a fat man, it is a feeling of physical inferiority that accounts for his impotence. Certainly, the "puffy, bloated, and rotund" carcass, to which he delivers a deprecatory obituary, is his own (M, II, 70). And the "gaunt, tall, and peculiar-looking form," which he holds by the nose in order that it assume a sitting position, may be his own penis, externalized as Mr. Windenough (M, II, 71).

It should be admitted finally that this *tour de force* tale defeats interpretation. It has the surrealist logic of a dream, and the connections suggested above may well be wrong or inadequate. Everything is made more equivocal by a deadpan, matter-of-fact style that turns comedy into tragedy and tragedy into comedy—a style today favored for black humor. Poe is literally exploding the possibilities of language by taking words to their philological roots and associative limits and going beyond those limits to create new contexts. To appreciate the tale, the reader must adopt "that indiscriminate philosophy," which is referred to four times (M, II, 75). The reader is in the position of Scissors, who is unaware that the "subterranean noises," about which he expounded an elaborate theory, emanate from Mr. Lackobreath and Mr. Windenough (M, II, 74). Consequently, the reader must be prepared to entertain every possibility and follow the

18. See the chapter entitled "The Confession of Impotence," in Bonaparte, *The Life and Works of Edgar Allan Poe: A Psycho-Analytic Interpretation*, 373–410.

hedge-betting advice of Laertius: "the *erection* of a shrine and temple 'to the proper God,' " who is one of many, all nameless (italics added; M, II, 75).

"King Pest," which first appeared in the September, 1835, *Southern Literary Messenger*, is apparently a burlesque upon the "Palace of the Wines" episode in Chapter 1, Book VI of Benjamin Disraeli's *Vivian Grey*, a work referred to approvingly in "Loss of Breath." However, the subtitle, "A Tale Containing an Allegory," would seem to indicate the need for further examination. Accordingly, William Whipple finds anti-Jacksonian political satire in the piece. William Goldhurst, however, argues that King Pest and his five courtiers amount to a disintegrated portrait of the grand duke (who presides over Disraeli's Palace of Wines), much as the current state of the universe, as described in *Eureka*, is attributable to the irradiated reality of God. Something of the metaphoric context of Disraeli's scene— the palace is suggestive of Valhalla—carries over into Poe's context. Thus, King Pest—who, Goldhurst claims, is successively associated with the devil, Dionysius, Bacchus, and even John Allan—shares with the grand duke the role of Odin, god of war and death.[19] Again, this fragmentation of identity makes most sense as anticipatory of Poe's cosmology. It has little to do with any literary or political target.

This, then, is another tale in which Poe questions the assumptions on which everyday life is based. Certainly, much in the tale is peculiar to Poe, including the pairing of short and tall characters as in "Bon-Bon" and "Loss of Breath." Each of the six grotesque characters, seated around a table in the middle of plague-country, represents a distorted aspect of one of man's perceptions: intellect (the ruler, King Pest the First), taste, smell, sensation, hearing, and sight. Their names all include the word *pest*, and they rule over pestilence. In other words, the pestilence, which should be compared with the plague in "The Masque of the Red Death," represents life. Thus, it is

19. R. L. Hudson, "Poe and Disraeli," *American Literature*, VIII (1937), 402–16; Whipple, "Poe's Political Satire," 84–88; William Goldhurst, "Poe's Multiple King Pest: A Source Study," *Tulane Studies in English*, XX (1972), 107–21. Goldhurst concludes that what seems to be an inconsequential exercise "contains elements of personal biography, political and social satire, history, myth, and unconscious imagery, as well as hints of the author's mature epistemology" (121).

the limitations, or distortions, of human perception that turn a potential arabesque existence into a confined, deathlike state. Predictably, access to the area is normally barred by "terrific barriers" (M, II, 243).

But Legs and his companion, Hugh Tarpaulin, are more at home in the arabesque world of the sea aboard the *Free and Easy.* The words "No Chalk," written in chalk—"that very mineral whose presence they purported to deny"—disturbs the two sailors who, although illiterate, sense the negation of arabesque whiteness (white being the fused omni-color), which the message implies (M, II, 241). The plague-ridden region into which they make their way is a kingdom of deception. As in the hold in *The Narrative of A. Gordon Pym,* which symbolizes the human condition, paths become "more narrow and more intricate" (M, II, 244). The "unearthly sovereign whose reign is over us all, whose dominions are unlimited, and whose name is death" is the same being who presides "over all" in "The Masque of the Red Death" (M, II, 250, 677). King Pest tries to initiate the two sailors by making them drink "Black Strap." But Tarpaulin recognizes King Pest as Tim Hurlygurly, stage player; and both he and Legs escape from this world of deception back to the sea and the *Free and Easy* with two of the three women present. The full import of this recognition is rather obscure. In terms of initials, Tim Hurlygurly is Hugh Tarpaulin reversed.[20] Perhaps, Hurlygurly is the false, grotesque aspect of Tarpaulin.

Apparently, "The Duc De L'Omelette," which first appeared in the March 3, 1832, Philadelphia *Saturday Courier,* is also a parody of the work of Disraeli—this time *The Young Duke*—as well as more directly a satire on N. P. Willis. But, like "King Pest," this tale (poor as it is) may be interpreted in accordance with Poe's general philosophy.[21] As in "Loss of Breath," the normal understanding of death is

20. This point is made in "The Poe Mystery Case," in Richard Wilbur, *Responses: Prose Pieces, 1953–1976* (New York: Harcourt Brace Jovanovich, 1976), 131. The piece originally appeared in the *New York Review of Books,* July 13, 1967, pp. 16, 25–28.

21. Hudson, "Poe and Disraeli," 407–11. Actually, Poe seems to have derived more from a review of *The Young Duke* than from the novel itself; see David H. Hirsch, "Another Source for Poe's 'The Duc De L'Omelette,'" *American Literature,* XXXVIII (1967), 534–36. For the Duc as N. P. Willis, see Kenneth L. Daughrity, "Poe's Quiz on Willis," *American Literature,* V (1933), 55–62. On the other hand, in relating the tale to Poe's more personal concern with metempsychosis, David H. Hirsch interprets the bird as a traditional symbol of the soul. See Hirsch, " 'The Duc De L'Omelette' as Anti-Visionary Tale," *Poe Studies,* X (1977), 36–38.

equivocated. If John Keats "died" as the result of a criticism, then the Duc De L'Omelette "perished of an ortolan" (M, II, 33). Given the Duc's refinement and titular connection with the bird world, it is not surprising that, seeing the bird served without feathers and paper, he should die in a "paroxysm of disgust" (M, II, 34). The object of the exercise is to convince the Duc to rearrange his attitudes and see himself in the same horrified terms as he saw the bird. This connection is anticipated by the initial description of the bird in its golden cage as "enamored, melting, indolent." Similarly, the Duc, reclining "languidly on that ottoman for which he sacrificed his loyalty in outbidding his king," is described as "the most enamored of men" (M, II, 33). It is the devil who is later found sitting "upon that ottoman" (M, II, 36). In other words, the Duc has neglected to give the devil his due, or, since the devil's apartment is clearly an arabesque environment, to see things in their correct relationships. Poe, like William Blake and Ambrose Bierce, often espouses the wisdom of the devil. Satan commands the Duc to strip and take his hair out of paper, in preparation for the frying pan and to point up his relationship with the naked paperless bird. Satan meets with some success; the Duc, "having become satisfied of his identity . . . took a bird's eye view of his whereabouts" (M, II, 35). Now correctly oriented and realizing that the devil never refuses a game of cards, the Duc persuades the devil to let his freedom depend upon the outcome. The Duc wins and is thus permitted to return to his ortolans.

"Four Beasts in One; The Homo-Cameleopard," originally entitled "Epimanes"—meaning madman (M, II, 126)—in the *Southern Literary Messenger* for March, 1836, is, of course, a satire on human dignity, possibly with a specific political application.[22] But it is also and most obviously a further demonstration of misguided response due to the limitations of space, time, and self. Poe begins by correcting a popular assumption that Antiochus Epiphanes is "the Gog of the prophet Ezekiel. This honor is, however, more properly attributable to Cambyses, the son of Cyrus" (M, II, 119–20). Epiphanes' fame rests upon his public acts, which are "more generally noticed by the historians of his time, than the impious, dastardly, cruel, silly

22. Once again President Andrew Jackson appears to be the target. Whipple, "Poe's Political Satire," 83–84.

and whimsical achievements which make up the sum total of his private life and reputation" (M, II, 120). In order to correct the balance, the narrator transports the reader back to the relevant time and place, being careful to distinguish Epiphanes' Antioch from sixteen other cities of the same name. Ever concerned with accuracy, the narrator admits "there is some dispute" about who actually built the city, and he attempts to eradicate "the advantages of a modern education" by apologizing for an anachronistic quotation from Shakespeare (M, II, 120, 121).

The balanced picture that now emerges takes account of "an infinity of mud huts, and abominable hovels," the narrow streets, and the appalling stench (M, II, 122). The object of worship in the Temple of the Sun is not the real sun but a stone representation of "Fire." Many of the ridiculous, painted, half-naked beings, "gesticulating to the rabble . . . belong to the race of philosophers" (M, II, 123). An image of the god Ashimah, it appears, "is neither a lamb, nor a goat, nor a satyr; neither has he much resemblance to the Pan of the Arcadians. Yet all these appearances have been given—I beg pardon—*will* be given—by the learned of future ages." The image is of a baboon. "What great fools are antiquarians," exclaims the narrator. The meaning of valor is equivocated by the song that the mob is singing. True, the king has killed a thousand, but "a thousand chained Israelitish prisoners" (M, II, 124). When the king does appear, it is in the form of a cameleopard, or giraffe, a just representation of the grotesque nature of man. Toward the conclusion, the "reader," who accompanies the narrator, describes the scene: "Surely this is the most populous city of the East! What a wilderness of people! what a jumble of all ranks and ages! what a multiplicity of sects and nations! what a variety of costumes! what a Babel of languages! what a screaming of beasts! what a tinkling of instruments! what a parcel of philosophers!" (M, II, 128). The "reader" is characterizing the contradictory, deceptive, and heterogeneous nature of the human state—a grotesque state. Consequently, Antioch is referred to as "that most grotesque habitation of man" (M, II, 120).

In "A Tale of Jerusalem," which first appeared in the June 9, 1832, Philadelphia *Saturday Courier*, the scene is again the past; and once again Poe is burlesquing another writer. An episode in Horace

Smith's *Zillah; a Tale of the Holy City* is the takeoff point.[23] But the piece makes most sense if interpreted in Poe's terms. The beleaguered city of Jerusalem is an emblem of man's imprisoned perceptions. From their perspective within the city the Philistines misinterpret the surrounding Romans, and the Romans from their perspective misinterpret the Philistines. The intervening layer of fog further symbolizes that impaired communication and understanding which accounts for the deceptive exchange on which the tale focuses.

There remain in the present category five tales that were not, it appears, intended for the Folio Club. They will be considered briefly and in chronological order. Significantly, "A Predicament" (to which attention now returns) or "The Scythe of Time," as it was originally entitled, is written "in the tone heterogeneous" (M, II, 347). And, as in "Loss of Breath," Poe is out to widen the reader's apprehension by bringing him up against the literal meaning of a phrase. With the clock hand—the "Scythe of Time"—biting into her neck, Zenobia discovers "the literal import of that classical phrase" (M, II, 354). Similarly, because the spiral ladder is seemingly endless, the literalistic Zenobia supposes that the top "had been accidentally, or perhaps designedly, removed." The dog, Diana, metaphorically and literally "*smelt a rat*" and is to be picked clean by the same (M, II, 350). At the beginning of the tale, Zenobia regrets her inability to dance or to smell a rat, like Diana. Dancing, it seems, "serene and god-like, and heavenly, and exalting," is symptomatic of harmony and unity (M, II, 348). As the clock hands prepare to meet around the figure V and decapitate Zenobia, the figure V proceeds to dance: "She was evidently a lady of breeding" (M, II, 354). This sentence serves to link the figure V and Zenobia with Diana. Then Zenobia, thinking in quite nonhuman terms, tries to hand the fatigued number a chair. Her sensations "grew indistinct and confused" as she feels herself about to be relieved from her "disagreeable situation," life: "And in this expectation, I was not at all deceived" (M, II, 354, 355). With the loss of her head, Zenobia is at one with the dog, whose attributes she so envied. Her severed head compensates for the dog's severed tail, "cut off exceedingly close";

23. J. S. Wilson, "The Devil Was in It," 219.

and now, "dogless, niggerless, headless," she is at one with everything (M, II, 348, 357).

A head is also lost in "Never Bet the Devil Your Head: A Tale with a Moral," first published in *Graham's Magazine*, September, 1841. Here it is the Transcendentalists, with their esoteric notions about the meaning of things, who are under attack. As a result of being flogged left-handedly, Toby Dammit grows up with an increasing propensity for evil, culminating in his compulsive tendency to bet the devil his head, thinking that the abstract nature of such a wager would not cost him money or anything tangible. His friend, the narrator, attempts to remonstrate with him, but his reply takes the form of a condescending lecture. The narrator, however, can only recall "the heads of his discourse" (M, II, 625). The pun here suggests that it is the basic abstract assumptions of the Transcendentalists that Poe wishes to demolish. Finally, the devil does take Dammit up on his bet, and Dammit does lose his head, first metaphorically then literally. He bets the devil his head that he can jump over a turnstile. But speculation is undercut by fact; an overhanging brace severs his head.

"Three Thursdays in One Week," a source of "Three Sundays in a Week," which Poe first published in the November 27, 1841, Philadelphia *Saturday Evening Post*, doubtless appealed to him as a demonstration that all may not be the way it seems.[24] Poe initiates the theme by having Bobby swear at his uncle in his imagination: "The fact is, some trivial discrepancy *did* exist, just then, between what I said and what I had not the courage to say" (M, II, 649–50). His uncle, possessed by the "whim of *contradiction*," refuses to consent to Bobby's marriage until "*three Sundays come together in a week*" (M, II, 651). However, two sailors who have just returned from trips around the world, but in opposite directions, are able to prove to him that the required condition has been fulfilled—because for one of them Sunday is expected tomorrow and for the other Sunday was yesterday, while for the uncle Sunday is that very day.

"The Oblong Box," which first appeared in *Godey's Lady's Book* for September, 1844, is both a transmogrified version of the ship,

24. For this identification see F. N. Cherry, "The Sources of Poe's 'Three Sundays in a Week,' " *American Literature*, II (1930), 232–35.

tomb, and premature burial motif in "The Premature Burial" (published the same year) and a further instance of idiopathic deception. The narrator, aboard the ship *Independence* comes to all the wrong conclusions about the contents of his artist friend's oblong box and the reason for the extra cabin. He supposes that the box contains a picture and that the extra cabin is to separate the artist from his ugly wife. It transpires that the woman whom the narrator supposed to be the artist's wife is only impersonating the wife, who actually lies dead in the box. Consequently, the nosy narrator confesses, "My own mistakes arose, naturally enough, through too careless, too inquisitive, and too impulsive a temperament" (M, III, 934). Because of personal idiosyncrasies, he is deceived about the nature of reality.

The equivocal distinction between appearance and reality occurs again in "The System of Doctor Tarr and Professor Fether," first published in *Graham's Magazine* for November, 1845. However, there is the additional twist that, as Harry Levin argues, the tale contains an allegory—albeit rather inconsistent—of the southern United States and asks the question: "What would happen if the slaves tired of slavery and dispossessed their masters?" But more generally, Poe is muddying the distinction between the sane and the insane. As a result of a revolution, made possible by the license of the Tarr and Fether "soothing system," it is claimed that the relationship between keeper and inmate has been reversed in the asylum described by the visiting narrator (M, III, 1021). The narrator is not entirely taken in by the supposedly cured lunatics. Nor should the reader be taken in by the narrator who, in all probability, is not a visitor but an inmate. His companion introduces him to the superintendent, Monsieur Maillard, and then leaves. Thus, it is not surprising that, when the ten keepers (who have been subjected to a tar-and-feather treatment) break out, the narrator identifies with the lunatics and gets beaten up.[25]

25. Harry Levin, *The Power of Blackness* (New York: Alfred A. Knopf, 1958), 122. For an alternative interpretation, see Richard Wilbur, "The House of Poe," in Robert Regan (ed.), *Poe: A Collection of Critical Essays* (Englewood Cliffs, N.J.: Prentice-Hall, 1967), 117–18. For the argument that the narrator is Charles Dickens, see William Whipple, "Poe's Double-edged Satiric Tale," *Nineteenth Century Fiction*, IX (1955), 121–33. But see also Richard P. Benton, "Poe's 'The System of Dr. Tarr and Prof. Fether': Dickens or Willis?" *Poe Newsletter*, I (1968), 7–9.

V

Among Poe's grotesques there exists a related group of tales—the fourth category of grotesques—that deal with the psychological condition of the schizophrenic.[26] Undoubtedly, in these works that emphasize the doppelgänger theme and illustrate a theory about the imp of the perverse, Poe is revealing aspects of his own personality. In these tales the narrator is a split personality and thus deceived about the nature of his true identity. More often than not, he desires to destroy his double, a projected aspect of his own personality that he does not wish to acknowledge. These tales, it should be observed, constitute the best of the grotesques.

The most explicit of the doppelgänger tales is "William Wilson," which first appeared in 1839 in the *Gift: A Christmas and New Year's Present for 1840*. It has received ample commentary and the remarks here will therefore be brief.[27] The William Wilson who dogs the narrator's footsteps is the narrator's conscience; in killing the undesirable shadow, he kills himself. In view of the deceptions that the narrator practices (toward the tale's conclusion, he is savoring the possibility of an adulterous relationship with the wife of his host) and the deception he experiences concerning his own nature, it is fitting (not less for being common in Poe's work) that the denouement takes place against the background of a masquerade.

In "The Man of the Crowd," first published in both George R. Graham's *The Casket* and in the *Gentleman's Magazine* (that Graham had recently bought from William E. Burton) for December, 1840, the narrator is the pursuer, not the double. The figure of the old man in the crowd, with whom the narrator feels an inexplicable

---

26. Patrick F. Quinn was the first critic to isolate the doppelgänger theme in Poe. See the chapter entitled "That Spectre in My Path," in Quinn, *The French Face of Edgar Poe* (Carbondale: Southern Illinois University Press, 1957), 216–56.

27. See, for example, three articles by James W. Gargano: "The Question of Poe's Narrators," *College English*, XXV (1963), 179; " 'William Wilson': The Wildest Sublunary Visions," *Washington and Jefferson Literary Journal*, I (1967), 9–16; and "Art and Irony in 'William Wilson,' " *Emerson Society Quarterly*, no. 60 (1970), 18–22. Ruth Sullivan intriguingly suggests that it is Wilson's superego who narrates the tale and not, as might appear, the sinful Wilson. She claims that the style is not that of instinctual license and points to Wilson's pleasure in recalling the restrictive character of Bransby's school. Sullivan, "William Wilson's Double," *Studies in Romanticism*, XV (1976), 253–63.

affinity, is compared to "pictural incarnations of the fiend" and seems to be a representative of unacknowledged guilt (M, II, 511). What is at issue is the affinity between the doppelgänger theme and the theme of human perversity. The narrator cannot explain why he feels obliged to follow the old man. In terms of Poe's philosophy, the answer resides in man's inherent desire for integration and unity. The human condition is that of division both externally and psychically. Notions of contrast and opposition exist only because of man's unnatural or perverse state. In a certain sense, it is man's imp of the perverse that leads him to distinguish between things and a sense of ideality that inspires him to pull things together. The doppelgänger, then, exists because of man's perverse condition. Duality and duplicity are opposed to unity. But at the same time, as Baudelaire realized, it is the nature of that which is perverse to unite or fuse contradictory elements.[28] Thus, the imp of the perverse may also be viewed as a function of man's aspirations toward unity. Poe's use of the term is richly paradoxical, reflecting as it does the elusive perceptual distinction between the grotesque and the arabesque. Correspondingly, it is in the nature of the doppelgänger tales that they ultimately subvert all attempts at rational analysis.

It is the narrator's fortune to gain some intimation of this state of affairs. He is in one of those "moods of the keenest appetency, when the film from the mental vision departs," unlike the gamblers among the crowd who are distinguishable by "a filmy dimness of eye" (M, II, 507, 509). With his enhanced perception, the narrator sees external reality—the crowd rushing by the window—in terms of duality: "Two dense and continuous tides of population were rushing past the door" (M, II, 507). He distinguishes "two large classes" among the upper echelon of society, and among the clerks "I discerned two remarkable divisions" (M, II, 508). The gamblers display "two other traits . . . by which I could always detect them," and "they seem to prey upon the public in two battalions" (M, II, 509).

28. Lois Hyslop and Francis E. Hyslop, Jr. (eds.), *Baudelaire on Poe* (Philadelphia: Bald Eagle Press, 1952), 125–26. Elsewhere it is argued that the perverse "is at bottom not an evil sentiment but a beneficient one"; see Joseph J. Moldenhauer, "Murder as a Fine Art: Basic Connections Between Poe's Aesthetics, Psychology, and Moral Vision," *PMLA*, LXXXIII (May, 1968), 295.

References to "pick-pockets" and "gamblers" connect duplicity and deception with the general duality. This description of mundane reality, "full of a noisy and inordinate vivacity, which jarred discordantly upon the ear, and gave an aching sensation to the eye," anticipates Poe's ideas about the heterogeneity of the irradiated universe as outlined in *Eureka* (M, II, 510).

The old man (enveloped in "a closely buttoned and evidently second-handed *roquelaire*," through a rent in which the narrator, unless "my vision deceived me," glimpses a diamond and a dagger) is most at ease when moving "to and fro" in the crowd (M, II, 512, 513, 514, 515). He spends all his time seeking out the crowd and is intensely disturbed when the crowd disperses. The old man is participating in man's idealist aspirations toward unity. Just as the imp of the perverse may be oriented toward both the mundane world and the ideal sphere, so the old man's function as a representative of earthly guilt does not contradict his idealistic role. Arabesque reality in Poe (or more accurately the contingent arabesque-grotesque relationship) is frequently symbolized by seas and lakes, and in this tale the crowd is likened consistently to a body of water. The old man "turned in the direction of the *river*, and, *plunging* through a great variety of devious ways, came out, at length, in view of one of the principal theatres. . . . I saw the old man *gasp as if for breath* while he *threw* himself amid the crowd" (italics added). The italicized words are all consistent with the water metaphor. Toward the tale's conclusion, "wooden tenements were seen tottering to their fall" (M, II, 514). The imminent collapse here intimated, as in "The Fall of the House of Usher," is clearly the centripetal collapse into unity.

Like the double in "The Man of the Crowd," the double of the narrator of "The Tell-Tale Heart," first published in the Boston *Pioneer* for January, 1843, is an old man. And just as William Wilson spies by lamplight on his sleeping double, so does the narrator in "The Tell-Tale Heart." The narrators in both tales are in a superacute state. In "The Tell-Tale Heart" the relationship between the old man and the narrator is made fairly explicit. The old man sits up in bed, "listening;—just as I have done, night after night"; and the old man's groan, "many a night, just at midnight . . . has welled up from my own bosom" (M, III, 794). What disturbs the narrator about the old man is his eye: "One of his eyes resembled that of a vulture—a pale blue eye with a film over it" (M, III, 792). On the basis of the vulture simile, Richard Wilbur identifies the old man as representative of "Science! true daughter of Old Time," which is called a "Vulture" in "Sonnet—To Science" (M, I, 91). The old man represents that aspect of the narrator which restricts him to conventional reality. It will be recalled that certain members of the everyday-world crowd in "The Man of the Crowd" possess "a filmy dimness of eye" (M, II, 509). Nor is it inconsistent that the "Evil Eye" may mean punningly, as one critic suggests, "an evil I" (M, III, 793).[29]

In killing the old man, the narrator is trying to escape from grotesque reality into arabesque reality. His method is actually suicide, although on a literal level he will die in accordance with the processes of justice. When the narrator congratulates himself "with what dissimulation I went to work," he does not realize that the dissimulation is at his own expense (M, III, 792). Although he desires unity, there is evidence to suggest that he is deceived or confused about the means of attaining it. He believes that by annihilating the earthly part of himself he may attain ideality. Consequently, in accordance with his need to distinguish, he uses only "a single thin ray" of light, "like the thread of a spider"; and, having killed the old man, "I dismembered the corpse" (M, III, 793, 794, 796). Further deceived at the tale's conclusion, he gives himself away to the police and to the reader. The police and the ringing sound are a further projection: "The ringing became more distinct:—it continued and became more distinct: I talked more freely to get rid of the feeling: but it continued and gained definiteness—until, at length, I found that the noise was not within my ears" (M, III, 797). The narrator appears to be exemplifying the paradoxical perverse and displaying a conflict between means and ends. He knows what he wants to get away from, but he does not see clearly what state it is that he wishes

29. Notes to Richard Wilbur (ed.), Poe: Complete Poems (New York: Dell, 1959), 132; E. Arthur Robinson, "Poe's 'The Tell-Tale Heart,' " Nineteenth Century Fiction, XIX (1965), 377.

to attain. The means that he uses betray his commitment to the earthly condition that he wishes to deny, to distinction rather than fusion. The narrator is in such a confused state that, ironically, at the tale's conclusion he again projects and disowns an aspect of himself when he accuses the police of deceiving *him* in pretending not to hear the heartbeats: " 'Villains!' I shrieked, 'dissemble no more!' " (M, III, 797).

What most displeases the narrator about earthly reality is its temporal nature. His real quarrel is with time, and his objective is the attainment of eternity. E. Arthur Robinson has paid tribute to Poe's pioneering use of subjective time in this tale.[30] In a sense, the narrator does almost succeed in stopping time because of his keyed-up condition: "It took me an hour to place my whole head within the opening. . . . A watch's minute hand moves more quickly than did mine" (M, III, 793). The old man is a product of and identified with time. He listens "to the death watches [literally a species of insect] in the wall" and "groans" at midnight—at midnight because then, at the edge of a new day, the passing of time is especially palpable (M, III, 794). The sound of the old man's heart is twice likened to the sound "a watch makes when enveloped in cotton" (M, III, 795, 797). The narrator speaks of death as having "enveloped the victim," and he kills the old man by suffocating him, although for a while his "heart beat on with a muffled sound" (M, III, 794, 795). But the narrator does thwart time, and not just subjectively, because in killing his double, like William Wilson, he kills himself. This tale is one of Poe's masterpieces, a *tour de force* of suggestiveness and compactness. Even the title, "The Tell-Tale Heart," betrays the sinister ticktock of time. Fyodor Dostoevski was much more prolix in *Crime*

30. Robinson, "Poe's 'The Tell-Tale Heart,' " 369. See also James W. Gargano, "The Theme of Time in 'The Tell-Tale Heart,' " *Studies in Short Fiction*, V (1968), 378–82. For an intriguing, if eccentric, analysis of Poe as "the maniac of time," see Jean-Paul Weber, "Edgar Poe or the Theme of the Clock," in Regan, *Poe: A Collection of Critical Essays*, 79–97. Further perspectives are provided by the Poe chapter in Georges Poulet, *The Metamorphosis of the Circle*, trans. Carley Dawson and Elliott Coleman (Baltimore, Md.: Johns Hopkins University Press, 1966), 182–202; and by "The Death of the Present: Edgar Allan Poe," in John F. Lynen, *The Design of the Present: Essays on Time and Form in American Literature* (New Haven, Conn.: Yale University Press, 1969), 205–71.

and *Punishment,* which is similar in theme and undoubtedly was influenced by Poe's tale.[31]

Perhaps "The Black Cat," first published in the Philadelphia *United States Saturday Post* for August 19, 1843, and often lumped with "Berenice" as the most distasteful of Poe's tales, is a more remarkable achievement. Once again, although this time more covertly, the theme is that of the doppelgänger.[32] As in "The Tell-Tale Heart," there is some doubt about the narrator's sanity. In the earlier tale, the narrator "dismembered the corpse" (M, III, 796). In this tale, he considers "cutting the corpse into minute fragments" (M, III, 856). After the deed in both tales, the narrator experiences a false sense of security. And, as before, he will not acknowledge that his actions are psychologically explicable. Everything is beyond normal human understanding. The narrator can only attribute the strange events to the "spirit of PERVERSENESS"—"one of the primitive impulses of the human heart. . . . It was this unfathomable longing of the soul *to vex itself*—to offer violence to its own nature—to do wrong for the wrong's sake only—that urged me to continue and finally to consummate the injury I had inflicted upon the offending brute" (M, III, 852). These words syntactically imply that, in injuring the cat, he is offering violence to his own nature. Although the narrator claims, "I am above the weakness of seeking to establish a sequence of cause and effect, between the disaster and the atrocity," he does admit that "some intellect may be found which will reduce my phantasm to the common-place . . . which will perceive, in the circumstance I detail with awe, nothing more than an ordinary succession of very natural causes and effects" (M, III, 853, 850).

The truth is that the narrator's violence toward his once muchadmired black cat *amounts* to an attempt to exorcise a recently activated aspect of his own personality—his intemperance and lost do-

31. Fyodor M. Dostoevski, "Three Tales of Edgar Poe: 'The Tell-Tale Heart,' 'The Black Cat' and 'The Devil in the Belfry,' " *Wremia,* I (1861), 2, 30, reprinted in Eric Carlson (ed.), *The Recognition of Edgar Allan Poe* (Ann Arbor: University of Michigan Press, 1966), 60–62; and Vladimir Ostrov, "Dostoievsky on Edgar Allan Poe," *American Literature,* XIV (1942), 70–74.

32. Again, a sensitive analysis is that of James W. Gargano, " 'The Black Cat': Perverseness Reconsidered," *Texas Studies in Literature and Language,* II (1960), 172–78.

cility. The link between the narrator's intemperance and the cat can be documented. The cat takes its name from Pluto, ruler of the underworld; and the narrator's superstitious wife regards "all black cats as witches in disguise" (M, III, 850). Correspondingly, the narrator "through the instrumentality of the Fiend Intemperance" is possessed by "the fury of a demon" and "a more than fiendish malevolence" (M, III, 851). Fiends, of course, belong in Pluto's underworld. In this state, the narrator opens his "penknife" and gouges out one of the cat's eyes: "I blush, I burn, I shudder, while I pen the damnable atrocity" (M, III, 851). The repetition of "pen" gives the reader the impression that, in writing about the experience, the narrator is actually reliving it. While "in a den of more than infamy," the narrator comes upon a second cat, "reposing upon the head of one of the immense hogsheads of Gin, or of Rum" (M, III, 854). This description anticipates the tableaux at the tale's conclusion, but it also underlines the connection between the cat and intemperance. And, in "a rage more than demoniacal," the narrator wields an axe above his wife's head (M, III, 856). Then, after the narrator asks that God deliver him "from the fangs of the Arch-Fiend," there occurs the telltale shriek "such as might have arisen only out of hell" (M, III, 859).

The narrator hangs the first cat, only to discover the image of a hanged cat imprinted upon the wall above his bed the following night after the rest of the house has been consumed by fire. The second cat is identical with the first, except for "an indefinite splotch of white, covering nearly the whole region of the breast" (M, III, 854). Thus black on white is followed by white on black. What is white and indistinct in Poe represents arabesque reality, and it is not surprising that the narrator's wife should be linked with the white splotch because the women with whom Poe's protagonists *fall* in love also represent arabesque reality: "My wife had called my attention, more than once, to the character of the mark of white hair" (M, III, 855). This mark, "originally very indefinite . . . assumed a rigorous distinctness of outline" (M, III, 855). It forms a gallows and reverberates backward and forward, linking the first cat, which the narrator hung, with the narrator's own forthcoming death by hanging. The changing outline of the splotch from indistinct to distinct and the "accidental" but symbolically codetermined death of his wife imply that the narrator, because of his penchant for distinguishing and disowning, has lost all potential for achieving arabesque reality.

There are two cats to mirror the two sides of the narrator's personality, two sides that gradually give way to one. The second cat hangs like "an incarnate Nightmare that I had no power to shake off —incumbent eternally upon my heart! . . . The feeble remnant of the good within me succumbed. Evil thoughts became my soul intimates—the darkest and most evil of thoughts" (M, III, 856). Since the house has burnt down, he now lives in the cellar, Pluto's underworld, where he finally walls up his dead wife and, unintentionally, the second cat "as the monks of the middle ages are recorded to have walled up their victims" and as Montresor is to wall up Fortunato (M, III, 857). Because the cellar is the underworld and the narrator is now all fiend, he and the building are specifically connected. The corpse is immured in "a false chimney, or fireplace," which has been bricked up. As to the efficacy of "this calculation I was not decieved," boasts the narrator (M, III, 857). He is, however, deceived in most other ways. Symbolically and traditionally, the chimney is the heart of the house; so when the narrator says, "I folded my arms upon my bosom," the reader is encouraged to suspect that this seemingly irrelevant gesture is, in fact, part of a symbolic design (M, III, 858). The tableau of the shrieking cat upon the head of the dead wife "of my bosom" entombed in the chimney can be seen as a projection of the narrator's self—the reality of the condition of his heart that his folded arms attempt to conceal (M, III, 858). His intemperance has extinguished whatever spark of ideality he may have possessed.

In some ways "The Imp of the Perverse," which first appeared in Graham's Magazine for July, 1845, is more an exercise in definition than a tale. The "mad" narrator, introducing his death-cell confession, is at his most perverse in supposing that the imp of the perverse lies outside of man's reason, whereas it is, in one sense, a consequence of it. Awareness of the unifying aspect of the perverse, however, is another matter: "In the pure arrogance of the reason, we have all overlooked it," the narrator reflects. "The intellectual or logical man, rather than the understanding or observant man, set himself to imagine designs—to dictate purposes to God. Having thus fathomed to his satisfaction the intentions of Jehovah, out of these intentions he built his innumerable systems of mind" (M, III, 1219).[33] In Poe's terms, the narrator is correct in criticizing man for this activity; but the narrator, by abnegating self-responsibility and defining some exclusively external imp of the perverse, is also deluded.

Yet, in giving instances of the perverse, he does betray an awareness of a schizoid condition. Concerning procrastination: "We tremble with the violence of the conflict within us,—of the definite with the indefinite—of the substance with the shadow. But, if the contest has proceeded thus far, it is the shadow, which prevails,—we struggle in vain" (M, III, 1222). Concerning the desire to fall: "By slow degrees our sickness, and dizziness, and horror, become merged in a cloud of unnameable feeling. By gradations, still more imperceptible, this cloud assumes shape, as did the vapor from the bottle out of which arose the genius in the Arabian Nights. But out of this our cloud upon the precipice's edge, there grows into palpability, a shape, far more terrible than any genius, or any demon of a tale, and yet it is but a thought" (M, III, 1222–23). This is reminiscent of the black cat's white splotch, but the association to be stressed is that between the perverse and thought: "To indulge for a moment, in any attempt at *thought*, is to be inevitably lost; for reflection but urges us to forbear, and *therefore* it is, I say, that we *cannot*" (M, III, 1223).

Finally comes the narrator's own story. It is very like "The Tell-Tale Heart." He has murdered his victim in bed by means of a poisoned candle. "For a very long period of time" he feels secure, "but there arrived at length an epoch, from which the pleasurable feeling grew, by scarcely perceptible gradations, [like the "cloud of unnameable feeling"] into a haunting and harrassing thought" (M,

33. These assertions may profitably be related to *Eureka*, published three years later.

III, 1224). The syntactical convolutions of the following sentence suggest, once more, that the murderer and his victim are one: "And now my own casual self-suggestion, that I might possibly be fool enough to confess the murder of which I had been guilty, confronted me, as if the very ghost of him whom I had murdered—and beckoned me on to death." As with the black cat, he tries "to shake off this nightmare of the soul" and to stem "every succeeding wave of thought. . . . I well, too well understood that, to *think*, in my situation, was to be lost." Nevertheless, he fails and confesses after experiencing "all the pangs of suffocation" (M, III, 1225–26). This moment and the murder are symbolically simultaneous. (Presumably, the poisoned candle affected the air that his victim breathed, so he died of asphixiation). But "the pangs of suffocation," coupled with the sense that he has been struck with a "broad palm upon the back," imply that this "death" is also a form of birth (M, III, 1226).

"The Cask of Amontillado," which appeared in *Godey's Lady's Book* for November, 1846, and "Hop-Frog," which appeared in the Boston *Flag of Our Union* for March 17, 1849, are unique among the doppelgänger tales in that the protagonist gets away with his murder, more unequivocally in the latter than in the former. In "The Cask of Amontillado," the doppelgänger theme is so well disguised as to be almost invisible, and in "Hop-Frog" it does not appear to be there at all. In between these two tales Poe wrote and published *Eureka*. This chronology is at least suggestive.

The evidence that identifies Montresor with his victim, Fortunato, is subtle, but it does exist.[34] Fortunato is a connoisseur of wines, and Montresor reveals, "In this respect I did not differ from him *materially*" (italics added; M, III, 1257). The three names in the story suggesting fortune, treasure, and lucre (Luchresi) all add up to much the same thing. In the following sentence as originally published (Mabbott's text follows Griswold's in placing a period after "arm"), Montresor and Fortunato are inextricably confused: "Thus

34. The pioneering work here has been done by James W. Gargano, who seems to have claimed the territory of the perverse in Poe as his own. Gargano, " 'The Cask of Amontillado': A Masquerade of Motive and Identity," *Studies inn Short Fiction*, IV (1967), 119–26.

speaking, Fortunato possessed himself of my arm; and putting on a mask of black silk and drawing a *roquelaire* closely about my person, I suffered him to hurry me to my palazzo" (M, III, 1258). More revealing, Montresor says of Fortunato: "You are happy, as once I was" (M, III, 1259). As in "The Black Cat," the narrator is taunted by the image of his former self.

The truth is that Montresor, although a rich man, is jealous of Fortunato because he believes him to be both rich and happy because of his name and his "motley," the dress of a jester. But Fortunato turns out to be unfortunate, not only because of his constant cold, but also because of his death. He is dressed in motley only because it is "the supreme madness" of the carnival masquerade. Montresor, then, is doubly deceived: first, in hoping that he can eradicate the memory of a formerly happier self and, second, in believing his former self to be happier than his present self. The relationship between the two of them is like that between Amontillado and sherry, between which Luchresi cannot distinguish for the very good reason that Amontillado is a sherry. When Montresor tells Fortunato that he has "a pipe of what passes for Amontillado," he is placing the drink in the context of the general masquerade. The tale is rich in such deceit. It is the "enthusiasm" of the Italians "to practise imposture upon the British and Austrian *millionaires*," and so Montresor smiles hypocritically in the face of Fortunato who, "like his countrymen, was a quack." (M, III, 1257).

Just as the different names may refer to the same object, so the same name may refer to two different objects. A cask may be a barrel or a casket: "We had passed through long walls of piled skeletons, with casks and puncheons intermingling" (M, III, 1260). Fortunato makes a grotesque gesture, which indicates that he is a member of the Masonic brethren. Montresor produces the trowel, with which he is to wall up Fortunato (in what may be viewed as the catacomb labyrinth of his mind), to indicate that, as a stonemason, he is similarly affiliated. Montresor can split things; he can see dual meanings in words, but he cannot see that the two names, Fortunato and Montresor, refer to one person. The peculiar conclusion—with Fortunato laughing hysterically and Montresor yelling—is intended to indicate a reversal of roles: Montresor turning into Fortunato and discovering that Fortunato is not so fortunate as he jealously thought. Then, Montresor discovers, "My heart grew sick; it was the dampness of the catacombs that made it so." He is sick with remorse and Fortunato's cold. "For the half of a century no mortal has disturbed" the area (M, III, 1263). In other words, as "definitely settled," he has punished with impunity as far as legal retribution is concerned, but not as far as peace of mind is concerned (M, III, 1256). After fifty years the event still bothers him. Perhaps the reader is listening to a deathbed confession. The symbolism of the Montresor coat of arms should now be clear: "A huge human foot d'or, in a field azure; the foot crushes a serpent rampant whose fangs are imbedded in the heel" (M, III, 1259). Such is the relationship between Montresor and Fortunato, and similarly symbiotic is the relationship of the parts that constitute this story.

"Hop-Frog" is unique among the doppelgänger tales because it is narrated by an outsider, as if to ensure objectivity. Indeed, it has not previously been included in this grouping. Hop-Frog does succeed in expelling his alter ego to the extent that there appears to be absolutely no relationship between Hop-Frog and his double in the first place. His alter ego takes plural form—the king and his seven ministers (compare King Pest and his court)—until the tale's conclusion when they form "a fetid, blackened, hideous, and indistinguishable mass" (M, III, 1354). Actually, the ministers are only extensions of the king and are like him in appearance, fat and oily and therefore good for candle wax. Of the king it is said, "He seemed to live only for joking. . . . Thus it happened that his seven ministers were all noted for their accomplishments as jokers" (M, III, 1345). But almost immediately following, it is explained that this king, unlike his fellow kings, has retained his jester because "he required something in the way of folly—if only to counterbalance the heavy wisdom of the seven wise men who were his ministers—not to mention himself" (M, III, 1345). The king and his ministers are divided beings, divided between jocularity and solemnity.

In consideration of their exalted positions, their frivolity must be externalized and kept as a form of scapegoat. It is Hop-Frog's function to act as a "counterbalance." The relationship between these luminary persons and Hop-Frog is like that between the chandelier in the circular grand salon and its counterbalance: "At night (the season for which the apartment was especially designed,) it was illuminated principally by a large chandelier, depending by a chain from the centre of the sky-light, and lowered, or elevated, by means of a counterbalance as usual; but (in order not to look unsightly) this latter passed outside the cupola and over the roof" (M, III, 1351). Like the counterbalance, Hop-Frog, a dwarf and a cripple, is similarly unsightly. The "protracted grating sound," which Hop-Frog appears to make when the king insults his friend Trippetta but which Hop-Frog attributes to a parrot "outside the window," might equally originate from the machinery that controls the elevation of the chandelier (M, III, 1349). The silence that accompanies the ascent of the king and his minister "was broken by just such a low, harsh, *grating* sound, as had before attracted the attention of the king and his councillors, when the former threw the wine in the face of Trippetta" (M, III, 1353). The king and his ministers, then, correspond both figuratively and, finally, literally to the artificial light of wisdom that the chandelier casts around the grand salon, which represents grotesque reality.

Hop-Frog and his more graceful friend Trippetta originate from faraway "adjoining provinces"; and, at the story's climax, Hop-Frog "disappeared through the sky-light" to join Trippetta in "their escape to their own country," which may be associated with the natural light of the sun (M, III, 1346, 1354). Actually, Trippetta is not seen after the episode with the king, perhaps because she is an aspect of Hop-Frog's side of things and represents his potential ability to attain arabesque reality—a potentiality that he realizes in extinguishing the wisdom of the king and his ministers. Both Trippetta and the king are aspects of Hop-Frog. When the king says, "he possessed a triplicate treasure in one person," referring to Hop-Frog as fool, dwarf, and cripple, he speaks more truly than he knows. Unwittingly, he is referring to himself as the fool, Trippetta as the dwarf, and Hop-Frog as the cripple. Hop-Frog is in an intermediate condition and hence his "interjectional gait" and his indeterminate appearance, which "much more resembled a squirrel, or a small monkey, than a frog" (M, III, 1346). After the indecision of the king and his ministers "as to what rôles they should assume" to give them "characters," Hop-Frog makes them reveal themselves as the fools they are by suggesting that they dress up as "Eight Chained Ourang-Outangs . . . one of my own country frolics" (M, III, 1347, 1349, 1350). If Hop-Frog is ultimately to turn into the beautiful princess Trippetta of the fairy story, the king and his cohorts are to turn into hop-frogs.

In the seven tales in this section the doppelgänger connection becomes progressively more debatable. In the final tale, the connection between Hop-Frog and the king is so tenuous that the division appears to be complete and the immolation of the outcast a mere formality. This progression may reflect Poe's own increasingly schizophrenic condition. Throughout his life, Poe was divided about his attitude toward man's reason. As an obstacle in the way of ideal perception, Poe condemned it. But, because he himself was a highly intellectual being, he was forced to come to terms with his own reason. In the tales of ratiocination, Poe supposes two types of reason. However, when he wrote *Eureka*, although the work clearly displays the mark of a reasoning intellect, Poe attributes his findings to an ambiguously defined intuition which reveals that beauty which is truth. Had Poe assimilated his double, or was he experiencing a total schizophrenic dissociation? The qualified success that Montresor enjoys in disposing of his double in the tale written just before *Eureka* and the total success enjoyed by Hop-Frog in the tale written just afterward may reflect Poe's splitting psyche. In *Eureka*, Poe does claim to be able to see the distinct truth; and Hop-Frog likewise, identifying the king and his ministers, says, "I now see *distinctly*" (M, III, 1354). In much of Poe's work, what is seen distinctly is a deception. Has Poe himself become the victim of such deception?

VI

In Poe's estimation, poetry and drama are antithetical modes, the former concerning itself with supernal reality and the latter with everyday reality. At one point Poe declares, "We are not too sure, indeed, that 'a dramatic poem' is not a flat contradiction in terms" (H, XIII, 73). And elsewhere he says, "The object of poetry, in general, is beauty—the object of the drama, which has nothing to do with poetry . . . is the *portraiture of nature in human action and earthly incident*" (H, XIII, 112). Thus, a dramatic product may be valued according to its degree of naturalism and verisimilitude. By definition, therefore, the drama will deal with deception since, for Poe, "earthly incident" is characterized by deception. Accordingly, the theme of deception does indeed appear to form the basis of his own play, *Politian—A Tragedy*, different scenes from which were first published in the *Southern Literary Messenger* for December, 1835, and January, 1836, and in 1845 in *The Raven and Other Poems*. But *Politian* is that anomaly, a "dramatic poem," being written in blank verse; and so it might be argued that, axiomatically, Poe found himself unable to finish it.

In accordance with his theory, Poe based his plot on an actual incident. J. O. Beauchamp, a young lawyer, murdered S. P. Sharp, a Kentucky politician, for betraying the woman who later became his wife.[35] Beauchamp was hanged on July 7, 1826, and his wife committed suicide. Politian corresponds to Beauchamp (while also corresponding to Poe), Castiglione to Sharp, and Lalage to the woman involved. In Poe's version of the story everything happens because of the misunderstanding of identity and intention. In a deceptive world nothing is known or fixed. Uncannily, in this drama of altered personalities, changing relationships, and reversed roles, Poe anticipates the theater of Jean Genet. The play's tragedy results from man's defective perception. Extended play on the word *see* in scene 1 serves the same undermining function as extended play on the word *perceive* in scene 10.

Politian is a man so subject to alteration that he appears to be two or three different people. Intimations of a schizoid Politian gradually

35. For a fuller account of the historical details and the play itself, see N. Bryllion Fagin, *The Histrionic Mr. Poe* (Baltimore, Md.: Johns Hopkins University Press, 1949), 75–86. The notes to the text in Thomas Ollive Mabbott (ed.), *Collected Works of Edgar Allan Poe* (6 vols. projected; Cambridge, Mass.: Belknap Press of Harvard University Press, 1969–), I, 288–98, reveal most of the play's many literary echoes.

accumulate. When Politian and Baldazzar, his companion, are talking in scene 6, Baldazzar instructs Politian to "be thy self!" (M, I, 267). But Politian complains, "There is an imp would follow me" (M, I, 268). Clearly, the reader is to intuit Poe's imp of the perverse and the doppelgänger theme. Perhaps Baldazzar, who has known Politian since childhood and who constantly attempts to recall Politian from the world of dreams into the world of practical realities, is Politian's double. By scene 7, Politian has met Lalage and confesses his love. Momentarily, their privacy is destroyed by Lalage's feeling that they are being watched:

> Hist! hush! within the gloom
> Of yonder trees methought a figure past—
> A spectral figure, solemn, and slow, and noiseless—
> Like the grim shadow Conscience, solemn & noiseless.
>
> (M, I, 273–74)

Is it Politian's double pulling him back to reality? In the play's unfinished form, it is impossible to tell. The final extant scene has Politian in the coliseum awaiting Lalage and awaiting the opportunity to kill Castiglione. The wedding between Castiglione and Alessandra, the woman for whom he has jilted Lalage, is to take place in the coliseum. Lalage enters and sees the bride but not the bridegroom. Politian answers, "Tis true where am I?" (M, I, 287). Shortly after this point, the manuscript ends, but there is here an implied identification between Lalage and the bride, Alessandra, and Politian and the bridegroom, Castiglione.

It is evident that, if *Politian* were a tale, it would belong among those dealing with the imp of the perverse. In all the perverse tales the doppelgänger theme is important. But this theme has dramatic complications that Poe chose to skirt. As now extant, the play concludes with Politian's soliloquy on time and the transience of fame —in fact, the theme of alteration, which so much of the play has been about.

> Here where on golden throne the monarch lolled
> Glides spectre-like into his marble home
> Lit by the wan light of the horned moon
> The swift and silent lizard of the stones. (M, I, 286)

"Lolled," in context applied to the monarch, might apply equally well to the lizard's tongue. "Spectre-like," applied to the lizard, might even more accurately describe the dead monarch. "Horned," applied to the moon, equally suits the lizard. The separate reality of the monarch, the moon, and the lizard is a slippery, deceptive thing. It is at this point that the theme of deception gives way to the possibilities of fusion, and it is therefore appropriate that Poe included Politian's apostrophe to the coliseum among his poems, where it will presently be discussed. The next chapter, however, will deal with the sea tales and other pieces that attempt the transition from grotesque to arabesque perception.

4

Sybils of the Future

The sea exercised an especial fascination over Poe. Killis Campbell writes: "Again and again, Poe introduces into his writings glimpses of the sea, with which he, beyond doubt, had an intimate and sympathetic acquaintance."[1] And Poe writes in his "Omniana": "I wonder any being who affects *taste* would venture to assert that this immense body of water presents only sameness and monotony. To me it seems that even the colors and sounds are little less varied than those we see or hear in the midst of the most luxuriant landscape."[2] This establishes a connection between the sea and the "natural" arabesque environments of such landscape pieces as "The Domain of Arnheim," as opposed to the "artificial" interior arabesque environments of the Poe rooms. More than likely, it was the everchanging fluidity of the sea that appealed to Poe. Its unstructured state makes it a perfect symbol of that marginal awareness which occurs when a quicksand grotesque reality gives way to arabesque reality. Certainly, two of Poe's most successful tales and his only complete novel concern sea voyages. And these works play a significant role in the design of his vision.

1. Killis Campbell, The Mind of Poe and Other Studies (1933; rpr., New York: Russell & Russell, 1962), 21; Charles Lee Lewis, "Edgar Allan Poe and the Sea," Southern Literary Messenger, n.s., III (1941), 5–10.
2. This appeared in Burton's Gentleman's Magazine for May, 1840, and is quoted by Campbell, The Mind of Poe, 21.

II

It should be apparent by this time that Poe construed reasoned, logical thought as a barrier to understanding. The "author" of "MS. Found in a Bottle," which first appeared in the Baltimore *Saturday Visitor* for October 19, 1833, is presented almost as a symbol of restrictive thought. His "contemplative turn of mind enabled" him (the past tense is significant) "to methodize the stores which early study very diligently garnered up." His "habits of rigid thought," directed at the works of "the German moralists," equipped him "to detect their falsities." A "relish for physical philosophy," combined with "a deficiency of imagination," he admits, has "tinctured my mind with a very common error of this age—I mean the habit of referring occurrences, even the least susceptible of such reference, to the principles of that science" (M, II, 135).

Although the writer ostensibly proffers this information as a guarantee of verisimilitude for what follows, there is more to it than this. The experience to be described is aimed directly at showing up the limitations of conventional reason. "A Descent into the Maelström," which first appeared in *Graham's Magazine* for May, 1841, and which will be treated parenthetically with "MS. Found in a Bottle," includes an epigraph conveying the same ideal in the slightly misquoted words of "Joseph Glanvill[e]":[3] "The ways of God in Nature, as in Providence, are not as our ways; nor are the models that we frame any way commensurate to the vastness, profundity, and unsearchableness of His works, *which have a depth in them greater than the well of Democritus*" (M, II, 577). Both tales may be read as allegorical journeys through life and into death, where the deceptions of reason are traumatically exposed.

The writer of "MS. Found in a Bottle" is an Ishmael, compelled to travel by a "nervous restlessness which haunted me as a fiend." He is aboard a cargo ship when, one evening, he notices "a very singular, isolated cloud." It spreads out until it looks deceptively "like a long line of low beach" (M, II, 135). A similar "singular copper-

3. Arthur Hobson Quinn, *Edgar Allan Poe: A Critical Biography* (New York: Appleton-Century-Crofts, 1941), 313.

colored cloud" presages the approaching whirlwind in "A Descent into the Maelström" (M, II, 585). Both clouds partake weirdly of the solidity of either a beach or copper. The subversion of reality is underway. The sea also undergoes "a rapid change, and the water seemed more than usually transparent. Although I could distinctly see the bottom, yet, heaving the lead, I found the ship in fifteen fathoms" (M, II, 136). In "A Descent into the Maelström" the sea undergoes "radical alteration" (M, II, 580). Appearances are treacherous. What follows is in both tales described repeatedly as beyond mortal understanding and perception.

"In the next instant," in "MS. Found in a Bottle," the simoon is upon them; but paradoxically "the extreme fury of the blast proved, in a great measure, the salvation of the ship" (M, II, 137). The import of this statement may reflect the contretemps in Poe's own life and certainly characterizes the movement in much of Poe's fiction, which very often depends upon the device of the red herring. What appears to be a situation of extreme hopelessness, or a state of complete security, almost immediately proves to be otherwise. Survival or acceptance depends on a recognition of this contrary principle and, *ipso facto*, of the fluid arabesque state of which the ocean, the uncertain element, is a symbol. Thus, the writer's despair is apparently confirmed by the appearance of a vast ship bearing down upon the smaller vessel, but instead the impact throws him "upon the rigging of the stranger." The writer's successful exchange from the ship of life to the ship of death depends upon a momentary adoption of the correct attitude: "At this instant, I know not what sudden self-possession came over my spirit. Staggering as far aft as I could, I awaited fearlessly the ruin that was to overwhelm" (M, II, 140).

Similarly, the Norwegian in "A Descent into the Maelström" actually succeeds in cheating death by taking the proper attitude or viewpoint. Caught "in the belt of surf that always surrounds the whirl," on the verge of the abyss, "down which we could only see indistinctly on account of the amazing velocity with which we were borne along," the Norwegian concentrates on the side of the whirlpool, which "stood like a huge writhing wall between us and the horizon" (M, II, 588). In other words, the wall of water has the same properties as an arabesque tapestry: "It may appear strange, but now, when we were in the very jaws of the gulf, I felt more composed than when we were only approaching it" (M, II, 588). Accordingly, like Noah, the Norwegian is provided with a covenant as the light of the moon and the dark of the abyss attempt a polarized synthesis: "The rays of the moon seemed to search the very bottom of the profound gulf; but still I could make out nothing distinctly, on account of a thick mist in which everything there was enveloped, and over which there hung a magnificent rainbow, like that narrow and tottering bridge which Mussulmen [Mussulmans or Mahometans] say is the only pathway between Time and Eternity" (M, II, 591). This is to imply that the traveler may cross either way; and the Norwegian, unlike the writer in "MS. Found in a Bottle," travels back from eternity into time.

In trying to estimate which of the objects caught in the whirlpool will be sucked under first, the Norwegian is continually mistaken; but the exercise is profitable: "At length, after making several guesses of this nature, and being deceived in all—this fact—the fact of my invariable miscalculation, set me upon a train of reflection that made my limbs again tremble, and my heart beat heavily once more" (M, II, 592). This sentence should serve to confirm the interpretation that it is the Norwegian's realization of the nature of reality which saves him, rather than the special behavior of "a cylinder, swimming in a vortex" (M, II, 593). This is a nice instance of Poe's deceptive technique. The information about cylinders and the reference to Archimedes is deliberately bogus.[4] To believe it is to apply "physical philosophy" to a strange occurrence, "a very common error of this age" (M, II, 135). Much more relevant is the element of perversity involved in the Norwegian's decision to abandon his boat in favor of a mere barrel.

"A Descent into the Maelström" is embedded in the discussion of "MS. Found in a Bottle" because it is likely that the Norwegian's story may be similar to that of the Swedish companion of the writer in "MS. Found in a Bottle." In both tales there are two characters un-

4. Killis Campbell, "Marginalia on Longfellow, Lowell, and Poe," *Modern Language Notes*, XLII (1927), 520.

dergoing the experience, but only the story of one of the participants is completely developed: in one case he presumably "dies," and in the other he "lives." If the parallel be extended and the Scandinavian common ground be taken into account, it is possible that in "A Descent into the Maelström" Poe is telling something like the story of the Swede, presumed dead, in "MS. Found in a Bottle." Certainly, the experience of the writer in "MS. Found in a Bottle" goes beyond that of the Norwegian and hence is here given subsequent consideration.

Once aboard the second ship, the writer is technically dead. Since the appearance of the second ship coincides with the loss of the first, it is likely that the two ships are closely related. The difference in size is proportionate, the one being "four hundred tons" and the other "four thousand tons" (M, II, 135, 140). Later, the writer examines the timber of the larger ship:

There is a peculiar character about the wood which strikes me as rendering it unfit for the purpose to which it has been applied. I mean its extreme porousness, considered independently of the worm-eaten condition which is a consequence of navigation in these seas, and apart from the rottenness attendant upon age. It will appear perhaps an observation somewhat over-curious, but this wood would have every characteristic of Spanish oak, if Spanish oak were distended by any unnatural means. (M, II, 142–43).

The vast size of the ship could, then, be explained as a result of its being stretched in the transfer from time into infinity. After all, Poe asserts in "Mesmeric Revelation" that spirituality is not a state apart but consists of unparticled matter. Conceivably, the stretching, somewhat solid cloud, which "spread all at once to the eastward and westward," is the narrator's vague adumbration of the spectral ship (M, II, 136).

Other details suggest that the spectral ship is a composite vessel. In spite of the "single row of brass cannon" and the "innumerable battle-lanterns," she "is not, I think, a ship of war" (M, II, 140, 142). She is a fusion of details past and present. "The crew glide to and fro like the ghosts of buried centuries"; and the narrator notes that "there will occasionally flash across my mind a sensation of familiar things, and there is always mixed up with such indistinct shadows of recollection, an unaccountable memory of old foreign chronicles and ages long ago" (M, II, 142, 144). In fact, the ship is a further image of that mediating arabesque condition in which things move "to and fro" and combine inexplicably. As in the case of the stranger's room in "The Assignation," the ship subverts those "proprieties of place, and especially of time . . . which terrify mankind from the contemplation of the magnificent" (M, II, 165–66). Later, random daubs with a tarbrush on a sail form the word "DISCOVERY" (M, II, 142). The use of such mystic script, incidently, is one of the elements common to four of the six pieces examined in this chapter.

Unadjusted to his new state, the writer's first reaction is to hide, but as the epigraph (taken from Philippe Quinault's play *Atys*) points out, "Qui n'a plus qu'un moment à vivre / N'a plus rien à dissimuler" (M, II, 135). Dissimulation, or deception, is only a function of man's mundane state. Nevertheless:

With little difficulty I made my way unperceived to the main hatchway, which was partially open, and soon found an opportunity of secreting myself in the hold. Why I did so I can hardly tell. An indefinite sense of awe, which at first sight of the navigators of the ship had taken hold of my mind, was perhaps the principle of my concealment. I was unwilling to trust myself with a race of people who had offered, to the cursory glance I had taken, so many points of vague novelty, doubt, and apprehension. I therefore thought proper to contrive a hiding-place in the hold. This I did by removing a small portion of the shifting-boards. (M, II, 140–41)

Those "shifting-boards" are particularly appropriate. Following his unnecessary concealment, the narrator experiences that extra sensation "which will admit of no analysis. . . . To a mind constituted like my own, the latter consideration is an evil. I shall never—I know that I shall never—be satisfied with regard to the nature of my conceptions. Yet it is not wonderful that these conceptions are indefinite, since they have their origin in sources so utterly novel. A new sense—a new entity is added to my soul" (M, II, 141). (In "A Descent into the Maelström," reference is made to "the wild bewildering sense of *the novel* which confounds the beholder" [M, II, 581].) As a consequence, the writer of the "MS. Found in a Bottle" recognizes that "concealment is utter folly on my part, for the people *will not see*" (M, II, 141). Because he is aboard a ship of the "dead," there is no reason why his arrival should attract particular attention. In attempting to deceive, he is acting as if he were still "alive."

An unspecified but considerable amount of time is allowed to pass, presumably while all aboard await the day of universal apocalypse. This is the first indication of a distinction between a presently attainable arabesque state and a superior version of the same to be attained in the future. The captain of the ship—whose balanced description like that of Usher and Augustus Bedloe in "A Tale of the Ragged Mountains" marks him as a medium between time and eternity—is not short, not tall, "about five feet eight inches . . . neither robust nor remarkably otherwise. . . . His forehead, although little wrinkled, seems to bear upon it the stamp of a myriad of years.—His gray hairs are records of the past, and his grayer eyes are Sybils of the future" (M, II, 144). (Poe was five feet eight inches tall.) Darkly, the narrator speculates, "It is evident that we are hurrying onward to some exciting knowledge—some never-to-be-imparted secret, whose attainment is destruction." He adds, anticipating The Narrative of A. Gordon Pym: "Perhaps this current leads us to the southern pole itself" (M, II, 145). Finally, the "quivering" ship goes down, but upon the countenance of the crew there is "an expression more of the eagerness of hope than of the apathy of despair" (M, II, 145–46).

The note of spurious factual corroboration appended to the tale, concerning the "holes at the poles" theory, is a typical Poe touch, akin to Hawthorne's "device of multiple choice," in Matthiessen's words, or "formula of alternative possibilities," Yvor Winter's phrase.[5] The effect, of course—if the information in the note were to be taken as the key truth—might be to sabotage the interpretation outlined above. However, as a part of Poe's strategy of fusion, the intention is that a naturalistic interpretation should be allied with, or kept in suspension with, a symbolic interpretation to create a sense of fluid form. And it should be remembered again that the tendency to refer strange occurrences to the science of physical philosophy is

5. F. O. Matthiessen, American Renaissance (New York: Oxford University Press, 1941), 276–77; Yvor Winters, In Defense of Reason (Denver: University of Denver Press, 1947), 170.

"a very common error of this age" (M, II, 135). It would not explain a porous ship.

III

The Narrative of A. Gordon Pym was first published in part in the Southern Literary Messenger for January and February, 1837, and as a book in 1838. Any interpretation of this densely multiplex work must now take some account of the findings detailed in the article, "Chartless Voyage: The Many Narratives of A. Gordon Pym," by J. V. Ridgely and Iola S. Haverstick. These two investigators discern five stages in the composition of the work: (1) the Messenger text— Chapter I through the end of the third paragraph of Chapter III (late in 1836), (2) the rest of Chapter III through Chapter IX (April–May, 1837), (3) Chapter X through Chapter XV (1837–1838), (4) Chapter XVI to the final chapter (March and May, 1838), (5) Chapter XXIII and the endnote (July, 1838). On the basis of these findings, Ridgely and Haverstick extravagantly deduce that any unified reading of the story is necessarily mistaken.[6]

It is hoped that the following pages will clearly demonstrate the error of this conclusion. As shall become apparent, Pym is a highly unified work—structured, in fact, to a quite extraordinary degree. Some guidance is provided here by the prior existence of "MS. Found in a Bottle," which thematically is a microcosm of Pym. The narrator journeys through the mundane world of multiple deception toward an apocalyptic vision of arabesque reality. There can be no question of Poe's beginning Pym unaware of the way in which it was

6. J. V. Ridgely and Iola S. Haverstick, "Chartless Voyage: The Many Narratives of A. Gordon Pym," Texas Studies in Literature and Language, VII (1966), 63–80. It should be noted, however, that the available evidence does not necessarily support only the extended composition theory. Ridgely and Haverstick's case depends largely on the hypothesis that a copyright entry for a half-written version of Pym recorded on June 10, 1837, was corrected over a year later to accord with the title page of the published volume. But it is quite possible that the Pym manuscript was essentially complete before June 10, 1837. See Alexander Hammond, "The Composition of The Narrative of Arthur Gordon Pym: Notes Towards a Re-evaluation," American Transcendental Quarterly, no. 37 (Winter, 1978), 9–20. Critics who, like Ridgely and Haverstick, attack unified readings of Pym include Sidney P. Moss, "Arthur Gordon Pym, or the Fallacy of Thematic Interpretation," University of Kansas City Review, XXIII (1967), 299–306; L. Moffitt Cecil, "The Two Narratives of Arthur Gordon Pym," Texas Studies in Literature and Language, V (1963), 231–41.

to end. There are also fairly direct verbal similarities and plot parallels between "MS. Found in a Bottle" and *Pym*. Pym's extraordinary transference from the *Ariel* to the *Penguin* is reminiscent of the miraculous exchange from one ship to the other in "MS. Found in a Bottle." Once aboard the strange new ship, the writer of "MS. Found in a Bottle" finds it necessary to conceal himself as does Pym aboard the *Grampus*. In addition, *Pym* concludes with a reference to "some immense and far-distant rampart in the heaven," which matches talk of "ramparts" at the end of "MS. Found in a Bottle" and in "A Descent into the Maelström" (M, II, 145, 597). But more importantly, even if the staggered timetable is accurate, *Pym* was written in less than two years. If the five stages of development occurred over a period of, for example, five years, Ridgely and Haverstick might have a stronger case.

However, Ridgely and Haverstick are probably correct in their analysis of the Introductory Note. The *Narrative* was planned as a hoax to appear under the authorship of A. G. Pym; but the first two episodes in the *Southern Literary Messenger* were attributed on the contents page to Poe, possibly as a result of the bungling of Thomas W. White, the editor. It seems likely that the reversals and convolutions of "Pym's" Note are largely an attempt to salvage the story's credibility by explaining how Poe came to write the first parts of Pym's story. The effect of this curious "*exposé*," as Pym ironically calls it, is to multiply confusion concerning the truthfulness of the narrative and give a further twist to the turns of deception (H, III, 3). Indeed, as Patrick Quinn and Edward H. Davidson conclusively demonstrate, deception is the dominant theme in *Pym*.[7] There is thus no need to rehearse in detail all the incidents and maneuvers involving deception: the hoodwinking of relatives by Pym and his friend Augustus; Pym's concealment in the hold of the *Grampus*; the mutiny and countermutiny including Pym's masquerade as a corpse;[8] the treachery of the natives from whom Pym and his second

7. Patrick F. Quinn, *The French Face of Edgar Poe* (Carbondale: Southern Illinois University Press, 1957), 169–218; Edward H. Davidson, *Poe: A Critical Study* (Cambridge, Mass.: Harvard University Press, 1957), 156–80.
8. Compare the strikingly similar episode in Herman Melville's *Israel Potter*. This parallel is also noted by Charles N. Watson, Jr., "Premature Burial in *Arthur Gordon Pym* and *Israel Potter*," *American Literature*, XLVII (1975), 105–107.

companion, Dirk Peters, conceal themselves. Not only is every turn of the plot motivated by, or illustrative of, deception; but the word itself constantly recurs. The following analysis will concentrate instead on Poe's deceptive technique, including what is perhaps the most illusive element in the work—its structural integrity.

An important aspect of Poe's technique of deception is the pseudocrisis, or red herring: all those occasions in Pym (and elsewhere) when a dire situation is survived, almost magically. In Chapter I, which is a microcosm of the whole, Pym and his friend Augustus quickly regret their decision to go for a night sail in Pym's boat, the Ariel: "A fierce wind and strong ebb-tide were hurrying us to destruction" (H, III, 9). Pym is ready to die: "I recommended myself to God" (H, III, 10). However, the next moment he is safely aboard the Penguin, as is Augustus, who expresses his relief with "alternate laughter and tears" (H, III, 11). Apparently, "our deliverance seemed to have been brought about by two of those almost inconceivable pieces of good fortune which are attributed by the wise and pious to the special interference of Providence" (italics added; H, III, 12). Pym was discovered fastened (almost umbilically) against the hull (perhaps it should be flanks) of the Penguin, whereas Augustus was still attached to the floating deck of the cuddy where Pym had tied him. The theme of rebirth, the sense that all may be a dream (Pym is in bed on the verge of a drunken sleep just before the escapade) or a hoax, the equation of survival or sustenance with descent (the area below deck, or the subconscious, and Pym's "down under" destination) are elements that appear throughout the entire narrative.[9] Pym can be read consistently and convincingly in a number of different ways. Some of these readings are complementary; where they

9. For the rebirth interpretive slant, see Marie Bonaparte, The Life and Works of Edgar Allan Poe: A Psycho-Analytic Interpretation, trans. John Rodker (London: Imago Publishing Co., 1949), 290–352. For an account of the dream quality, see Gaston Bachelard's 1942 Introduction to a French edition of Pym reprinted in Bachelard, The Right to Dream, trans. J. A. Underwood (New York: Grossman, 1971), 113–26; and Walter G. Bezanson, "The Troubled Sleep of Arthur Gordon Pym," in Rudolf Kirk and C. F. Main (eds.), Essays in Literary History, Presented to J. Milton French (New Brunswick, N.J.: Rutgers University Press, 1960), 145–75. For the above-below dichotomy, see Richard A. Levine, "The Downward Journey of Purgation: Notes on an Imagistic Leitmotif in The Narrative of Arthur Gordon Pym," Poe Newsletter, II (1969), 29–31.

are not—where the nature of the reality of the narrative is in dispute —Poe requires his reader not to choose but to maintain such interpretations in a state of fluid coexistence on the basis of a deceptive unity. It must, however, be admitted that this is a position which makes it often impossible to distinguish between what is Poe's deliberately deceptive technique and what is plain error.

Pym's explanation as to why, after his nightmarish experience, he still longed for the sea, is fraught with reversal and contradiction. "In no affairs of mere prejudice, pro or con," he writes, "do we deduce inferences with entire certainty" (H, III, 17). The one week after the adventure "proved amply long enough to erase from my memory the shadows, and bring out in vivid light all the pleasurably exciting points of colour, all the picturesqueness, of the late perilous accident." Augustus' stories, "more than one half of which I now suspect to have been sheer fabrications," appeal to Pym's "enthusiastic temperament, and somewhat gloomy, although glowing imagination." It now appears that it is precisely "the shadows . . . which most strongly enlisted my feelings":

> For the bright side of the painting I had a limited sympathy. My visions were of shipwreck and famine; of death or captivity among barbarian hordes; of a lifetime dragged out in sorrow and tears, upon some gray and desolate rock, in an ocean unapproachable and unknown. Such visions or desires—for they amounted to desires—are common, I have since been assured, to the whole numerous race of the melancholy among men—at the time of which I speak I regarded them only as prophetic glimpses of a destiny which I felt myself in a measure bound to fulfil. (H, III, 17–18)

In anticipation of this perverse destiny, Augustus is represented as fusing with Pym, having "thoroughly entered into my state of mind" to the extent of involving "a partial interchange of character" (H, III, 18).[10]

Thus driven, Pym arranges with Augustus to hide in the afterhold of the *Grampus*, a ship commanded by his friend's father. The afterhold appears to symbolize both the subconscious and Poe's view of the human state, containing, as it does, "a complete chaos of

10. The element of the perverse is also evident throughout the narrative. See Joseph J. Moldenhauer, "Imagination and Perversity in *The Narrative of Arthur Gordon Pym*," *Texas Studies in Literature and Language*, XIII (1971), 267–80.

almost every species of ship-furniture, together with a hetero-geneous medley of crates, hampers, barrels, and bales" (H, III, 23). The "iron-bound box . . . nearly four feet high, and full six long" in which Pym hides is, of course, suggestive of a tomb and takes its place in that reading of Pym which sees it as an oneiric drama moving from death to rebirth, or a series of such cycles. The actual narrative covers nine months, from mid-June, 1827, to February, 1828, although Pym's entire adventure (which the reader does not hear about) covers "nine long years" (H, III, 109). (From this point of view, it is significant that the island of Tsalal in the vicinity of the South Pole is reached on January 19, Poe's birthday.)[11] In the after-hold, Pym is necessarily deceived about what is going on around and above him and has to grope his way through innumerable "windings" (H, III, 25, 31, 37). He loses track of time because Augustus' watch runs down, as does the watch of the Norwegian in "A Descent into the Maelström."

During this period Pym dreams of "calamity and horror." Limitless deserts give way to "wide-spreading morasses," which "concealed" the roots of "immensely tall . . . trees." These "strange trees seemed endowed with a human vitality; and, waving to and fro their skeleton arms," they seemed to be crying in despair (H, III, 28). Later, in a different but equally unhappy situation, this dream state recurs—"a state of partial insensibility, during which the most pleasing images floated in my imagination; such as green trees, waving meadows of ripe grain, processions of dancing girls, troops of cavalry, and other phantasies. I now remember that, in all which passes before my mind's eye, motion was a predominant idea" (H, III, 102). When he recovers, he imagines himself back in the hold, the situation of the earlier dream. Both dreams involve visions of fluid arabesque reality, but they also support the possibility that much of what happens in Pym may be a dream. Safely aboard the Jane Guy, much later, Pym looks back on the past events with ambiguous feelings:

11. Richard Wilbur, Responses: Prose Pieces, 1953–1976 (New York: Harcourt Brace Jovanovich, 1976), 209. The Pym essay reprinted in this collection originally appeared as the Introduction to Edgar Allan Poe, The Narrative of Arthur Gordon Pym (Boston: David R. Godine, 1973), vii–xxv.

We began to remember what had passed rather as a frightful dream from which we had been happily awakened, than as events which had taken place in sober and naked reality. I have since found that this species of partial oblivion is usually brought about by sudden transition, whether from joy to sorrow or from sorrow to joy—the degree of forgetfulness being proportioned to the degree of difference in the exchange. (H, III, 150)

In conjunction with the pattern of reversal in Pym, this sounds very much like a statement of Poe's artistic intention.

To return to Pym's dream in the hold: he fancies that a "fierce lion of the tropics" is about to attack him and awakes to find "the paws of some huge and real monster were pressing heavily upon my bosom—his hot breath was in my ear—and his white and ghastly fangs were gleaming upon me through the gloom" (H, III, 28). Pym "breathed a faint ejaculation to God" and resigned to die. But, once again, this is a false alarm, a red herring. The animal is Pym's "Newfoundland [to be understood literally] dog Tiger," who at least has a dangerous name: "I experienced a sudden rush of blood to my temples—a giddy and overpowering sense of deliverance and reanimation" (H, III, 29). But shortly afterward, the dream does become a reality. Tiger emits "a slight snarl," then a "singular hissing sound," and suddenly "sprang with a loud growl towards my throat" (H, III, 43–44).[12] Pym hurls the animal, presumed to be dying, from him. Soon afterward, without reason, Tiger "appeared to have recovered in some measure his faculties" (H, III, 73). However, during the countermutiny, Tiger does in fact kill. The next related detail occurs when, drifting and starving, the sailors agree to hold a lottery to decide on a victim to be cannibalized. Pym confesses: "At this moment all the fierceness of the tiger possessed my bosom, and I felt towards my poor fellow-creature, Parker, the most intense, the most diabolical hatred" (H, III, 128). This strange metamorphosis suggests that Tiger's reality is a metaphorical indication of the unreliable or perverse tigerism of the world.

Because Tiger had not been mentioned previous to his appearance in the hold and because he is not accounted for concretely later, critics like Ridgely and Haverstick, who find the work totally dis-

12. The name—met with later—of the savages' king, Tsalemon, and the name of their island, Tsalal, commenced "with a prolonged hissing sound . . . which was precisely the same with the note of the black bittern" (H, III, 239).

organized, include him among the "loose ends." There are other examples of "errors," which may be aspects of Poe's deceptive
technique. At one point, Pym refers to information received from
Augustus after "many years elapsed," but Augustus dies in Chapter
XIII. There would appear to be a contradiction here, unless it is precisely Augustus' death that allows for "a more intimate and un-
reserved communion" (H, III, 64). Episodes are anticipated but do
not take place. However, in view of the picture of reality that Poe is
building, it is not special pleading to maintain that promises of actions which never occur, confusing shifts in characterization (on a
par with the paradoxical dog Tiger), and discrepancies in factual detail all contribute, although perhaps not intentionally, to the desired
effect. Like the writer of "MS. Found in a Bottle" and the Norwegian
of "A Descent into the Maelström," Pym discovers that rational
explanations are not forthcoming. The reader makes a similar
discovery.

An example of inconsistent characterization may be the fearsome
figure of Dirk Peters, who replaces Augustus as Pym's companion
and doppelgänger.[13] He is a hybrid, whose bowed arms and legs
"appeared to possess no flexibility whatever" and whose extended
lips seemed "to be devoid of natural pliancy" (H, III, 52). At least two
critics cannot reconcile his displeasing appearance and role in the
mutiny with his basically benevolent role in the remaining action.[14]
But Poe's technique depends on defeating expectations, and the issue is that of appearance versus reality, as in the case of Herman
Melville's Queequeg. Furthermore, there is evidence to link Peters
with the sea and, since the unstructured fluidity of the sea approxi-
mates the real nature of things, to reveal that Peters has a special
awareness. As well as being ugly, he is short, "not more than four
feet eight inches high" (H, III, 51). Two paragraphs later, the reader
learns that "a short and ugly sea was running" (H, III, 54). Like the
elements, his conduct "appeared to be instigated by the most arbitrary caprice alone" (H, III, 73). If Augustus represents the use-

---

13. The name Dirk Peters, in combination with *Arthur* Gordon Pym, evokes King
Arthur and the sword Excalibur buried in stone.
14. Ridgely and Haverstick, "Chartless Voyage," 73.

lessness of Augustan reason, Peters represents the power of imagination.

As Pym and Peters journey toward the South Pole, the deceptive nature of reality appears to resolve itself into the contraries of black and white. Charles O'Donnell's interpretation of the color symbolism is useful.[15] White is "the omni-color" and represents unity (H, XIV, 170). But since the attainment of unity involves death, and perhaps bloodshed, white is often associated with red. Black, a noncolor and the antithesis of white, represents the deceptiveness of man's mundane existence. The association of red and white is apparent from this description of a dead bear: "His wool was perfectly white, and very coarse, curling tightly. The eyes were of a blood red" (H, III, 176). Subsequently, they come across

a bush, full of red berries . . . and the carcass of a singular-looking land animal. It was three feet in length, and but six inches in height, with four very short legs, the feet armed with long claws of a brilliant scarlet, and resembling coral in substance. The body was covered with a straight silky hair, perfectly white. The tail was peaked like that of a rat, and about a foot and a half long. The head resembled a cat's, with the exception of the ears—these were flapped like the ears of a dog. The teeth were of the same brilliant scarlet as the claws. (H, III, 179–80)

In keeping with the connotations of whiteness, the animal, as Patrick Quinn notes, is "a fusion of fidelity and perfidy."[16] As a hybrid, Peters is able to mediate between the black and the white. Within this symbolic color scheme, the reference to Peters and Pym as "the only living white men upon the island" is perhaps not the error it may at first appear (H, III, 209).

Like Moby-Dick, Pym contains a good deal of factual ballast. Poe derived this from a number of sources, including A Voyage to the Pacific, published in 1784 by Captain James Cook and James King; Archibald Duncan's The Mariner's Chronicle, published between 1804 and 1808; Jane Porter's Sir Edward Seaward's Narrative of His Shipwreck, published in 1831; Benjamin Morell's 1832 Narrative of

15. Charles O'Donnell, "From Earth to Ether: Poe's Flight into Space," PMLA, LXXVII (1962), 87.

16. P. F. Quinn, The French Face of Edgar Poe, 191. Compare this creature to the delicacy, biche de mer, which is not quite fish, animal, or bird but a bit of each: "By their elastic wings, like caterpillers or worms, they creep in shallow waters" (H, III, 197).

Four Voyages to the South Seas and the Pacific, 1822–1831; Jeremiah N. Reynolds' 1835 Voyage of the Potomac and his 1836 Address, on the Subject of a Surveying and Exploring Expedition to the Pacific Ocean and South Seas; R. Thomas' Remarkable Events and Remarkable Shipwrecks of 1836; Washington Irving's 1836 Astoria; J. L. Stephens' 1837 Arabia Petraea; and possibly John Cleves Symmes's 1820 account of a subterranean polar world, Symzonia.[17] A certain amount of the "factual" material is simply used to help the hoax along, but some of it can be justified punningly or allegorically—the section on the "shifting" cargo for example (H, III, 69–72). The same may apply to the practice of "lying to," which Poe spends time explaining (H, III, 82–84). Certainly, as Joel Porte argues, the six paragraphs describing the albatross, one "of the gull species," and the nest, or "rookery," which it shares with the penguin, are not without their hidden significance (H, III, 154–55).[18]

The incident involving Augustus' fragmented message is extremely labored unless it can be taken as somehow allegorical of Poe's narrative technique in Pym. Upon first finding the paper strung around Tiger's neck, Pym does not know how to read it. Finally, he illuminates the paper with the aid of phosphorus, only to find it blank. There would appear to be a further inconsistency here. It subsequently transpires that Augustus used "a duplicate of the forged letter from Mr. Ross" (H, III, 60). Presumably, then, there would have been writing on both sides. Pym tears the paper into "three pieces" and throws them away, before realizing that the message may be on the other side (italics added; H, III, 39). But all is not lost. Tiger noses out the three pieces of paper; and after feeling for

17. Robert Lee Rhee, "Some Observations on Poe's Origins," University of Texas Studies in English, X (1930), 135–45; D. M. McKeithan, "Two Sources of Poe's Narrative of Arthur Gordon Pym," University of Texas Studies in English, XIII (1933), 116–37; J. O. Bailey, "Sources for Poe's Arthur Gordon Pym, 'Hans Pfaal' and Other Pieces," PMLA, LVII (1942), 513–22; Keith Huntress, "Another Source for Poe's Narrative of Arthur Gordon Pym," American Literature, XVI (1944), 12–25; Randel Helms, "Another Source for Poe's Arthur Gordon Pym," American Literature, XLI (1970), 572–75; Daniel J. Tynan, "J. N. Reynolds' Voyage of the Potomac: Another Source for The Narrative of Arthur Gordon Pym," Poe Studies, IV (1971), 35–37; Burton R. Pollin, "The Narrative of Benjamin Morrell: Out of 'The Bucket' and into Poe's Pym," Studies in American Fiction, IV (1976), 157–72.

18. Joel Porte, The Romance in America: Studies in Cooper, Poe, Hawthorne, Melville, and James (Middletown, Conn.: Wesleyan University Press, 1969), 92.

the uneven surface, Pym makes out "*three* sentences . . . for I saw there were *three*" (italics added). In his anxiety, however, he only reads "the seven concluding words, which thus appeared—'*blood*— *your life depends upon lying close,*' " written (the reader is later informed) in Augustus' blood (H, III, 41). In view of the extreme amount of deception in *Pym*, it is very likely that the phrase "lying close" contains a pun. The mystifying business of Pym's reading only seven words constitutes a further red herring. As it is, he is filled with "indefinable horror" by the fragmentary warning, "particularly" by the word "blood"—"how *trebly* full of import did it now appear—how chilly and heavily (disjointed, as it thus was, from any foregoing words to qualify it or render it *distinct*) did its vague syllables fall, amid the deep gloom of my prison, into the innermost recesses of my soul" (italics added; H, III, 41). To a considerable extent, the disjointedness of the narrative accounts for its effectiveness. An act of imaginative completion is required from the reader.

This piece of paper deserves further scrutiny. Poe's three key colors are present: presumably the paper is white, the message is red, and the duplicate letter is written in black ink. The figure "three" is emphasized in this commentary because Poe also emphasizes it in an attempt to prod the attentive reader into solving the problem of the phosphorus at first revealing a blank sheet of paper. (Note particularly that the paper is torn into three pieces rather than the more natural four.) This is a three-sided piece of paper. Pym and the reader are encouraged to entertain this illogical reality as analogous to the ultimate realm beyond reason and writing where Pym is headed. This instance of deceptive language may be related to other details in the text. Jean Ricardou has argued that the strange water of Tsalal, "made up of a number of distinct veins" and claimed as "the first definite link in that vast chain of apparent miracles, with which I was destined to be at length encircled," represents the printed page (H, III, 187). This water is presumably responsible for the formation of the hieroglyphic gorges—a problematic message which should be paired with that from Augustus. The emphasis on black and white, especially black characters (the natives), gains obvious new meaning in this context. Thus it is possible to read *Pym* as a journey through the illusory solipsistic world of print to the end of the page, which is, of course, arabesque white.[19] Pym must see beyond the writing on the wall.

Returning to the chronicle of pseudocrises, it is apparent that the circumstances of Pym's release from the hold abound in the generation of unjustified anxiety. With a "single gill of liqueur" remaining, "I felt myself activated by one of those fits of perverseness which might be supposed to influence a spoiled child in similar circumstances, and, raising the bottle to my lips, I drained it to the last drop, and dashed it furiously upon the floor" (H, III, 44). But what is really perverse about this action is that it does not lead to the expected consequences. The next minute Augustus is on the scene. However, when Pym hears someone calling his name, he is unable to reply: "Had a thousand words depended upon a syllable, I could not have spoken it" (H, III, 45). But fortunately a carving knife drops to the floor with a rattle and Augustus hears it.

During the period between Peters' gaining control of the *Grampus* and the appearance of the *Jane Guy*, the pseudocrisis comes into its own. Chapter VIII ends with a huge wave "sweeping the companion-way clear off, bursting in the hatchways, and filling every inch of the vessel with water" (H, III, 98). All are safe, however, because, in the opening words of Chapter IX, "luckily, just before night, all four of us had lashed ourselves firmly to the fragments of the windlass" and Pym now realizes "a vessel with a cargo of empty oil-casks would not sink." He records that "hope revived within me" (H, III, 99). Until Chapter XIV, hope and despair oscillate repeatedly. The main problem is food; and Peters, with a rope around his waist, attempts to swim through "a narrow passage" into the storeroom (H, III, 107). After nearly drowning, Peters discovers

19. Jean Ricardou, "Le caractère singulier de cette eau," *Critique*, CCXLIII–IV (1967), 718–33. A translation by Frank Towne appears in *Poe Studies*, IX (1976), 191–96. It should be noted that the land is also stratified and that the natives make use of this fact in their treachery. See also a review of Ricardou's article, Patrick F. Quinn, "*Arthur Gordon Pym*: 'A Journey to the End of the Page'?" *Poe Newsletter*, I (1968), 13–14; Claude Richard, "L'Ecriture D'Arthur Gordon Pym," *Delta*, I (1975), 95–124; Daniel A. Wells, "Engraved Within the Hills: Further Perspectives on the Ending of *Pym*," *Poe Studies*, X (1977), 13–15.

that the door is locked. The company gives way to despair and then prays to God.

Suddenly an incident occurs "replete with the extremes first of delight and then of horror" (H, III, 109). Augustus is agitated and Parker distressed by the appearance of "a large hermaphrodite brig, of a Dutch build, and painted black, with a tawdry gilt figurehead." Presumably, the element of fusion implied by the word *hermaphrodite* prepares for the hermaphroditically named *Jane Guy*. The company do not realize at first that it is a death ship which is bearing down on them. They account for the ship's erratic course "by supposing the helmsman to be in liquor" (H, III, 110). Suddenly, they become aware of an awful stench, and the truth is evident. A sound, "so closely resembling the scream of a human voice that the nicest ear might have been startled and deceived," emanates from a sea gull fastened upon the back of a corpse, "busily gorging itself with the horrible flesh, its bill and talons deep buried, and its white plumage spattered all over with blood" (H, III, 112). The now-exposed teeth give the appearance of a smile. The scene is fateful: black brig, red blood, white teeth. The sea gull drops "a portion of clotted and liver-like substance" at Parker's feet (H, III, 113). Parker is shortly to urge that one of their number be a victim of cannibalism; and when the straws are drawn, he turns out to be the candidate.

Two days after eating Parker, Pym has "an idea which inspired me with a bright gleam of hope" (H, III, 130). He remembers that he had taken an axe into the forecastle, and with this, the storeroom door could be cut through. The attempt is successful "beyond our utmost expectations" (H, III, 131). Clearly, the act of cannibalism was unnecessary. But two days later, "to our great grief," much of the food is washed overboard, and the brig is about to overturn (H, III, 136). The discovery that there is no more food in the storeroom "filled us with despair" (H, III, 137). And the brig does roll over: "I scarcely made a struggle for life, and resigned myself, in a few seconds, to die. But here again I was deceived, not having taken into consideration the natural rebound of the hull to windward" (H, III, 142). Nevertheless, all the provisions have now been swept overboard; and, accordingly, "we gave way both of us to despair" (H, III,

143). However, "the accident . . . proved a benefit rather than an injury." It is an example of sustenance below. The keel was "*thickly covered with large barnacles, which proved to be excellent and highly nutritious food*" (H, III, 144). Three days later, a sail is sighted; it is the *Jane Guy*. Before the rescue, Poe raises an additional red herring: "We now became alarmed, for we could hardly imagine it possible that she did not observe us, and were apprehensive that she meant to leave us to perish as we were. . . . In this instance, however, by the mercy of God, we were destined to be most happily deceived" (H, III, 146–47).

The *Jane Guy's* meandering course is apparently without purpose until it is decided, in Chapter XVI, to head for the South Pole. Time is spent describing Desolation Island with its "deceitful appearance" and its penguins whose "resemblance to a human figure is very striking, and would be apt to deceive the spectator" (H, III, 152, 154). It is likely that Leslie Fiedler and Harry Levin are correct and that such indirections serve to disguise an allegory of the southern United States.[20] Hence the description of Captain Guy as "a gentleman of great urbanity of manner, and of considerable experience in the southern traffic, to which he had devoted the greater portion of his life" and this reference to a strange land: "In approaching it from the northward, a singular ledge of rock is seen projecting into the sea, and bearing a strange resemblance to corded bales of cotton" (H, III, 148, 176). Moreover, after passage through ice fields, the farther south they voyage the warmer it gets. And there are black men. Poe, who approved of slavery, is apparently issuing a direct warning of Negro insurrection and making the Negro emblematic of man's treacherous nature. At the same time, if Poe's ideal region is a sphere where opposites are united, the existence of heat where cold is expected and the confusion of place are also aspects of Poe's fusion strategy.

While Pym and Peters are entombed under fallen rock (a consequence of the natives' treachery), the pattern of hope and despair

20. Leslie Fiedler, *Love and Death in the American Novel* (rev. ed.; New York: Stein & Day, 1966), 397–400; Harvy Levin, *The Power of Blackness* (New York: Alfred A. Knopf, 1958), 120–23.

continues. They finally extricate themselves; and Pym, looking at the flames leaping from the *Jane Guy*, says, "We now anticipated a catastrophe, and were not disappointed" (H, III, 216). Such precision of prediction is only possible this once in the novel. The ship does blow up, killing large numbers of the savages. The narrative ends gnomically with Pym and Peters in a canoe moving through milky water and "a chaos of flitting and indistinct images" toward the white figure in the chasm (H, III, 241–42).

The writer of the endnote takes up the matter of the mysterious hieroglyphics and deduces the Ethiopian, " 'To be shady'—whence all the inflections of shadow or darkness," the Arabic, " 'To be white,' whence all the inflections of brilliancy and whiteness," and in Egyptian, "The region of the south" (H, III, 244). "To be shady" is also an equivalent of "to be deceptive." The note concludes with the biblical tones, *"I have graven it within the hills, and my vengeance upon the dust within the rock"* (H, III, 245). It seems likely that Poe's interest in such veiled biblical pronouncements received an impetus from his reading of J. L. Stephens' *Arabia Petraea*, which Poe discussed in the *New York Review* for October, 1837. The previous year, it may be noted, Poe had written the article "Palaestine" for the *Southern Literary Messenger*. Is there then an explanation in Poe's reading for why, once out of the chasms, the country reminds Pym "of those dreary regions marking the site of degraded Babylon" (H, III, 230–31)? Is there evidence here to suggest that Pym is destined to discover an interior world (Pymzonia?) like that described by John Symmes in *Symzonia* and inhabited by the lost tribes of Israel?[21]

Two of the more problematical aspects of *Pym* are the question of its overall structure, if any and if complete, and the mechanism of Pym's ultimate rescue.[22] Clearly, he must survive the apocalypse at the conclusion of the book if he is to write the narrative. That he has died since then is merely convenient. These two problems are, in fact, related; the solution to the one provides the solution to the other.

21. See J. O. Bailey, "Sources for Poe's *Arthur Gordon Pym*," 513–22; Sidney Kaplan, Introduction to *The Narrative of Arthur Gordon Pym* (New York: Hill & Wang, 1960), vii–xxv.

22. The endnote maintains that the manuscript is incomplete. Jules Verne and H. P. Lovecraft wrote sequels entitled, respectively, *The Sphinx of the Ice Fields* and *At the Mountains of Madness*.

Edward Davidson discerns five structural divisions, whereas there are actually seven because Davidson's fifth division includes three distinct parts. By overlooking this, Davidson misses an important clue to Poe's intention in *Pym*. Charles O'Donnell first revealed the basic structure of the book. The following table corroborates his hypothesis that *Pym*, after the prologue chapter, divides into parallel halves:[23]

CHAPTERS	NO. OF CHAPTERS		THEME	VESSEL CONCERNED
1. I	1		Microcosm of whole	*Ariel / Penguin*
2. II–VI	5		Confinement and release	
3. VII–IX	3	12	Treachery	*Grampus*
4. X–XIII	4		Lack of direction and privation	
5. XIV–XVII	4		Lack of direction and security	
6. XVIII–XX	3	12	Treachery	*Jane Guy*
7. XXI–XXV	5		Confinement and release	

The second half of the novel does not balance the first in length; but, as the table indicates, there is an exact balancing, episode for episode, in terms of chapter allotment and theme. It is also worth noticing that the *Grampus* overturns at the end of Chapter XIII. The underside of a boat saved Pym in the first chapter, and now the underside of another boat is topside. This movement suggests the moment of *bouleversement*, described in "Hans Pfaal" and in *Eureka*, when the force of repulsion gives way to the force of attraction. And it is this moment that forms the hinge whereby the second half of *Pym* may be folded back over the first half.

O'Donnell notes some of the episodic parallels. In the first half of the book and noted as a log entry, Simms, "being very much in liquor," falls overboard while "taking in the fore-top sail" of the *Grampus* and drowns (H, III, 76). In the second half, also in a log entry, Peter Vredenburgh—the second Vredenburgh in the narrative—slips "over the bows" of the *Jane Guy* and dies "between two cakes

23. Davidson, *Poe: A Critical Study*, 163–64; O'Donnell, "From Earth to Ether," 89. Harry Levin also notes the division at Chapter XIII, in *The Power of Blackness*, 114–15.

of ice" (H, III, 174). More frequently remarked upon is the parallel between Pym's confinement in the afterhold of the *Grampus* and the entrapment of Pym and Peters after the landfall. Both experiences are a kind of burial. Then there is Augustus' mysterious message and later the mysterious message graven in rock. But granted this rigid parallelism, to what purpose is it directed? O'Donnell's view is convincing.[24] Poe wished to conclude his novel with a vision of the apocalypse. At the same time, it is necessary that his hero survive to write his story. Poe had already used the implausible manuscript-in-a-bottle device and was later to use the expedient of a return from the brink. Moreover, the second of these options is not quite consistent with the sense or hope that arabesque reality is a desirable state.

This time Poe's solution is altogether more ingenious and satisfactory. Rather than spoil a climax by explaining how Pym survives yet another catastrophe, Poe's thematic and structural parallels—plus the pattern of miraculous escape—allow the reader to infer the means of Pym's deliverance. If the structural parallelism is to be complete, the reader must, in his imagination, supply an epilogue chapter to balance the prologue chapter. There is already the canoe at the end of Chapter XXV, which corresponds to the *Ariel*.[25] In the prologue Pym "tumbled headlong and insensible upon the body of my fallen companion" before being, incredibly, transferred to the *Penguin* (H, III, 10). As O'Donnell argues, Poe attempts to trigger a series of associations in the reader's head enabling him to envision or manufacture that unwritten final chapter containing a similar reversal after the book's ostensible conclusion. A few pages before the end, in a passage that culminates the theme of perversity and draws together the use of deception as content and as technique, Pym falls into Peters' arms, recalling the earlier occasion when he fell on top of Augustus and pointing, by means of the vague description of Peters, toward the "filmy figure" of the conclusion:

24. P. F. Quinn, *The French Face of Edgar Poe*, 187–88; O'Donnell, "From Earth to Ether," 89.

25. Gertrude P. Stevenson observes that there is a progression in the degree of control Pym is able to exercise over the vessels with which he is associated. At the end he is able to "paddle his own canoe," so to speak. Stevenson, "The Sea Tales of Edgar Allan Poe" (M.A. thesis, Sir George Williams University, 1973), 24.

For one moment my fingers clutched convulsively upon their hold, while, with the movement, the faintest possible idea of ultimate escape wandered, like a shadow, through my mind—in the next my whole soul was pervaded with *a longing to fall;* a desire, a yearning, a passion uncontrollable. . . . But now there came a spinning of the brain; a shrill-sounding and phantom voice screamed within my ears; a dusky, fiendish, and filmy figure stood immediately beneath me; and, sighing, I sank down with a bursting heart, and plunged within his arms. I had swooned, and Peters caught me as I fell. (H, III, 229–30)

If the reader is alert, he should have the earlier episode in mind when he reads of the figure blocking Pym's path, whose skin "was of the perfect whiteness of the snow" (H, III, 242). It may be that Pym is seeing a sail.[26]

IV

"The Journal of Julius Rodman," which appeared in *Burton's Gentleman's Magazine* from January to June, 1840, is clearly a companion piece to *Pym* and should be read in the light of that work. Like *Pym*, Rodman is motivated by visions of gloom, or what is referred to as "an hereditary hypochondria. . . . He was possessed with a burning love of Nature; and worshipped her, perhaps, more in her dreary and savage aspects, than in her manifestations of placidity and joy" (H, IV, 10, 13). This trait provides the main reason for the voyage. As in the case of *Pym*, the movement is through layers of deception into an unexplored region. "Julius Rodman" is unquestionably an unfinished work, but the same concluding black-white opposition appears in Chapter VI. The voyagers come across "a high wall of black rock on the south," beyond which was "another wall of a light color" and beyond that another wall "composed of a very white soft sandstone" (H, IV, 90).

However, the succession of idyllic retreats suggests that the conclusion of the voyage might be an Island of the Fay similar to the one described in the tale of that title, which appeared a year later. On Au-

26. A fragment entitled "The Lighthouse" (discovered by Thomas Ollive Mabbott in 1942 and published in *Notes and Queries,* April, 1942) belongs with the three sea voyages and like *Pym* breaks off with an image of whiteness. Although the narrator-diarist of the piece is relieved to have escaped society through appointment to a lighthouse, he is disturbed to find that the lighthouse is built on chalk.

gust 17, 1791, Rodman describes the first of such retreats; it is a fluid arabesque landscape: "The prairies exceeded in beauty anything told in the tales of the Arabian Nights. On the edges of the creeks there was a wild mass of flowers which looked more like Art than Nature, so profusely and fantastically were their vivid colors blended together. . . . Every now and then we came to a kind of green island of trees, placed amid an ocean of purple, blue, orange, and crimson blossoms, all waving to and fro in the wind" (H, IV, 42). Their ultimate destination is suggested by the twice-repeated image of the fusion of sea and sky. Early in the narrative, Rodman describes the vision that gave an impetus to his travels: "As I looked up the stream (which here stretched away to the westward, until the waters apparently met the sky in the great distance) and reflected on the immensity of territory through which those waters had probably passed, a territory as yet altogether unknown to white people, and perhaps abounding in the magnificent works of God, I felt an excitement of soul such as I had never before experienced" (H, IV, 33–34). In the last chapter, Rodman writes: "The two rivers presented the most enchanting appearance as they wound away their long snake-like lengths in the distance, growing thinner and thinner until they looked like mere faint threads of silver as they vanished in the shadowy mists of the sky. We could glean nothing, from their direction so far, as regards their ultimate course" (H, IV, 94). But on the basis of the succession of fairy-tale landscapes, it is evident what form that realm beyond the vanishing point would take.

The arabesque landscape is one of the controlling symbols in the work. The countersymbol is the shifting sandbars, repeatedly mentioned, which stand for the treacherous nature of grotesque reality. Their role is given its fullest statement in Chapter IV, after the larger of the two boats has run aground on one of them: "We were relieved, very unexpectedly, by the sinking of the whole sand-bar from under the boat, just as we were upon the point of despair. The bed of the river in this neighborhood is much obstructed by these shifting sands, which frequently change situations with great rapidity, and without apparent cause. The material of the bars is a fine hard yellow sand, which, when dry, is of a brilliant glass-like appearance, and almost impalpable" (H, IV, 69). Earlier, "we met with several quick-sand bars, which put us to trouble; the banks of the river here fall in continually, and, in the process of time, must greatly alter the bed" (H, IV, 36–37). Later, "we had not proceeded far before we found the very character of the stream materially altered, and very much obstructed by sandbars" (H, IV, 96). The very term *sandbar* is particularly appropriate, since Poe is concerned with crossing barriers that he claims do not actually exist. Sometimes the mounds of sand appear above the water so that "I could not make up my mind whether these hillocks were of natural or artificial construction" (H, IV, 40). As well as being of indeterminate origin, above sea level they are a barrier to vision: "Passed a creek on the south, the mouth of which is nearly concealed by a large sand-island of singular appearance" (H, IV, 43).

To make sense of the narrative, the inconsequential action must be read as serving a function analogous to the sandbars that unaccountably rise and fall to save or to destroy. The unifying principle of deceptive action and circumstance is as much at work in "Julius Rodman" as in *Pym*. However, Poe's success in "Julius Rodman" is much diminished, perhaps due to the increased use of material taken from other sources. Much of the narrative is an almost direct transcript from Washington Irving's *Astoria* and the accounts of the expeditions of Lewis and Clark and of Captain B. L. E. Bonneville, all of which Poe has the grace to mention in the introductory chapter.[27] Once again, Poe wanted the impression of verisimilitude for the purpose of a hoax.

Among the voyagers were five brothers "by the name of Greely" (H, IV, 25). It may be remembered that a man named Greely figures in *Pym* and Horace Greeley figures in Poe's biography. Alexander Wormley has been a preacher and is subsequently referred to as the Prophet because of his visionary habits: "This hallucination was now diverted into another channel, and he thought of nothing else

27. Hervey Allen, *Israfel: The Life and Times of Edgar Allan Poe* (rev. ed.; New York: Farrar & Rinehart, 1934), 372; H. Arlin Turner, "A Note of Poe's 'Julius Rodman,'" *University of Texas Studies in English*, X (1930), 147–51; Polly Pearl Crawford, "Lewis and Clark's Expedition as a Source for Poe's 'Journal of Julius Rodman,'" *University of Texas Studies in English*, XII (1932), 158–70.

than of finding gold mines in some of the fastnesses of the country" (H, IV, 26). Rodman adds, "I counted much upon this recruit, on account of his enthusiastic character, and in the end I was not deceived" (H, IV, 26). Rodman, wanting a "friend to whom I could converse freely, and without danger of being misunderstood," feels himself in especial sympathy with another voyager, Andrew Thornton, who "participated in all my most visionary projects" (H, IV, 34, 77). Thornton is inexplicably ill during most of the voyage, but he recovers just as inexplicably. This and other elements in the narrative anticipate Melville's *Typee*. While in the Happy Valley, Melville's Tommoo suffers from an unaccountable leg injury. In "Julius Rodman," someone called Toby is a Negro, but a Toby also figures in *Typee* as Tommoo's initial companion. Even more important as evidence that Melville read "Julius Rodman" before writing *Typee* is the ambiguous nature of the Indians—friendly or hostile. There are two tribes in *Typee*, one good and one bad, and Tommoo makes a mistake as to which is which.

The Sioux Indians are at one with the treacherous reality symbolized by the sandbars. They exist in a state of division, "subdivided into numerous clans . . . four divisions of regular Sioux [and] five tribes of seceders. . . . These seceders were often at war with the parent or original Sioux" (H, IV, 56, 57). In dealing with the Sioux, customary methods of deception are employed: "That the enemy might perceive no semblance of fear or mistrust, the whole party joined the Canadians in an uproarious boat-song at the top of their voices" (H, IV, 55). When they encounter the Indians, the voyagers are caught between two steep banks, but there is a characteristic reversal: "Either good luck upon our parts, or great stupidity on the part of the Indians, relieved us very unexpectedly from the dilemma" (H, IV, 61). The voyagers refuse to come ashore, and the Indians ride away. It is just possible that they are friendly after all. They leave in order to return with an interpreter, who explains that it is the Ricarees, not the Sioux, who are hostile. Rodman responds by giving the command to fire, killing six of the Indians. Later, Rodman feels guilty about shedding blood, perhaps as a tardy and futile attempt on Poe's part to fill out his character.[28] However, the interpreter did lie. The Ricarees do turn out to be friendly; and when the voyagers leave them, it is with "unfeigned regret" (H, IV, 71).

The unfriendly Saonie Sioux capture John Greely, the Prophet, and a Canadian. They have also captured a large herd of antelopes by enticing them into an enclosure. Greely and the Prophet are disarmed, but the Canadian "was suffered, for some reason not perfectly understood, to remain unbound" (H, IV, 72–73) and to retain possession, perhaps accidentally, of his knife. His being unbound seems to be just a part of the inconsequential nature of things. The escape of the antelopes reverses the situation and gives the human prisoners a chance to escape too. They come across one of the antelopes, burnt and with a broken leg: "It was no doubt one of the herd which had been the means of deliverance. Had there been even a chance of its recovery the hunters would have spared it in token of their gratitude, but it was miserably injured, so they put it at once out of its misery, and brought it home to the boats, where we made an excellent breakfast upon it next morning" (H, IV, 75). Between seeing the animal and eating it, there are at least three turnabouts of attitude!

The remaining episodes all have a pointlessness that seems not quite accidental. In fact, the narrative drift from pseudocrisis to pseudocrisis is akin to the action of the sandbars and the nature of reality. Concern is aroused only to be dispelled. Incidents are anticipated but do not actually happen. Clearly, inconsequence and pointlessness are pertinent thematically, and the truncated conclusion leaves paradise, as ever, beyond the horizon.

V

Poe's use of cabalistic script, present in "MS. Found in a Bottle" and *Pym*, finds further expression in "Shadow—A Parable," which first

28. Stuart Levine argues, not altogether convincingly, that Poe demonstrates a new interest in character development in "Julius Rodman." See the section entitled "Judaism, Plagiarism and the Wild West," in Levine, *Edgar Poe: Seer and Craftsman* (De Land, Fla.: Everett/Edwards, 1972), 252–60.

appeared in the September, 1835, *Southern Literary Messenger*, and "Silence—A Fable," which was originally published as "Siope: In the Manner of the Psychological Autobiographists" (Edward Bulwer and Thomas De Quincey) in the *Baltimore Book* for 1837. These two pieces mark the appearance of what might be called a metaphysical vein in Poe's writing, the other examples being the 1839 "Conversation of Eiros and Charmion," the 1841 "Colloquy of Monos and Una," the 1845 "Power of Words," and *Eureka* in 1848. In each case, the prose style verges on poetry; indeed, Poe wished that *Eureka* be considered a poem. It is apparent that these six pieces fall neatly into groups of two; and considered as separate pairs, they represent a convenient method for tracing the evolution of Poe's thought. They stand out from the rest of Poe's work as evidence of a certain order and chronological development. Consequently, a part of Chapters 4, 7, and 10 will be devoted to an examination of each successive pair.

Clearly, in the voyage tales Poe is pushing against the frontiers of mortality in an attempt to glimpse what is beyond. But in order to make an impression on the beyond, the narrator needs to die in the process, which creates problems of verisimilitude in the written account. The narrator of "Shadow—A Parable," the Greek Oinos (whose name means One), is already dead; but in that state he has been able to etch his story "in the characters here graven with a stylus of iron." The tale he tells is an anticipation of "The Masque of the Red Death." He describes the entrance of the shadow of death while he and six companions are in an arabesque chamber with the corpse of a friend "in a dim city called Ptolemais" (M, II, 189). The abysslike "depths of the ebony mirror" table around which the company is seated is the major agential factor. This "parable" is generally admired for its evocative power of effect. However, the oracular biblical tones tend to convey a strong element of pastiche and dubious sincerity.[29] The sentence, "Yet we laughed and were merry in our

29. Many of the details in "Shadow" derive from Jacob Bryant's *Mythology* (1774, 1776). See Stuart Levine and Susan Levine, "History, Myth, Fable, and Satire: Poe's Use of Jacob Bryant," *Emerson Society Quarterly*, XXI (1975), 197–214. An additional source appears to be a chapter of Thomas Moore's *The Epicureans* (1827). See Burton R. Pollin, "Light on 'Shadow' and Other Pieces by Poe; Or, More of Thomas Moore," *Emerson Society Quarterly*, XVIII (1972), 166–73. The reference to Ptolemais suggests that the reality transformation may be analogically related to the supplanting of the Ptolemaic cosmology by the Copernican. See J. M. De Falco, "The Source of Terror in Poe's 'Shadow—A Parable,' " *Studies in Short Fiction*, VI (1969), 643–48.

proper way—which was hysterical; and sang the songs of Anacreon —which are madness; and drank deeply—although the purple wine reminded us of blood," is uncomfortably overwritten (M, II, 190). But this evidence of an uneasy relationship between the serious and the comic in Poe should probably be attributed to his desire to disconcert the reader.

"Silence—A Fable," involving a conversation with "the Demon," is even more Blakean than "Shadow—A Parable." Given the enigmatic nature of the "fable," any interpretation is necessarily conjectural. Nevertheless, there is room to read it as the devil's version of Christ's temptation in the wilderness.[30] With his hand commandingly upon the narrator's head, the demon tells of "a dreary region in Libya, by the borders of the river Zäire. And there is no quiet there, nor silence" (M, II, 195). What is there, as the "characters engraven in the stone" tell the demon, is "DESOLATION" (M, II, 196). The description of the sluggish waters, the lurid light from "the red eye of the sun" and the crimson moon, and the "indistinct murmur" of the lilies as they "sigh one unto the other" is reminiscent of the poem, "The City in the Sea." The low underwood of the surrounding forest, agitated in spite of the lack of wind, is "like the waves about the Hebrides"—a phrase similar to one in the poem, "The Valley of Unrest" (M, II, 195). The whole tone of the piece is poetical, not just the allusions but also the refrainlike use of lulling repetition.

The being upon the rock is thought to be clothed in "the toga of old Rome," but "the outlines of his figure were indistinct." Possibly he is Christ, although he is also reminiscent of the sibylline captain of the phantom ship in "MS. Found in a Bottle": "His features were the features of a deity. . . . And his brow was lofty with thought, and his eye wild with care; and, in the few furrows upon his cheek I read the fables of sorrow, and weariness, and disgust with mankind, and a longing after solitude" (M, II, 196). The demon conjures up three temptations to fear and despair. Neither the wild animals—the hippopotami and the behemoth among "the wilderness of the lilies"— nor the second incentive to fear—the tempest—achieves the desired effect (M, II, 197). They are merely a part of the general desolation.

30. "Silence" is also Poe's version of Edward Bulwer's "Monos and Daimonos, A Legend" (1830). See A. H. Quinn, Edgar Allan Poe: A Critical Biography, 215.

Finally, growing angry, the demon says that he has cursed the area "with the curse of *silence*"; and consequently, the characters on the rock "were SILENCE" (M, II, 197–98). Confronted with this condition of nada, the man on the rock turns and flees. Apparently, the demon is positing two conditions—the human condition of desolation and a subsequent state of total nothingness, the secondfold silence of the "Sonnet—Silence." The intention is that the narrator despair. But "the lynx which dwelleth forever in the tomb, came out therefrom, and lay down at the feet of the Demon, and looked at him steadily in the face" (M, II, 224). The action of the lynx gives the lie to the demon's story if the reader remembers Poe's dictum that "it is only the philosophical lynxeye that, through the indignity-mist of Man's life, can still discern the dignity of Man" (H, XVI, 161).

In the six related works examined in this chapter, Poe is disentangling himself from the meshes of deception that cloud mortal vision and standing "upon the brink of eternity," to use a phrase from "MS. Found in a Bottle" (M, II, 143). But the term *brink* still implies the existence of a barrier. In the works discussed in Part II under the heading of "Fusion," Poe demonstrates that the barriers are down, that they never actually existed.

Part Two

FUSION

5

A Sort of Runic Rhyme

In spite of the fact (noted by Lewis Chase) that Poe's public saw him as a critic and current readers see him mainly as a short story writer, Poe thought of himself primarily as a poet; and it was as a poet that he began his literary career.[1] An explanation of this self-estimate is not hard to fathom. The best poetry, according to Poe's formulation, provides an outlet from the world of deception into a realm of supernal beauty and truth. Poetry, for Poe, was a means of communicating the "fancies" that arise "at those mere points of time where the confines of the waking world blend with those of the world of dreams," by transferring the "recollections" of the "impressions" of that point "into the realm of Memory," where such "fancies" can be surveyed "with the eye of analysis," since "thought is logicalized by the effort at (written) expression" (H, XVI, 88–90). This view of the creative process, as a fusion of imagination and analysis, informs Floyd Stovall's assertion that "the early poems, even after revision, were dominated by the conceptual and imaginative faculty of the mind, whereas the later poems reflect primarily the analytic and constructive faculty."[2] Yet, the late "Ulalume" is a far more evocative poem than the early "Tamerlane,"

1. Lewis Chase, Poe and His Poetry (London: Harrap, 1913), 63. In the preface to the 1845 volume of his poems, Poe described his poetry as "not a purpose, but a passion" (M, I, 579).
2. Floyd Stovall (ed.), Introduction to The Poems of Edgar Allan Poe (Charlottesville: University of Virginia Press, 1965), xxvi.

and in poems like "Ulalume" Poe goes furthest in his efforts to disperse the fabric of deception and thus justify his conception of the artist's role.

The body of Poe's poetry may best be conceived as a writhing arabesque tapestry. As the following titles indicate—"Dreams," "A Dream Within a Dream," "Dream-Land," "Eulalie—A Song," and "Ulalume—A Ballad"—it can be extremely difficult to separate one poem from the rest. Similar images and themes permeate the ninety-odd poems as they do the arabesque tales. Several of the poems originally appeared in arabesque tales, and almost all of them underwent extensive revision. "The Coliseum" was originally part of *Politian*, and "The Lake—To—" was once part of "Tamerlane." So in what context and in what version should a poem be examined? Clear-cut chronological divisions are impossible; indeed, any attempt to structure Poe's poetry rigorously cannot but lead to distortion.

It is extremely likely that Poe thought of his poetry as an organic whole, much like Walt Whitman's *Leaves of Grass*. Whitman revised old material to bring it in line with the new in successive editions of *Leaves of Grass*, as did Poe in new editions of his poetry. "The Bells," which concludes most editions of the poetry, may be viewed as a microcosm of the whole. While Poe was alive, his poetry appeared in four editions: *Tamerlane and Other Poems* (1827), *Al Aaraaf, Tamerlane, and Minor Poems* (1829), *Poems* (1831), and *The Raven and Other Poems* (1845). "The Bells" went through what seems to be four stages. The first version of seventeen lines was written in May, 1848, and probably lost. A second short version was published in *Sartain's Union Magazine* (Philadelphia) for December, 1849. A long version written on February 6, 1849, was sold to John Sartain, although it appears to be a revised version of the same which was published in *Sartain's Union Magazine* for November, 1849.

Poe's object in "The Bells," in Anthony Caputi's terms, is "to synthesyse [sic] the ambivalences of experience by underscoring heavily the multifaced complexity of a single object."[3] In each of the

3. Anthony Caputi, "The Refrain in Poe's Poetry," *American Literature*, XXV (1954), 176.

four sections of the poem, the sound of the bells assumes a different character. They appear first as merry sleigh bells, second as mellow wedding bells, third as "loud alarum bells," and finally as "iron bells" solemnly tolling.[4] The analogy with the human cycle of birth, marriage, struggle, and death is readily apparent. But there is more. By making each section progressively longer than the preceding section, Poe is assimilating one section into the next, or syncopating the sequential cycle, to indicate that a complete understanding of the nature of the bells, or of the nature of life, requires the ability to hold in equilibrium, or to fuse, alternative possible meanings.

An appreciation of Poe's poetry demands a similarly prestigiatory ability. In much the same way as stanza four of "The Bells" incorporates stanza three, stanza three incorporates stanza two, and stanza two incorporates stanza one, so The Raven and Other Poems absorbs Poems, Poems absorbs Al Aaraaf, Tamerlane, and Minor Poems, and Al Aaraaf, Tamerlane, and Minor Poems absorbs Tamerlane and Other Poems. In its final form, as will become apparent, Poe's poetry appears to be structured in terms of four sequentially assimilative cycles centering on "Tamerlane," "Al Aaraaf," "The Raven," and "Ulalume." The condition of stasis, fusion, or equilibrium is augmented in "The Bells" by associating childhood with winter—the traditional season of death—and by the reference to the "merry bosom" of the king of the ghouls and the word "happy" in the final section. "The moaning and the groaning of the bells," symbolic of death, is paradoxically described as "a happy Runic rhyme."

By circling around a subject, temporally and spatially, over and over again, always on a slightly different path, Poe hopes to dizzy himself and his reader into that moment of understanding and breakthrough which justifies art. The effect may be likened to a psychedelic discothêque—an appropriate simile for an arabesque room —where the euphoric sensation is all-important. Poe simulates the kaleidoscopic outline-effacing effect of the alternating and revolving strobe lights by circling around his subject. Poe's poetic output on a theme may be visualized as an arabesque globe with each poem and

4. All quotations from Poe's poetry are taken from Thomas Ollive Mabbott (ed.), Collected Works of Edgar Allan Poe, Cambridge, Mass.: Harvard University Press, 1969–), I, and may be located by poem title.

each version of each poem describing a slightly different circle upon it. If sufficient lines are drawn around a globe, a gradual fusion will take place and an arabesque fluidity will result.

Poe's increasing use of repetition and the refrain becomes an integral part of this fusing process.[5] Almost by definition, and certainly in Poe's terms, the repeated line of the refrain accrues meaning each time it is used. To separate one circumstantial meaning, as does the student in "The Raven," is to exist in a state of deception. In addition to the use of repetition and the refrain, notable characteristics of Poe's poetry are the moment of *trompe l'oeil* reversal, as one possible line of interpretation gives way to another, and the use of paradox, oxymoron, synesthesia, pathetic fallacy, metaphor, and other devices of fusion, leading to the quality of indefiniteness that Poe so admired in poetry. The poetry is also highly symbolic; and symbolism, of course, involves fusion. Other aspects of Poe's method of removal—including the hypnotic use of sound, the luxuriance of language, and the elimination, or diminution, of intellectual and dramatic content—have been sufficiently observed and so will not figure in the ensuing analysis.[6] Rather, Poe's strategy of fusion will be explored, the strategy that he uses to eradicate the everyday world.

II

To move from "The Bells," among Poe's latest poems, to "Tamerlane," his first major poem, may be warranted by the anticipation of the later poem in Tamerlane's admission that the past "With its interminable chime / Rings in the spirit of a spell, / . . . a knell" upon his empty heart. The text of "Tamerlane," first published in 1837 as introductory to *Tamerlane and Other Poems*, was not finalized until 1845 when it was reprinted in *The Raven and Other Poems* (the version analyzed here). It provides the clearest index to the entirety of Poe's poetry. Most of the poems, if not literally discarded fragments of "Tamerlane," amplify various aspects of that poem. Although in

5. See Caputi, "The Refrain in Poe's Poetry," 169–78.
6. For example, Richard Wilbur (ed.), Introduction to *Poe: Complete Poems* (New York: Dell, 1959), 7–39.

subsequent versions of the poem Poe toned down the auto-biographical element, Tamerlane is clearly Poe in a Byronic mood. The narrative concerns Poe's failure to realize on earth his arabesque vision and his reconciliation to that failure. Neither the historical Tamerlane nor the hero of Christopher Marlowe's play is particularly relevant to this work.

The poem takes the form of a dramatic monologue, the silent party being, as indicated in the 1827 text, a "holy friar." It is a death-bed confession. The note of reconciliation, which concludes the work, is anticipated by the parenthetical qualification in Tamerlane's assurance that "Kind solace . . . is not (now) my theme." Thus, the form of "Tamerlane" is characteristically circular. Tamerlane acknowledges the paradox that "the undying voice of that dead time," the happiness he experienced in youth, blights his present glory, turning his crown into a "halo of Hell" and a "fever'd diadem." Like his crown, which was "claim'd and won usurpingly," Tamerlane is the victim of his passions, which "Usurp'd a tyranny" internally.

In lines 35 to 64, Tamerlane claims that his overwhelming passion—ambition—was ignited externally by his childhood exposure to the forces of nature. He was born on a mountain where, he argues, "I believe, the winged strife / And tumult of the headlong air / Have nestled in my very hair." Paradoxically, the dew, "So late from Heaven," is described as falling upon him "with the touch of Hell." To his "half-closing eye"—the eye of fused, corrected vision—a thunderstorm took upon the aspect "Of human battle"; and the clouds, "like banners," seemed "the pageantry of monarchy." Tamerlane apparently found his own passions formed by, then identified and fused with, those of the elements and not of his "innate nature." Similarly, in "Alone," Poe states that his entire being, "the mystery which binds me still," derives from natural phenomena, including "the cloud that took the form / (when the rest of Heaven was blue) / Of a demon in my view—."

Coincidental with his ambition exists a second passion, that of love. In the third major revision of "Tamerlane" (1831), a shortened version of the poem subsequently entitled "The Lake—To—" was inserted after what is line 74 in the final version of "Tamerlane."

Once again water, now associated with death, symbolizes the potential of a fluid arabesque reality. Consequently, the darkening of the lake evokes a terror that is "not fright, / But a tremulous delight." Characteristically, the poet "trembles," or feels "tremulous," when about to merge with the arabesque state. The reversal is really part of an extended paradox. Many of Poe's poems are of this kind and may be compared to the novelty object that reveals two different pictures depending on the angle of the light—except that in this case one picture is true, the other is false. The fluid, formless description of Tamerlane's lady confirms the interpretation, suggested by the lake, that the loved object is actually a vision of arabesque reality:

> I have no words—alas!—to tell
> The lovelines of loving well!
> Nor would I now attempt to trace
> The more than beauty of a face
> Whose lineaments, upon my mind,
> Are—shadows on th' unstable wind.

To Tamerlane she was "the shrine / On which my every hope and thought / Were incense."

Gradually, "she" becomes fused with nature, presumably the same nature that fostered Tamerlane's ambition. Her identification is prepared for by this pathetic fallacy:

> And, when the friendly sunshine smil'd,
> And she would mark the opening skies,
> I saw no Heaven—but in her eyes.

Indeed, " 'mid that sunshine, and those smiles," Tamerlane's cares evaporate, as does his independence: "I had no being—but in thee." The immediacy of the transference from indirect to direct, from "her" to "thee," points to the crucial nature of this admission. Nature was the controlling factor; now "she," or his love for her, is in charge. But "she" is nature incarnate:

> The world, and all it did contain
>
> . . . .
>
> That was new pleasure—the ideal,
> Dim, vanities of dreams by night—
> And dimmer nothings which were real—

> (Shadows—and a more shadowy light!)
> Parted upon their misty wings,
> And, so, confusedly, became,
> Thine image and—a name—a name!
> Two separate—yet most intimate things.

In other words, love has been equated with ambition. Since she is the world, Tamerlane must conquer it to attain her; her "image," the arabesque dream, is fused with Tamerlane's need for "a name," the status of ruler. By attributing Tamerlane's ambition to nature and identifying the object of Tamerlane's love with nature, Poe has succeeded, within the context of the poem, in making love and ambition one. She sustains his dream during the day by oppressing his mind "with double loveliness," that of her and that of the world she represents.

Lines 139 to 164 correspond to lines 35 to 64. From "the crown / Of a high mountain" where they walk, "The dwindled hills . . . shouting with a thousand rills" simulate applause. The fallacy inherent in Tamerlane's ambition to achieve the arabesque condition in mortal terms may be intuited in Tamerlane's need to deceive his companion:

> I spoke to her of power and pride,
>   But mystically—in such guise
> That she might deem it nought beside
>   The moment's converse; in her eyes
> I read, perhaps too carelessly—
>   A mingled feeling with my own—

Tamerlane is too eager to implement his vision of arabesque fusion. In line 165, Tamerlane reverts to the present and refers to his city, Samarcand, as "queen of Earth." Samarcand is Tamerlane's attempt to make his arabesque vision (as symbolized by his lady) concrete. Hence, Samarcand is female. But human love, "thou spirit given, / On Earth, of all we hope in Heaven," which "fall'st into the soul like rain / . . . leav'st the heart a wilderness." Now that he has attempted and, consequently, failed to realize his vision, the rain, originally inspiring, has a withering effect; and the wilderness, which Tamerlane converted into Samarcand, is now within. "The sound of the coming darkness," with its synesthesic fusion, signifies the approaching death that depresses the eagle, Hope. The moon, with whom the feminine arabesque principle is now identified, carries the same associations: "Her smile is chilly—and her beam / . . . will seem / . . . A portrait taken after death." But on returning to his old home, he recalls the vision of his youth; and the lines, "I have no words—alas! —to tell / The loveliness of loving well," find their transmogrified parallel in the following:

> O, I defy thee, Hell, to show
> On beds of fire that burn below,
> An humbler heart—a deeper wo.

The paradoxical hellish touch of heavenly dew, which Tamerlane experienced in childhood, is microcosmic of the poem's total and fused action.

In the epilogue, Tamerlane affirms his belief in a world elsewhere, away from material deception:

> Father, I firmly do believe—
> I know—for Death who comes for me
> From regions of the blest afar,
> Where there is nothing to deceive,
> Hath left his iron gate ajar,
> And rays of truth you cannot see
> Are flashing thro' Eternity—
> I do believe that Eblis [Mahometan prince of evil spirits] hath
> A snare in every human path—

"Else how," he asks, did Ambition leap "In the tangles of Love's very hair," when Love, the snowy-winged eagle, surrounds himself only with the purest "incense of burnt offerings." This mixed metaphor conjuring up a hairy eagle is rather unfortunate, but if the images in these lines are tracked back into the poem, Tamerlane answers his own question. The incense was that of Tamerlane's pure and childish hopes and thoughts, the tangled hair was originally his own in which nestled the "tumult of the headlong air," and the eagle—here a symbol of love—was earlier equated with "Hope" or ambition. By implication, love and ambition ideally are one since the word hope is applicable to both of them. However, the identification of love and ambition is not possible in this world of distinction. Tragically, on earth love and ambition are separate and at war. The arabesque state is not presently attainable.

Much of the remainder of Poe's poetry is implicit in "Tamerlane"; but there is a group of poems that relate specifically to its themes. Like Tamerlane's lady, the bride in "Song" is identified with nature, with "The world all love before thee," so that she "Was all on Earth my aching sight / Of Loveliness could see." Tamerlane's arabesque vision fired thoughts of conquest and grandeur, much as the bride's "burning blush" and "a kindling light" in her eye ignited "a fiercer flame" in the breast of the poet.[7] But this bride married another. As if to vindicate the poet's belief that his mistress cannot forget him, the heroine of "Bridal Ballad" is disturbed at having betrayed a past lover, now dead.

The painful memory of a happy moment is the subject of "The Happiest Day." The dark bird of mutability, a recurring symbol in Poe's work, is suggested in stanzas one, three, and six; and the bird's destructive "essence" is linked with pride's "venom."[8] In "To One in Paradise" (originally part of "The Assignation"), the object of the poet's love, now departed by marriage or death, is "a shrine," as in "Tamerlane." Poe's second "To Helen" presents Sarah Helen Whitman in the role of the lady who inspires arabesque vision, whose eyes "were the world to me." Although she has gone, her eyes, two "Venuses . . . illumine and enkindle—" like those of the bride in "Song."

The contrast between the youthful world of dreams, "when the sun was bright," and "the dull reality / Of waking life" in the poem "Dreams" repeats the "sunshine"–"white moon" antithesis in "Tamerlane." In the interests of fusion and the subversion of reality, dreaming is paradoxically equated with daytime and waking reality with the night. The poet's sensations when the "chilly wind" came

7. It should be noted that, in a review of Frances Sargent Osgood's poetry (*Godey's Lady's Book*, March, 1846), Poe admires a passage that begins, "I saw her on her bridal day" (H, XIII, 109). "Song" opens with the lines, "I saw thee on thy bridal day." And the "gleam of rosy fire" in the cheek of Osgood's Elfrida corresponds to the blush of the bride in Poe's poem.

8. Wilbur, Notes to *Poe: Complete Poems*, 123.

over his spirit, or when the moon or stars shone too coldly while he slept, are an intimation of that time when "the beam / Of an Eternity should bring the morrow," of the death which must intervene before he achieves the arabesque condition. Meanwhile, dreams provide relief:

> Dreams! in their vivid colouring of life—
> As in that fleeting, shadowy, misty strife
> Of semblance with reality which brings
> To the delirious eye more lovely things
> Of Paradise and Love—and all our own!
> Than young Hope in his sunniest hour hath known.

In these lines, Poe evokes the state of fusion.

The same opposition between waking reality and arabesque reality occurs in "Evening Star" with Venus, the evening star, representing the latter and the cold moon the former. The "fleecy cloud" that "pass'd, as a shroud" in the poem's exact center between the moon and the star indicates death, the point of transition from one world to the other. Poe's preference for median states determines the time of year and day: " 'T was noontide of summer, / And mid-time of night." In "A Dream," waking reality and dream reality are again contrasted but in the manner of "A Dream Within a Dream." The poet's absorption with the past turns waking reality into a "dream of life and light," thus allowing for the ambiguity of "Truth's day-star" in the final line. Similarly, the basic contrast between the clear sky of childhood and subsequent disturbance informs Morella's "Hymn." The transition from love to remorse, or from dream to reality, is also expressed in terms of a changing landscape, externalized in "The Valley of Unrest" and internalized in "The Haunted Palace." In "The Haunted Palace," originally part of "The Fall of the House of Usher," images of fluid, arabesque movement, banners that "float and flow," "gentle air that dallied," "Spirits moving musically, / To a lute's well-tunéd law," and "Echoes . . . flowing, flowing, flowing" give way to "Vast forms, that move fantastically / To a discordant melody." In "The Conqueror Worm," it is "vast formless things" that control earthly life.[9]

9. For a detailed discussion of convention in this poem, see Klaus Lubbers, "Poe's 'The Conqueror Worm,' " *American Literature*, XXXIX (1967), 375–77.

III

The poems that may be viewed as revolving around "Tamerlane" take as their underlying theme the displacement of dream reality in favor of waking reality. The poems circling around "Al Aaraaf" suggest a means by which the corrupting power of time may be avoided and the dream reality sustained. In the construction of poems directed toward the attainment of supernal beauty and divorced from didactic truth and passion, the conditions of the arabesque ideal may at least be approximated. As Cairns and Stovall have indicated, "Al Aaraaf," even in its unfinished state, is an allegory about the world of poetry.[10] In all but its length, "Al Aaraaf," with its exclusion of intellect and passion, anticipates Poe's critical pronouncements about the nature of true poetry.

Al Aaraaf, "a medium between Heaven & Hell" among the Arabians, is identified with the nova discovered by Tycho Brahe but converted by Poe into a wandering planet (*Letters*, I, 18). Its inhabitants, lesser angels and exceptional mortals, are charged with the business of mediating between heaven and the many worlds of God's universe. Poe conceived of poetry in similar terms. Since Al Aaraaf is an artistic realm, Poe indicates that Earth's artistic treasures have their home there: "You will see that I have supposed many of the lost sculptures of our world to have flown (in Spirit) to the star Al Aaraaf—a delicate place more suited to their divinity" (*Letters*, I, 33). As described in Part I, Al Aaraaf is composed of "all the beauty" of Earth with none of its "dross."

The ruler of Al Aaraaf, Nesace, basks in the light of the four suns of the constellation Cassiopeia after a visit to Earth. She kneels; and her song, by the miracle of synesthesia, is borne up to heaven "in odors"—the odors of the surrounding flowers, which include the hyacinth of Zante (whose transient beauty enrages Poe in "Sonnet. To Zante"). All the flowers exemplify the "Tamerlane" theme of reversal. In this way, the "Tamerlane" cycle of poems is absorbed

10. W. B. Cairns, "Some Notes on Poe's '*Al Aaraaf*,'" *Modern Philology*, XIII (1915), 35–44; Floyd Stovall, "An Interpretation of Poe's '*Al Aaraaf*,'" *University of Texas Studies in English*, IX (1929), 126–33, reprinted in Stovall, *Edgar Poe the Poet: Essays New and Old on the Man and His Work* (Charlottesville: University of Virginia Press, 1969), 102–25.

into the "Al Aaraaf" cycle, which elaborates on the alternate dream reality.

She assures God that her world has not overstepped its "barrier" and "bar" by seeking after knowledge, unlike the beings of Earth who "Have dream'd for thy Infinity / A model of their own" in devising, like Milton, an anthropomorphic God. In a later description of the seraphs in Part II, Poe points out that their happiness depends upon their lack of knowledge:

> ev'n with us the breath
> Of Science dims the mirror of our joy—
> To them 'twere the Simoon, and would destroy—
> For what (to them) availeth it to know
> That Truth is Falsehood—or that Bliss is Woe?

At this point, the "Sonnet—To Science," which Poe intended as a proem to "Al Aaraaf," is relevant. Science, offspring of mutability, "alterest all things with thy peering eyes" and, like a vulture, preys upon the poet's heart. Science distinguishes and separates fused elements:

> Hast thou not dragged Diane from her car?
> And driven the Hamadryad from the wood
> To seek a shelter in some happier star?
> Hast thou not torn the Naiad from her flood,
> The Elfin from the green grass, and from me
> The summer dream beneath the tamarind tree?

Al Aaraaf, of course, is that "happier star" of art.

Unlike Nesace's message which is conveyed synesthetically, God's reply is conveyed by oxymoron, a "sound of silence." This idea is elaborated in "Sonnet—Silence," which contrasts the "corporate Silence" of death with "his shadow," the silence not of nada (a concept introduced in "Silence—A Fable") but of ideality. Thus, the three poems Poe specifically designated sonnets are contained or suggested by "Al Aaraaf." God commands that Nesace and her train relinquish the Earth and, using the fate of Earth as an example, inform "other worlds" of the incompatibility of knowledge, the province of intellect, and art, the province of taste and imagination. The first part of "Al Aaraaf" is designed solely to advance an aesthetic doctrine. Part II illustrates the other half of that doctrine, the incompatibility of art and passion—the province of the moral sense.

The fall of Ianthe and Angelo through passion is prefigured in Part II by mention of "beautiful Gomorrah" and "Tenantless cities of the desert" and in Part I by the account of the lilies "On the fair Capo Deucato," which hung "Upon the flying footsteps of—deep pride—/ Of her who lov'd a mortal—and so died," and the account of the repentent "gemmy flower" whose "honied dew" fell from its exalted place in heaven upon an earthly flower in Trebizond. The fall here is metaphorical and therefore unfortunate, unlike the physical falls in Poe. Ianthe, a native of Al Aaraaf, and Angelo, originally of Earth, miss Nesace's summons and thus fall, because "Heaven no grace imparts / To those who hear not for their beating hearts." That Ianthe shares Angelo's sensuality is indicated by her unconscious echoing of John Donne's "Elegie XIX: To His Mistris Going to Bed" in this description: "around, above, below, / Gay fire-fly of the night we come and go." Love's kisses, as Nesace claims, are "lead on the heart" and serve to exclude Ianthe and Angelo from the realm of artistic ideality. Since Poe has indicated that Angelo is Michelangelo, it seems logical to construe the whole episode as a critique of Michelangelo's art (*Letters*, I, 19). Poe may be implying that the work of Michelangelo is limited by its sensuousness and its anthropomorphic conceptions of divinity.

The quality of fusion, indeed confusion, in "Al Aaraaf" is largely conveyed by images of things rising and falling and, by implication, merging at some intermediate point. Here are some examples. After mention of "gardens where the day / Springs from the gems of Circassy" and the "Earth, / Whence sprang the 'Idea of Beauty' into birth, / (Falling in wreaths thro' many a startled star . . .)," Nesace kneels down among "lilies such as rear'd the head / On the fair Capo Deucato, and sprang / So eagerly around about" and the Sephalica, which "uprear'd its purple stem," and the sad gemmy flower whose dew "fell on gardens of the unforgiven." Nesace's prayer is borne "up to Heaven" after a reference to Cupid floating "down the holy river." "High on a mountain / . . . that towering far away / . . . caught the ray / Of sunken suns at eve / . . . Uprear'd . . . a pile / Of gorgeous col-

umns on th' unburthen'd air," Nesace's palace. The rising and falling motions are combined in the image of the hypothetical "drowsy
shepherd / . . . Raising his heavy eyelid." The columns are reflected
"Far down" into the surrounding water, and the pavement is car-
peted with stars "such as fall / Thro' the ebon air." With a "falling
strain," Nesace makes a landing and calls on her subjects, whose
"wonder" makes stars "come down" to shine in their eyes, to "Up!"
and "Arise!" and shake off leaden kisses. After it is pointed out that
God refracted from Al Aaraaf the "keen light" of knowledge "That
fell," the remainder of the poem is concerned with the fall of Ianthe
and Angelo. Although he falls, Angelo is described as "A gazer on
the lights that shine above." Correspondingly, each star "looks so
sweetly down on Beauty's hair." But Angelo and Ianthe sit upon a
beetling "mountain crag" that "scowls on starry worlds that down
beneath it lie." Angelo recalls the moment of his death when "The
sun-ray dropp'd, in Lemnos" and the "heavy light" weighed upon
his eyelids, and "Thence sprang I—as the eagle from his tower . . . as
my pennon'd spirit leapt aloft."

The star Al Aaraaf embodies a fusion of earthly and nonearthly
elements. It is a place bound together by music, which "No magic
shall sever," containing a lake, "Where wild flowers creeping, / Have
mingled their shade." At the same time, there is a good deal of evidence to indicate that Al Aaraaf is Earth under another guise, or
Earth's true nature as seen through the half-closed eye. Certainly, its
inhabitants "ponder / With half closing eyes." In Part I when Nesace
leaves the helm of rulership, it is by no means clear where she goes.
And the following lines are not very helpful:

> Now happiest, loveliest in yon lovely Earth,
> Whence sprang the "Idea of Beauty" into birth,
> (Falling in wreath's thro' many a startled star,
> Like women's hair 'mid pearls, until, afar
> It lit on hills Achaian, and there dwelt)
> She look'd into Infinity—and knelt.
> Rich clouds, for canopies, about her curled—
> Fit emblems of the model of her world—
> Seen but in beauty—not impeding sight
> Of other beauty glittering thro' the light—

> A wreath that turned each starry form around,
> And all the opal'd air in color bound.

From this it would appear that Nesace, as the "Idea of Beauty," represents all that is best on Earth and is derived from Earth. The clouds symbolize her world, which is described as a wreath and a model. Presumably, Poe is referring to the Platonic conception of ideal forms. Al Aaraaf, as a world of art, is a model of such forms and is presented by Poe as a phosphor surrounding Earth. Nesace is kneeling on Al Aaraaf and Earth at the same time. There is a similar ambiguity when Nesace gets up:

> Up rose the maiden in the yellow night,
> The single mooned-eve!—on Earth we plight
> Our faith to one love—and one moon adore—
> The birth-place of young Beauty had no more.

Earth has already been described as the birthplace of the "Idea of Beauty." Both Al Aaraaf and Earth have one moon. Why not the same one? Thus, it is probable that Al Aaraaf and Earth are actually one.

This interpretation may be further substantiated by a passage in Part II. Angelo is speaking of his "death":

> Perhaps my brain grew dizzy—but the world
> I left so late was into chaos hurl'd—
> Sprang from her station, on the winds apart,
> And roll'd, a flame, the fiery Heaven athwart.

Syntactically, the flame could refer to Earth or Al Aaraaf. At first glance it may be thought to refer to Earth, but the subsequent description of Al Aaraaf and its "brazen rays" as a "red Daedalion" suggests otherwise. Poe conceived of the act of artistic creation in terms of the destruction of everyday reality. In other words, the existence of Al Aaraaf necessarily obliterates Earth. The "dizzy" sensation experienced by Angelo indicates, in terms of Poe's philosophy, that he is about to enter the arabesque state. Furthermore, Angelo falls toward Al Aaraaf with a "tremulous motion," another typical presentiment of the arabesque state. And in line 260, Earth "thy star trembled." It is much like the cinematic technique for introducing a flashback by rippling one frame and dissolving it into another. This would account for the coincidence of the arrival of Al Aaraaf and Earth's destruction with Angelo's death. It should also be noted that he dies at a median time of year, "that autumn eve," among "th' Arabesque carving of a gilded hall" and "the draperied wall." It seems necessary to conclude that evidence suggesting Al Aaraaf has destroyed Earth should be taken metaphorically.[11] What occurs is an apocalypse of mind.

In three other poems, art is experienced in terms of a "trembling wobble." The supernal song of Israfel, to the accompaniment of the "trembling living" strings of his lyre, entrances "the giddy stars" and causes the moon, "tottering above," to blush. The patently artificial yet admirable "painted paroquet" of the poem "Romance" is superceded by the grotesque reality of "eternal Condor years" in a variation of the "Tamerlane" theme of reversal. But it is art that prevails at the conclusion:

> And when an hour with calmer wings
> Its down upon my spirit flings—
> That little time with lyre and rhyme
> To while away—forbidden things!
> My heart would feel to be a crime
> Unless it trembled with the strings.

Unfortunately, the ugly word *flings* mars the final mood. The river in "To the River—" is an "emblem" of "the playful maziness of art" in Alberto's daughter. Just as the wave "trembles" when it embodies her reflection, so "her worshipper . . . trembles" in her sight.

Various other elements in "Al Aaraaf" occur in other poems. The image of "molten stars . . . besilvering the pall," part of the description of Nesace's palace, figures in "To—" (Elmira Royster Shelton?). The eyes of his heavenly mistress fall "on my funereal mind / Like starlight on a pall." In "Al Aaraaf" artistic ideality is identified with classical times and ruins—incomplete images of a former perfection. Consequently, in "To Helen," her "classic" beauty transports the

---

11. Stovall's view that Al Aaraaf has literally destroyed Earth ("An Interpretation of Poe's 'Al Aaraaf,'" 106–22), is ably refuted by Richard Campbell Pettigrew and Marie Morgan Pettigrew, "A Reply to Floyd Stovall's Interpretation of 'Al Aaraaf,'" *American Literature*, VIII (1937), 439–40.

poet, like Ulysses, to Greek glory and Roman grandeur, secular criteria of beauty. The agate lamp that she holds casts a variegated light and thus creates an arabesque effect. Given such an effect, polarities merge. Thus Helen can be a living person and a piece of classical sculpture at the same time. In her person, classical paganism and Christianity, "from the regions which / Are Holy-Land," may be reconciled. Poe draws on "To Helen" in the poem "To F—" (Frances Sarah Osgood), originally entitled "To Mary" (Winfree), whose "memory is to me / Like some enchanted far-off isle / In some tumultuous sea—." The classical standard appears again in "The Coliseum," a poem in blank verse and originally part of *Politian*. As a pilgrim, the poet prepares to "drink within / My very soul thy grandeur, gloom, and glory" and concludes that the classical spirit still influences the artist.

IV

The "Al Aaraaf" complex of poems emphasizes the dream reality half of the "Tamerlane" dichotomy and proposes artistic endeavor as a means of obliterating life's vicissitudes. The waking reality side of the dichotomy reaches its logical extension in those poems that consider the implications of death and that may be viewed as revolving around "The Raven." This theme, "dark thoughts of the gray tombstone," is announced in "Spirits of the Dead." At the moment of death, Poe envisages that the stars, instead of imparting hope, "shall seem / As a burning and a fever / Which would cling to thee forever"; that visions will not pass like the dew; and that the mist, "Shadowy—shadowy—yet broken, / Is a symbol and a token—" but of what? In "For Annie," the moment of death has arrived, "And the fever called 'Living' / Is conquered at last."

The successive cycles of themes considered so far are recapitulated in "Stanzas" where the poet explains that moments of communion with nature, habitual in youth but now as fleeting "As dew of the night-time," are "bid / With a strange sound, as of a harpstring broken / T'awake us—'Tis a symbol and a token, / Of what in other worlds shall be." The poet further incorporates the theme of "Al Aaraaf" by maintaining that such moments are God-given to those "Who otherwise would fall from life and Heav'n / Drawn by their heart's passion." As Poe takes up a new aspect of the same subject, he implicitly involves the angles he has already examined. Thus, the poems circling around death are dialectically complex because former issues are entwined. Consequently, more and more cross references are apparent.

"The Raven" begins familiarly with the student pondering "Over many a quaint and curious volume of forgotten lore." That such an occupation is futile and possibly dangerous is suggested by Poe's affirmation in "Stanzas" that he "will half believe" his intuitive moments "fraught / With more of sov'reignty than ancient lore / Hath ever told." And the following lines from "Tamerlane" are equally applicable:

> Thus I remember having dwelt
> Some pages of early lore upon,
> With loitering eye, till I have felt
> The letters—with their meaning—melt
> To fantasies—with none.

This is a reasonably accurate description of the movement of the later poem. Because of his reliance on the intellect, the student in "The Raven" loses an opportunity to regain his lost Lenore.

In "The Philosophy of Composition," Poe provides the best extant criticism of the poem, and what he says makes it clear that the student's conclusions about the bird are totally subjective. "I determined," claims Poe, "to produce continuously novel effects, by the *variation of the application* of the refrain—the refrain itself remaining, for the most part, unvaried" (H, XIV, 199). The application of the refrain, "Nevermore," is made in the student's own mind; "the effect of the *variation of application*" is the *raison d'être* of the poem (H, XIV, 201).[12] In these lines, Poe provides a clue to the organic

12. It should be noted that the raven invokes only the student's "fancy" not his "imagination." See Marvin Mengeling and Frances Mengeling, "From Fancy to Failure: A Study of the Narrators in the Tales of Edgar Allan Poe," *University of Kansas City Review*, XXXIII (1967), 297. Lynen makes the valuable point—not understood by the student in the poem—that "nevermore" premises "always." John F. Lynen, *The Design of the Present: Essays on Time and Form in American Literature* (New Haven, Conn.: Yale University Press, 1969), 266.

principle behind his entire poetic output. From this analysis it should be clear that each poem obeys this variation of application rule, a technique exemplified in miniature in "The Bells." Thus each poem contributes to Poe's "Runic" (interlacing) rhyme.

"The Raven" may be divided into three equal parts of six stanzas each. In the first six stanzas, the student's situation is outlined, and the entrance of the bird is anticipated. In the six stanzas following, as Poe indicates in "The Philosophy of Composition," the student's attitude toward the raven is one of mock seriousness. But in the final stanzas, the student tortures himself into believing that Lenore is gone forever and, *ipso facto*, loses an opportunity to regain her at precisely that moment. Poe is teasing the reader when he writes:

It will be observed that the words, "from out my heart," involve the first metaphorical expression in the poem. They, with the answer, "Nevermore," dispose the mind to seek a moral in all that has been previously narrated. The reader begins now to regard the Raven as emblematical—but it is not until the very last line of the very last stanza, that the intention of making him emblematical of *Mournful and Never-ending Remembrance* is permitted distinctly to be seen. (H, XIV, 208)

This is only a "distinctly" partial solution. The full sentence Poe is referring to reads, "Take thy beak from out my heart," and recalls the description of the vulture in "Sonnet—To Science," which preys "upon the poet's heart." Is it possible that the raven represents the quest of the intellectual for knowledge, and is it the student's desire for a mathematical certainty that leads to "*Mournful and Never-ending Remembrance*"? The emphasis on distinction in the first section of the poem characterizes the student's scientific cast of mind. He remembers the time "distinctly," as well as "each separate dying ember" and "each purple curtain."

There is much in the poem to substantiate such an interpretation of the raven. First, the bird settles upon the bust of Pallas, goddess of wisdom. The bust is stony, pallid, and totally dead—as dead as the student finally believes Lenore to be. Poe's assertion "that the bust was absolutely *suggested* by the bird" would support this correspondence (H, XIV, 205). Second, the description, "a stately Raven of the saintly days of yore," recalls the student's "many a quaint and curious volume of forgotten lore." The "ancient Raven" and the volumes share the qualities of antiquity and irrelevance. Like the books, the raven's reiterated answer "little meaning—little relevancy bore." It seems likely that Poe is equating the raven and the volumes. Certainly, if the experience is a dream, it is in all likelihood informed by the book the student was reading before "nearly napping." (In support of the dream possibility, there is the suggestion that the raven's "shadow, that lies floating on the floor" at the conclusion, bears some relation to the observation in stanza 2 that each "ember wrought its ghost upon the floor.") Presumably, the comic aspect that the "shorn and shaven" bird first presents is intended to ridicule the student's reliance on knowledge. It is ironic that the student mocks the raven's appearance without realizing the personal application of his laughter.

In the third section, the student's attitude toward the raven is much more serious and probing, just when Lenore is about to make an entrance:

Then, methought, the air grew denser, perfumed from an unseen censer
Swung by Seraphim whose foot-falls tinkled on the tufted floor.[13]

Wilbur makes the right associations here: "In 'Ligeia,' similar phenomena are the first indications that the dead beloved is to be rematerialized. 'I saw that there lay upon the golden carpet, in the very middle of the rich lustre thrown from the censer, a shadow—a faint, indefinite shadow of angelic aspect. . . . I became distinctly aware of a gentle foot-fall upon the carpet.'(M, III, 325)"[14] The implication, which Wilbur does not make, is that Lenore is about to appear. All the circumstances are correct. It is a median time, midnight, and December, mid-winter. The curtaining, presumably arabesque, moves with a "sad, uncertain rustling." And for a while, the student, "linking / Fancy unto fancy," adopts the correct attitude toward the bird of knowledge. But then, he suddenly rationalizes the phenomenon as God's means of letting him "forget this lost Lenore,"

13. Critics who are disturbed by the unlikely word "tinkled" have Poe's own quite adequate answer that he used the word for its "supernatural" effect (Letters, II, 331).
14. Wilbur, Notes to Poe: Complete Poems, 144.

the "surcease of sorrow" he had "sought to borrow / From my books." With this immediate loss of the perspective of the half-closed eye, the reader may assume that Lenore cancels her intended visitation.

An examination of light sources, or means of illumination, in the poem supports this reading. The information that "each separate dying ember wrought its ghost upon the floor" (stanza 2) allows for the possibility that all apparent materializations in "The Raven" derive from the subjective or dream experience of the student. But more importantly it infers the existence of a fire, much as other details infer the presence of Lenore. Nowhere is the existence of a fire directly confirmed, thus facilitating its metaphorical identification with Lenore. In stanza 13 natural firelight, now as a metaphor, is set against an artificial light source, mentioned here for the first time in a context that renders the symbolic import clear:

This I sat engaged in guessing, but no syllable expressing
To the fowl whose fiery eyes now burned into my bosom's core;
This and more I sat divining, with my head at ease reclining
On the cushion's velvet lining that the lamp-light gloated o'er.

Firelight is associated with the heart or the soul. There are two references to the student's agitated or inflamed heart, plus "all my soul within me burning" (stanza 6). The artificial lamplight is associated with the head or intellect. In stanza 14, the outcome of the conflict is clear, and the poem contains no further suggestions of fire. Lenore and the revelation she signifies have eluded the student. The poem concludes with the lamp, symbolically positioned somewhere over the head of Pallas, casting the artificial light of reason over the bird to create the "shadow on the floor." The reader may assume that the fire, indirectly suggested in stanza 2 and only fitfully glowing then, is now out.

Ironically, the student is probably correct in believing, at the poem's opening, that Lenore is knocking at his chamber door. Filled "with fantastic terrors never felt before," the student is in a state to perceive her. After throwing open the door, the student peers into the darkness: "And the only word there spoken was the whispered word 'Lenore?' / This I whispered, and an echo murmured back the word, 'Lenore!' " The syntax here is slightly ambiguous and does not positively confirm the likelihood that he first voiced the name "Lenore." The echo may have spoken first. However, the original "rapping"—it is explicitly stated—occurs "at my chamber door"; and unquestionably, the raven taps at his "window lattice." There the case rests. Read in this way, "The Raven" is much more than "an attenuated exercise for elocutionists"[15] and deserves its eminent place in the Poe canon. Every image plays its part in the brilliantly conceived drama in which a major part of the action and many of the directives for interpreting this action must be located offstage.

In "The Raven" Poe's attitude toward death—unlike that of the student—is positive, as it is in the poem "Lenore," which describes her funeral. Poe contrasts conventional and insincere grief, symbolized by "yon drear / And rigid bier," with the celebration of her lover, Guy de Vere, who rejoices in her ascension to heaven. In "The Sleeper," which Pope-Hennessy admires for its "audible quiet," Poe is less optimistic.[16] It is a June midnight, and Irene's sleep—not death—betokens a similar sleep of all that is beautiful in nature. The movement of "The bodiless airs" affects "the curtain canopy" so that "Like ghosts the shadows rise and fall," suggesting the arabesque moment in which the barrier between life and death is lifted. But in this poem, the best that the lover can hope for is that death may be an undisturbed sleep: "Soft may the worms about her creep!" In "The Conqueror Worm" death appears to end everything. However, this poem was written to be included in "Ligeia" to illustrate one possible attitude toward death, not necessarily Poe's.

V

The nodal point for the final sequence of poems is "Ulalume." The "Al Aaraaf" sequence and "The Raven" sequence take up and develop different sides of the dichotomy expressed in the "Tamerlane" sequence. In this final series the two sides are reintegrated. All the previous themes are gathered into the remaining poems, which make up the most difficult and confusing of the four cycles. One way

15. Yvor Winters, In Defense of Reason (Denver: University of Denver Press, 1947), 253.
16. Una Pope-Hennessy, Edgar Allan Poe (London: Macmillan, 1934), 119.

of illustrating the organic nature of Poe's poetry may be to picture it as four converging solar systems. (It will be recalled that Al Aaraaf rests in the illumination of the four suns in the constellation Cassiopeia.) To catch the mood of the whole, it is necessary to envisage the collapse of the four systems into one, preparatory to a final moment of arabesque release.

To borrow a line from "Dreams," the final cycle might be entitled "climes of mine imagining." This cycle represents Poe's furthest departure from the conventional world and his fullest attempt to envision the nature of a supernal world. The theme of fulfillment in an aesthetic or an amatory sense is equated with death. These poems provide the evidence for Poe's supposed necrophiliac desires. The ambiguity and extreme use of repetition, characteristic of these poems, are a corollary of their function. The reiterated refrain and other repetitions point both to the incorporation of previous themes and to a sense of the tightening, accelerating whirl of Poe's organic design.

A side-by-side analysis of "Fairy-Land" [I]—the revised version is virtually a new poem—and "Dream-Land" indicates the nature of the fusion that Poe is proposing between the art poems and the death poems. "Fairy-Land" [I] opens with the following lines:

> Dim vales—and shadowy floods—
> And cloudy-looking woods,
> Whose forms we can't discover
> For the tears that drip all over.

In "Dream-Land" occur the following lines:

> Bottomless vales and boundless floods,
> And chasms, and caves, and Titan woods,
> With forms that no man can discover
> For the tears that drip all over.

In both poems, the landscape is identical. However, in "Fairy-Land" [I], in spite of the element of parody noted by Richard Wilbur, Poe is describing a realm of poetry.[17] But in "Dream-Land," the landscape is beyond the grave. Poe is concluding that the true poet has moments of insight into the spiritual world.

17. Wilbur, Notes to Poe: Complete Poems, 131–32.

The numerous moons in "Fairy-Land" [I] recall the four suns in "Al Aaraaf," an "albatross" is rhymed with "loss" in both poems, and the final lines make it clear that Poe is talking about poetry. The tentlike drapery of one of the moons covers the area until the morning, at which time:

> Its atomies, however,
> Into a shower dissever,
> Of which those butterflies,
> Of Earth, who seek the skies,
> And so come down again
> (Never-contented things!)
> Have brought a specimen
> Upon their quivering wings.

In "The Poetic Principle," the aspiration of the poet is likened to the "desire of the moth for the star" (H, XIV, 273).

In "Dream-Land," the narrator has just returned from "an ultimate dim Thule / . . . Out of Space—out of Time." He describes it as a land in which the four elements of earth, water, air, and fire fuse into one another:

> Mountains toppling evermore
> Into seas without a shore;
> Seas that restlessly aspire,
> Surging, unto skies of fire;
> Lakes that endlessly outspread.

Poe is reading the creation back into its original chaos, or unity, as often symbolized throughout his work by lakes—this time a limitless lake. The rising and falling motion mirrors that in "Al Aaraaf." In this region live the "Ghouls . . . White-robed forms of friends long given, / In agony, to the Earth—and Heaven." Paradoxically, although the atmosphere seems to be one of terror, to the heavy-hearted "Tis a peachful soothing region"—an "Eldorado!" in fact. The knight in the poem "Eldorado" is told by the "pilgrim shadow" that the place lies beyond death, "Down the Valley of the shadow."[18] In affirmation, the word *shadow* occurs as the final word in the middle of each stanza. The fact that the knight is "Singing a song, / In

18. Apparently, before O. S. Coad, "The Meaning of Poe's 'Eldorado,' " *Modern Language Notes*, LIX (1944), 59–61, the poem was thought to be exclusively about the California gold rush.

search of Eldorado" suggests that art is a means of attaining arabesque reality. In "Dream-Land" the traveler "May not—dare not
openly view it." He must assume the perspective of the half-closed
eye because:

> Never its mysteries are exposed
> To the weak human eye unclosed;
> So wills its King, who hath forbid
> The uplifting of the fringed lid.

These lines are heavily paradoxical. "The human eye unclosed"
refers to the living; but the "fringed lid," as in "The Sleeper," is
closed and merges with the lid of the coffin. Poe is again insisting
that what is normally thought of as life is actually more like death.

Similar ambiguity pervades "The City in the Sea," perhaps Poe's
most enigmatic poem. The basic situation is that of "The Fall of the
House of Usher." It is important to realize that the image is not of a
sunken city but of a city about to sink: "There open fanes and gaping
graves / Yawn *level with* the luminous waves" (italics added). In a
manner comparable to the inexplicable illumination in Usher's
painting of a vault, "light from out the lurid sea / Streams up the turrets silently." But there is, as yet, no corresponding downward
movement into the final release that death should bring. The
inhabitants are artists living in an arabesque state that simulates
death but is not. Like "MS. Found in a Bottle," this poem suggests
two gradations of arabesque reality—one a limbo available in the
present, the other awaiting a day of apocalypse. The towers "tremble
not" but are "pendulous in air," poised on the brink between life and
death. An arabesque fusion is implied by the "turrets and shadows"
that "blend" and by:

> ... many a marvellous shrine
> Whose wreathéd friezes intertwine
> The viol, the violet, and the vine.

Northrop Frye comments on "a fusion of two opposed qualities"
in this last line, "paronomasia" or "verbal wit and hypnotic
incantation."[19]

19. Northrop Frye, *Anatomy of Criticism* (Princeton, N.J.: Princeton University
Press, 1957), 276.

In the last stanza, the city does sink, transporting its entranced dwellers from arabesque death into arabesque life. In other words, "The City in the Sea" describes the fulfillment of Poe's dream to lapse from mortal life while, and by means of, aesthetically living in an arabesque condition. In "The Masque of the Red Death," a similar attempt is made but with apparently less success. However, the poem has an added ambiguity resulting from the imagery of evil and blasphemy. As the city goes down, "Hell, rising from a thousand thrones, / Shall do it reverence." The House of Usher, likewise, sinks to the accompaniment of "a long tumultuous shouting sound like the voice of a thousand waters" (M, II, 417), presumably the same "voice of many waters" that in Revelation 14:2 precedes the fall of Babylon. The walls of the city are "Babylon-like," and there is much in the poem to suggest the submersion of Gomorrah in the Dead Sea, as imaged in the following lines from "Al Aaraaf":

> the stilly, clear abyss
> Of beautiful Gomorrah! O, the wave
> Is now upon thee—but too late to save!

In fact, the poem was earlier called "The Doomed City" and "The City of Sin." As Wilbur points out, "Overlooking certain inconsistencies (notably line 4) it is possible to see the poem as a fantastic picture of the wicked dead awaiting judgement during Jesus' thousand year reign on earth."[20]

But to read the poem in this way is to fall victim to Poe's deceptive art. Poe is ironically using conventional morality against itself, just as he frequently inverts the meaning of dream and reality, life and death. In Basler's words, the poem is a "symbolic avowal (come hell or high water!) of Poe's poetic creed that the function of the poet is to create beauty rather than to moralize."[21] The line between hell and heaven, life and death, can be made to disappear. The equation of "good" and "worst" and "bad" and "best" in the fourth line—"the good, and the bad, and the worst, and the best"—is intended to erase such distinctions. The poetic world can merge into

20. Wilbur, Notes to Poe: Complete Poems, 30.
21. Roy P. Basler, Sex, Symbolism, and Psychology in Literature (New Brunswick, N.J.: Rutgers University Press, 1948).

the world of the afterlife. For this reason, it is a little difficult at certain points to determine whether the city is in or out of the sea. Echoes from the first stanza—the repetition of "lo" and and the mention of "thrones" in the final stanza—are intended to make the poem a continuous circle.

The action of "Ulalume—A Ballad" is directed at instructing the narrator that only death will provide the fulfillment of his love.[22] This necessary coincidence is underlined by a dualism that directs the poem. The narrator is presented in duplicate, as Psyche—his soul—and as his emotional heart, between whom there is a sister-brother relationship. And the ten stanzas fall into two groups of five, the first ruled by the heart and the second ruled by Psyche. In the following lines, the narrator draws attention to the necessary combination of love and death, but without recognizing it at the time:

> These were days when my heart was volcanic
> As the scoriac rivers that roll—
> As the lavas that restlessly roll
> Their sulphurous currents down Yaanek,
> In the ultimate climes of the Pole—
> That groan as they roll down Mount Yaanek,
> In the realms of the Boreal Pole.

The narrator might think that he is saying that the world is too cold for his passions, as critics have affirmed;[23] but in fact he is connecting passion with death. The white "ultimate climes of the Pole" here, as in *Pym*, symbolize the world beyond.

This dualism determines the nature of Astarte, or Venus, which arose "Distinct with its duplicate horn." *Duplicate* functions as a pun. It means *two* and *the same* and thus implies the union of love and death. For this reason, the narrator ascribes to Venus apparently contradictory aspects, a sensual aspect:

> . . . She is warmer than Dian;
> She rolls through an ether of sighs—

22. For opposing interpretations, see J. E. Miller, Jr., " 'Ulalume' Resurrected," *Philological Quarterly*, XXXIV (1955), 197–205; Eric W. Carlson, "Symbol and Sense in Poe's 'Ulalume,' " *American Literature*, XXXV (1963), 22–37.
23. For example, Edward H. Davidson, *Poe: A Critical Study* (Cambridge, Mass.: Harvard University Press, 1957), 94–95.

> She revels in a region of sighs.
>
> And a spiritual aspect, since she comes
>
> > To point us the path to the skies—
> > To the Lethean peace of the skies—

This is equivalent to the "lava at the pole" dichotomy. But "duplicate" also suggests duplicity and deception because the narrator's
heart chooses to ignore one aspect of Astarte's dualism and to
assume that he can achieve fulfillment without dying. Psyche, realizing that the narrator has incompletely grasped the star's import,
says, "Sadly this star I mistrust." And the narrator, from the vantage
point of having completed the experience, admits, "Our memories
were treacherous." Moreover, Astarte, having come through the
Lion, is in an astrologically unfavorable position.[24] In other words,
this is not the night on which the narrator is to be united in death
with his "lost Ulalume." He is deluded in ascribing a "Sibyllic
splendor" to the star.

Naïvely expecting his love to be fulfilled, the narrator is
abruptly reminded of Ulalume's death and the mortal gap between
him and her, between deceptive existence and ideality. At this point,
the narrator recognizes a further dualism:

> . . . It was surely October,
> on this very night of last year,
> That I journeyed—I journeyed down here!—
> That I brought a dread burden down here—

But all the dualism in the poem—the "skies" and "leaves," "ashen
and sober," "crispéd and sere," the "night" and the "year," "Weir"
and "Auber," the virtual repetition of the last four lines of stanza 1
in the last four lines of the penultimate stanza, and the scenic
externalization of the narrator's mind—underlines the necessary
union of love and death. In the last stanza, Psyche and the narrator
speak as one, indicating that the narrator realizes the import of his
experience. They speculate that the "merciful ghouls," spirits of the

---

24. *Ibid.*, 95. There is some doubt about the accuracy of Poe's astrology here. See
Thomas Ollive Mabbott, "Poe's 'Ulalume,' " *Explicator*, VI (1945), item 57; Stovall,
Edgar Poe the Poet, 229; Mabbott, *Collected Works*, I, 422n44.

dead, arranged the appearance of Astarte, "the spectre of a planet," to shield the narrator from the unhappy knowledge that he must wait until death before his love may be fulfilled. As a "spectre," Astarte is a duplicate of the actual planet, and so the narrator may be pardoned for misunderstanding its significance.

"Eulalie—A Song" concerns the poet's happiness after death, since only in that state can he say, "Now Doubt—now Pain / Come never again." And only from a nonearthly perspective would Venus shine all day. Furthermore, the yellow-haired Eulalie appears to be the sun, and it is as a mother that she "upturns her matron eye" to Astarte. That the situation seems to refer to the bloom of life is precisely Poe's point. In "Annabel Lee" the poet celebrates a soul-love that death does not "dissever" but fulfills:

> And so, all the night-tide, I lie down by the side
> Of my darling, my darling, my life and my bride
> In her sepulchre there by the sea—

The kingdom by the sea represents that point of transition between life and death. In symbolic terms, lying alongside the sea and the dead bride amounts to the same thing. In "For Annie," the poet falls asleep on the breast of his dead mistress:

> And I lie so composedly,
> Now, in my bed,
> (Knowing her love)
> That you fancy me dead—

For Freudians, these lines brand Poe as a latent necrophiliac. Moreover, the mention in "Annabel Lee" of disapproving "high-born kinsmen" and those "older than we" might suggest parental opposition to the incestuous union of brother and sister such as that evoked in "Ulalume."[25] In these final poems, however, Poe's main concern is the denial of all conventional boundaries—between good and bad, between life and death, and those involving the incest taboo—in order to simulate the true arabesque.

It should be clear by now that each poem has its logical place in

25. One critic notes that incest involves "the merging of two who are already too nearly one." See Lynen, The Design of the Present, 233.

an organic structure. The four cycles of poetry find their parallels in the four stanzas and stages of "The Bells"—the wintry childhood corresponding to the "Tamerlane" group, the happy marriage to the "Al Aaraaf" group, the troubled alarum of adult life to "The Raven" group, and the "happy" "monody" of death to the "Ulalume" group. Although the divisions in this chapter are generally chronological, the poems do not appear in quite the order in which they have been treated here. Nor should they. Poe endeavors to eradicate divisions of any kind, including those posited here. It is Poe's extraordinary achievement that, in the context of his poetry, he succeeds in making the words ambition, love, art, death, and reality one.

6

Arabesques

Poe is probably best known for what might be distinguished as his tales of the arabesque. Although the arabesques constitute only a fraction of his total output, critics have generally concentrated their efforts on these ten tales. Chronologically listed, they fall roughly into pairs: "Metzengerstein" and "The Assignation," "Berenice" and "Morella," "Ligeia" and "The Fall of the House of Usher," "Eleonora" and "The Oval Portrait," "The Masque of the Red Death" and "The Pit and the Pendulum." "Ligeia" and "The Fall of the House of Usher" remain Poe's masterpieces. Their preeminence is highlighted by the four tales that lead up to, and away from, them.

In terms of development, the arabesques are a logical outgrowth of the poetry. Some of the arabesques include a poem, and many commentators have spoken of the poetic or evocative power of these tales. This evocative power can be attributed to a technique of fluid form. The meaning of an arabesque tale can only be tentatively fixed within certain limits. Almost all of them can be genuinely interpreted in a variety of ways, whether literal, parodic, psychological, or supernatural. It is a mistake to attempt to rank those elements as "levels" of meaning. A complete interpretation involves the ability to maintain these varying approaches and possibilities in a state of omnidimensional fusion. Consequently, the surface of an arabesque tale becomes as convoluted and fluid as an arabesque tapestry; the distinction between the literal narrative surface and the symbolic meaning disappears. Thus, the tales identified here as arabesques exhibit not only a concern with mind-expanding arabesque decor but also a fluidity of form, technique, or structure that seeks to approximate the arabesque condition.[1] With this in view, an unbiased appreciation of these tales may be possible.

II

In dealing with the cursed-house theme, "Metzengerstein," which first appeared in the January 14, 1832, *Saturday Courier*, anticipates "The Fall of the House of Usher"; but the focus is on metempsychosis. In a review of *Sheppard Lee*, published in the *Southern Literary Messenger* for September, 1836, Poe indicates that a tale of metempsychosis should be written "as if the author were firmly impressed with the truth, yet astonished at the immensity, of the wonders he relates" (H, IX, 138). This is true of Poe's practice in "Metzengerstein." Before beginning the tale, the narrator discusses the questionable belief that, after death, a person's soul may pass into some other body. The downtrodden Berlifitzing family gain their revenge on the Metzengersteins through the soul of the dead Count Berlifitzing, who uses the arabesque tapestry in Baron Metzengerstein's apartment to overcome the barrier between life and death. By this means, his soul passes into the powerful body of the horse depicted on the tapestry. The horse appears in the stable because that is where the count died, in a fire probably instigated by the baron. Thus, the borderline between art and reality becomes radically equivocal.[2] The baron is allied with the Metzengerstein in the tapestry who stabbed the Berlifitzing ancestor, and perhaps the soul

1. E. Arthur Robinson is concerned with a similar aspect of Poe's tales when he writes: "The point is that the peculiar quality of Poe's 'horror' stories stems in part from a fusion of commonly disparate elements, the union of haunting mood with rational form and style." See Robinson, "Order and Sentience in 'The Fall of the House of Usher,' " *PMLA*, LXXVI (1961), 80.

2. In the course of a detailed investigation of the elements of irony and parody in this tale, G. R. Thompson notes a series of puns on the *equ* of *equus*, including the word *equivocal*. See Thompson, *Poe's Fiction: Romantic Irony in the Gothic Tales* (Madison: University of Wisconsin Press, 1973), 62. For more on the equivocal nature of this tale, see Benjamin F. Fisher, "Poe's 'Metzengerstein': Not a Hoax," *American Literature*, XLII (1971), 487–94.

now inhabiting the horse is a combination of the count's soul and that of his slain ancestor in the picture. Presently, the horse arranges that the baron also die a fiery death. The ending of the tale is very similar to the ending of "The Fall of the House of Usher" with the addition that, after the whirlwind, "a white flame still enveloped the building like a shroud" (M, II, 29).

One of Poe's finest tales, originally entitled "The Visionary" in [Godey's] Lady's Book for January, 1834, is more popularly known by its later title, "The Assignation." (The assignation referred to is the arranged union, after death, of the Marchesa di Mentoni and her lover, the visionary.) What fluidity of form exists in this tale may be attributed to the "confused recollection" of the narrator (M, II, 151). Studies of "The Assignation" shed very little light on the relationship between the first part of the tale, in which the marchesa's lover rescues her child from drowning in the canal, and the second part, which deals with the suicide of the marchesa and her lover. David M. Rein attempts to reconcile the two episodes in terms of the Oedipal conflict. The rescuer is Poe; and the Marchesa Aphrodite is his mother, as well as the mother of the rescued child: "If the young man is the baby grown up, then, in craving the baby's mother is he not craving his own mother?"[3]

It makes more sense, however, to interpret the first section with its mingled implications of sex and death as an allegorical demonstration that the marchesa and her lover have discovered how to overcome mortality by simulating the arabesque condition. The knowledge of their success encourages them to proceed with the suicide pact. The tableau quality of the first section pictures the cycle of death and erotic rebirth. Thus the depths of the canal, described as "the abyss," are clearly equated with death. The narrator in a gondola compares his progress, "like some huge and sable-feathered condor," to Charon, ferrying the dead across the Styx: "I had myself

3. David M. Rein, Edgar A. Poe: The Inner Pattern (New York: Philosophic Library, 1960), 95. There are indeed different ways to read this tale. Richard P. Benton convincingly argues for a hidden parallel with the Byron-Guiccidi romance and identifies the narrator as Thomas Moore, who edited Byron's letters and journals. See Benton, "Is Poe's 'The Assignation' a Hoax?" Nineteenth Century Fiction, XVI (1963), 193–97.

no power to move from the upright position I had assumed upon first hearing the shriek, and must have presented to the eyes of the agitated group a spectral and ominous appearance, as with pale countenance and rigid limbs, I floated down among them in that funereal gondola" (M, II, 152, 153).

In retrieving the child from these waters, the stranger has retrieved the child from death. The marchesa acknowledges this: " 'Thou has conquered—' she said, or the murmurs of the water deceived me—'thou has conquered—one hour after sunrise—we shall meet—so let it be!' " (M, II, 155). (These words are subsequently echoed at the suicidal conclusion of "William Wilson": *"You have conquered, and I yield"* [M, II, 448].) The connection here between the child's rescue and the suicide assignation only makes sense given this allegorical interpretation. The water represents not only death but potential arabesque rebirth and life. During this episode, the marchesa undergoes a similar transformation. She is originally described, à la "To Helen," as an immobile statue. But in rejoining her child, "the statue has started into life!" (M, II, 154). Previously, the marchesa looked across at her lover and not into the canal because, as the tale's opening sentences imply, it is he who has actually discovered how to die and be reborn: "Ill-fated and mysterious man!—Bewildered in the brilliancy of thine own imagination, and fallen in the flames of thine own youth! Again in fancy I behold thee! Once more thy form hath risen before me! . . . in that city of dim visions, thine own Venice" (M, II, 150–51). The fall and the deliverance of the child are but an allegorical parallel to the possibility of resurrection. The marchesa agrees to the suicide pact because her lover has proved to her that death is not final.

The narrator asks, "Who does not remember that, at such a time as this, the eye, like a shattered mirror, multiplies the images of its sorrow, and sees in innumerable far off places, the wo which is close at hand?" (M, II, 153). Thus he prepares the reader for the passage in the second half of the tale describing the reflected multiplied passions of the stranger, each of which throws "its own distinct image upon the mirror of that face—but that the mirror, mirror-like, retained no vestige of the passion, when the passion had departed"

(M, II, 156). The two parts of the tale—one devoted largely to the marchesa and the other largely to the stranger—may be viewed as opposing mirrors, the one duplicating endlessly the images in the other. As a result the tale achieves a disorienting, kaleidoscopic effect similar to that experienced by the narrator in the apartment of the stranger: "I was shown up a broad winding staircase of mosaics, into an apartment whose unparalleled splendor burst through the opening door with an actual glare, making me blind and dizzy with luxuriousness" (M, II, 157).

The stranger, by means of the bizarre arabesque furnishings, particularly the censer, has succeeded in eradicating the barrier between life and death. His fluidity of expression—"the mingled tone of levity and solemnity," the gravity interweaving with the gaiety "like adders which writhe from out the eyes of the grinning masks in the cornices around the temple of Persepolis"—is perfectly in keeping with the room's state of constant flux (M, II, 161). The world of deception that the stranger is about to relinquish is introduced in relation to the stranger's poem of lament. After pointing out that the stranger delights in "concealing" his accomplishments, the narrator draws attention to the word London, overscored—"not, however, so effectually as to conceal the word from a scrutinizing eye"—as denoting the place of composition (M, II, 163). To pursue his devotion to the marchesa after her marriage, the stranger, an Englishman, was compelled to resort to subterfuge.

If it be granted that a writer's psychological drives determine what is most important in his work, Marie Bonaparte may well be correct in attributing Egaeus' obsession with the teeth of Berenice to Poe's preoccupation with the vagina dentata.[4] On the other hand, there is sufficient documentable evidence in "Berenice"—that most grisly of Poe's arabesques, first published in the March, 1835, Southern Literary Messenger—to support an alternative interpretation. Unquestionably for Egaeus, Berenice provides a physical connection

4. Marie Bonaparte, The Life and Works of Edgar Allan Poe: A Psycho-Analytic Interpretation, trans. John Rodker (London: Imago Publishing Co., 1949), 218–19. Poe would have pronounced Berenice as four syllables to rhyme with "very spicy" (M, II, 219).

with a dimly remembered arabesque state—"a memory like a shadow, vague, variable, indefinite, unsteady"—a connection that he hopes to strengthen by marriage. She is described as a "sylph amid the shrubberies of Arnheim," and that arabesque realm is where she truly belongs (M, II, 210). For Poe life is a plague, a plague from which Berenice dies: "Disease—a fatal disease—fell like the simoom upon her frame, and, even while I gazed upon her, the spirit of change swept over her" (M, II, 211). (The simoom, so vividly described in "MS. Found in a Bottle," brings about an analogous change.) When Egaeus sees her just before the wedding, she is already dissolving from material reality: "Was it my own excited imagination—or the misty influence of the atmosphere—or the uncertain twilight of the chanber—or the gray draperies which fell around her figure—that caused in it so vacillating and indistinct an outline" (M, II, 214). Egaeus' partial admission of responsibility here, the possibly causal connection between his "excited imagination" and her fuzziness, and the fact that he speaks of his "own disease" should be noted (M, II, 211).

Actually, Berenice is an externalization of Egaeus' own arabesque imaginings. In the attempt to materialize a dream, Egaeus, like Tamerlane, realizes that fulfillment involves death. Egaeus' arabesque cast of mind reveals itself in the paradoxical, hence fusion-oriented, nature of his responses. He explains, "The realities of the world affected me as visions, and as visions only, while the wild ideas of the land of dreams became, in turn, not the material of my every-day existence, but in very deed that existence utterly and solely in itself" (M, II, 210). Similarly, "In the strange anomaly of my existence, feelings, with me, *had never been* of the heart, and my passions *always were* of the mind" (M, II, 214). When he notices Berenice's changed condition, it is paradoxically a warm day in winter. This yoking of opposites betrays a concern with oneness, and Egaeus rightly speaks of his "monomania" (M, II, 211). The fact that Berenice and Egaeus, like Poe and Virginia, are cousins and that Berenice is indirectly linked with Egaeus' mother, who died in childbirth, suggests that the relationship is doubly incestuous. But for Poe the incestuous relationship, like the verbal paradox, is a way of dissolving illusory barriers. Poe's concern with incest further betrays his preoccupation with unity. Incest must have been one aspect of the primal human condition.

However, the most violent paradox occurs in the opening paragraph:

> Misery is manifold. The wretchedness of earth is multiform. Overreaching the wide horizon as the rainbow, its hues are as various as the hues of that arch—as distinct too, yet as intimately blended. Overreaching the wide horizon as a rainbow! How is it that from beauty I have derived a type of unloveliness?—from the convenant of peace a simile of sorrow? (M, II, 209)

This passage, with its rainbow simile, should be recalled when Egaeus speaks of his perverse fascination with the frivolous, specifically "the white and ghastly *spectrum* of the teeth": "In the multiplied objects of the external world I had no thoughts but for the teeth." The movement from unity to the state of heterogeneous dispersion is being compared to the prismatic refraction of white light. "Long, narrow, and excessively white," Berenice's teeth represent for Egaeus the culmination of that return to arabesque unity which she is undergoing (M, II, 215). When Egaeus says of the teeth, which are linked with ideas, "I turned them in every attitude," he might as well be talking about Poe's Neoplatonic ideas, which are surveyed from different aspects in his various compositions. Day after day, Egaeus sits in his psychedelic room; " and still the *phantasma* of the teeth maintained its terrible ascendancy as, with the most vivid and hideous distinctness, it floated about amid the changing lights and shadows of the chamber" (M, II, 216). As with his prenatal memories, Egaeus has "no definite comprehension" of Berenice's burial; "yet its memory was replete with horror—horror more horrible from being vague, and terror more terrible from ambiguity" (M, II, 217). This parallel and an excised passage would suggest that, with Berenice's death, Egaeus does return momentarily to that prenatal region. He cannot rid himself of this shadowy memory of ideality with which he may not be truly reunited "while the sunlight of my reason shall exist" (M, II, 210). In an attempt to preserve the experience, he extracts Berenice's teeth, an action that previously he had falsely rationalized: "I felt that their possession could alone ever restore me to peace, in giving me back to reason" (M, II, 216). The ambiguous references to "reason" as a hurdle to be crossed or as a protection from the terrors of insanity, or death, reflect Poe's own dilemma.

Like the paradoxical Egaeus, the passions of the unnamed admirer of "Morella," first published in the April, 1835, *Southern Literary Messenger*, appear to be of the mind—"the fires were not of Eros"—although his interest in Morella's mystical studies concerning pantheism and identity is more passionate than intellectual (M, II, 229). But eventually, his joy at being with Morella gives way to horror. Again, as in "Berenice" and "A Descent into the Maelström," the image of a rainbow occurs: "There was a dim mist over all the earth, and a warm glow upon the waters, and, amid the rich October leaves of the forest, a rainbow from the firmament had surely fallen" (M, II, 232). The rainbow is a convenant that Morella recognizes: "I am dying, yet shall I live." Morella, like Berenice, represents an ideal arabesque state. The narrator, looking into her eyes, "became giddy with the giddiness of one who gazes downward into some dreary and unfathomable abyss." In other words, as the echo of "MS. Found in a Bottle" intimates, he is drawn toward death; and actually he longs for Morella's decease. Morella's daughter is born at the moment of her mother's death, recalling Egaeus' birth. There is, however, no mention of Morella being pregnant. The entire event, presumably, is symbolic of the meaningless distinction between life and death. The time of the event, "one autumnal evening," is significant (M, II, 232). It is the evening of the year and the autumn of the day.

In other respects this tale anticipates "Ligeia." In both cases there is much talk about human identity; and the heroine, after death, is able to assert her identity through a surrogate, in this case the apparently aged child. At the christening, when the narrator compulsively calls the child Morella, the words "I am here!" fall "distinct, coldly, calmly distinct" within the narrator's ear (M, II, 235). What makes for the "distinct" here is the antagonistic attitude of the narrator, who uses cold reason to protect himself from the arabesque reality that Morella, or his imagination, holds out to him. The original Morella dies because of the narrator's "gradual alienation" in his attitude toward her (M, II, 231). But in naming the child Morella, he briefly and reluctantly capitulates to the dictates of the imaginative world of unified truth.

III

The themes introduced in the four early arabesques culminate and coalesce in "Ligeia," which Poe thought to be his best tale, and "The Fall of the House of Usher," the tale for which Poe is best known.[5] Within "Ligeia," first published in the American Museum for September, 1838, a conflict exists between the arabesque ideal, as represented by Ligeia, and the mundane world, as represented by the narrator's second wife, the Lady Rowena Trevanion of Tremaine; between the putative Joseph Glanvill quote, "Man doth not yield himself to the angels, nor unto death utterly, save only through the weakness of his feeble will," which is used as an epigraph and repeated in the tale three times, and that poetic expression of death's finality (first included in the New York New World version, February 15, 1845), "The Conqueror Worm" (M, II, 310, 314, 319–20). A conflict also exists between critics who read the tale literally as an account of Ligeia's usurpation of the body of Rowena by force of will and critics, like Roy P. Basler and George Snell, who argue that the narrator—a madman—poisons Rowena and hallucinates Ligeia's return.[6]

This difference of opinion does exist in the interests of fluid form, but the contradiction may be intellectually resolved if the

5. Writing to Evert A. Duyckinck (January 8, 1846), Poe characterizes "Ligeia" as "undoubtedly the best story I have written" (Letters, II, 309). In a later letter, Poe says, " 'Ligeia' may be called my best tale" because it exhibits "the highest imagination" (Letters, II, 329).
6. Roy P. Basler, Sex, Symbolism, and Psychology in Literature (New Brunswick, N.J.: Rutgers University Press, 1948), 143–59; George Snell, The Shapers of American Fiction, 1798–1947 (New York: E. P. Dutton, 1947), 54–55. This reading is opposed by James Schroeter, "A Misreading of Poe's 'Ligeia,' " PMLA, LXXVI (1961), 397–406. Other studies include the satirical reading, in Clark Griffith, "Poe's 'Ligeia' and the English Romantics," University of Toronto Quarterly, XXIV (1954), 8–25; Claudia C. Morrison, "Poe's 'Ligeia'—An Analysis [Freudian]," Studies in Short Fiction, IV (1967), 234–44 ; James W. Gargano, "Poe's 'Ligeia': Dream and Destruction," College English, XXIII (1962), 337–43.

reader recognizes, with Richard Wilbur, that Ligeia and Rowena can be understood as symbolic of the narrator's apprehension of the nature of reality.[7] During the period of the narrator's association with Ligeia, he is able to appreciate arabesque reality. In describing the "expression" of her eyes, the narrator points out:

I found, in the commonest objects of the universe, a circle of analogies to that expression. I mean to say that, subsequently to the period when Ligeia's beauty passed into my spirit, there dwelling as in a shrine, I derived, from many existences in the material world, a sentiment such as I felt always aroused within me by her large and luminous orbs. . . . I recognized it . . . sometimes in the survey of a rapidly-growing vine— in the contemplation of a moth, a butterfly, a chrysalis, a stream of running water. (M, II, 314)

Two particular stars, certain musical sounds, and the Glanvill passage elicit the same response. In further describing the nature of the Ligeia perception, Poe acknowledges the transcendental basis of his philosophy: "Her presence, her readings alone, rendered vividly luminous the many mysteries of the transcendentalism in which we were immersed" (M, II, 316). Since Ligeia's beauty is specifically linked with a supernal world, it is quite appropriate that the details of Ligeia's biography should be vague and that the narrator can "but indistinctly recall" their marriage (M, II, 311).

With the passage of time and an increasing intellectual curiosity, the narrator loses the ability to maintain his arabesque vision and Ligeia dies. Basler is on the right track in stressing that it is his will to conquer death that motivates the story, not hers, and that it is the narrator who is obsessed with the Glanvill quotation, since Ligeia is representative of the narrator's dwindling powers of imagination.[8] A more limited awareness, which supersedes the apprehension of arabesque reality, is symbolized by the Lady Rowena. The scene switches from a decaying city on the Rhine to a decaying abbey in England. As usual, and in accordance with Poe's conviction that localized time and place make for deception, the year and the area are not specified.

7. Richard Wilbur (ed.), Introduction to Poe: Complete Poems (New York: Dell, 1959), 7–28.
8. Basler, Sex, Symbolism, and Psychology in Literature, 148.

If previously the narrator's arabesque vision (Ligeia) faded in favor of diminished vision (Rowena), he now attempts to destroy the latter in order to regain the former. He arranges the arabesque decor in order to obliterate the distinction between life and death and to facilitate the reappearance of Ligeia. The following sentence may be construed as a guilty admission by the narrator of his intention to murder Rowena: "Where were the souls of the haughty family of the bride, when, through thirst of gold, they permitted to pass the threshold of an apartment so bedecked, a maiden and a daughter so beloved?" (M, II, 321). The bridal room resembles a death chamber. Moreover, the narrator is being perfectly honest in his admission that the disturbances—sounds and "unusual motions among the tapestries"—which Rowena experiences have their origin "perhaps in the phantasmagoric influences of the chamber itself," influences for which he is responsible (M, II, 323–24).

The decor does have the designed effect. He sees "a faint, indefinite shadow of angelic aspect." He becomes "distinctly aware of a gentle foot-fall upon the carpet." And then—the sentence which forms the basis of Basler's and Snell's argument—as Rowena raises a container of wine to her lips, "I saw, or may have dreamed that I saw, fall within the goblet, as if from some invisible spring in the atmosphere of the room, three or four large drops of a brilliant and ruby colored fluid" (M, II, 325).[9] Upon drinking the liquid, her condition instantly deteriorates. In order to assist Ligeia's return, the narrator (like the stranger in "The Assignation") attempts to identify with the furnishings: "I gazed with unquiet eye upon the sarcophagi in the angles of the room, upon the varying figures of the drapery, and upon the writhing of the parti-colored fires in the censer overhead." He is rewarded by the sound of a "low, gentle, but very distinct" sob. He feels sure he "could not have been deceived" (M, II 326). Nor is he. The corpse is animated: "I saw—distinctly saw— a tremor upon the lips" (M, II, 327–28). When the coverings are loosened, the

9. Rather than or aside from poison, the red drops may be "a primary corporeal form attained by Ligeia's spirit; and in themselves the elixir of life" (M, II, 308, 334n31).

figure, whether real or a "distinct" hallucination, is discovered to be that of Ligeia.

The attainment of arabesque vision, consequent upon the destruction of earthly vision, implies that from an earthly point of view the narrator should die. And there is evidence to suggest that he does: "Through a species of unutterable horror and awe, for which the language of mortality has no sufficiently energetic expression, I felt my heart cease to beat, my limbs grow rigid where I sat" (M, II, 327). A little later, he states that the now animate figure "had chilled me into stone" (M, II, 329). The implication is that the narrator has turned into a statue. When it is recalled that Ligeia is among Poe's statuesque maidens—her hand was originally likened to "marble"— her identification with the narrator should be readily apparent (M, II, 311). Of course, the fact that the narrator is telling the story implies that the condition does not last. In a letter to Philip Pendleton Cooke, after agreeing with Cooke's criticism that "the gradual perception of the fact that Ligeia lives again in the person of Rowena is a far loftier and more thrilling idea [because with no harsh outlines it would be more suggestive of fusion?] than the one I have embodied," Poe admits that the tale should have ended with a final relapse (Letters, I, 118). Nevertheless, the tale, as it is, is among his best.

No single-minded interpretation of "The Fall of the House of Usher," which first appeared in Burton's Gentleman's Magazine for September, 1839, can be adequate. This tale may be viably interpreted in natural or supernatural terms, but it can only be fully appreciated if the reader is able to maintain various readings in a state of suspension.[10] "The Fall of the House of Usher" is a sentient ideo-

---

10. Among the nonnaturalistic readings of "The Fall of the House of Usher" are the following: Maurice Beebe, "The Universe of Roderick Usher," Personalist, XXXVII (1956), 147–60; Maurice Beebe, "The Fall of the House of Pyncheon," Nineteenth Century Fiction, XI (1956), 1–6; Robinson, "Order and Sentience in 'The Fall of the House of Usher,' " 68–81. The naturalistic readings would include Darrel Abel, "A Key to the House of Usher," University of Toronto Quarterly XVIII (1949), 176–85; I. M. Walker, "The Legitimate Sources of Terror in 'The Fall of the House of Usher,' " Modern Language Review, LXI (1966), 585–92. An argument for a synthesis of the transcendent and the naturalistic is made by David W. Butler, "Usher's Hypochondriasis: Mental Alienation and the Romantic Idealism in Poe's Gothic Tales," American Literature, XLVIII (1976), 1–12.

gram and Poe's finest experiment in the technique of fluid form. Although the tale exhibits an apparently simple five-part development, the relationships between the various episodes are so equivocal and intricate that it is quite impossible to impose any fixity upon so shifting an arabesque surface. The factually minded narrator attempts to view the scene more favorably by changing his perspective, looking at the reflection of the house instead of the actual construction:

It was possible, I *reflected*, that a mere different arrangement of the particulars of the scene, of the details of the picture, would be sufficient to modify, or perhaps to annihilate its capacity for sorrowful impression; and, acting upon this idea, I reined my horse to the precipitous brink of a black and lurid tarn that lay in unruffled lustre by the dwelling, and gazed down —but with a shudder even more thrilling than before—upon the remodelled and inverted image of the gray sedge, and the ghastly tree-stems, and the vacant and eye-like windows. (Italics added; M, II, 398)[11]

No reassuringly tidy viewpoint is possible because the tale is "one of the phantasmagoric conceptions" of Poe (M, II, 405). *Phantasmagoric* may be defined as "a fantastic series of illusive images or real forms." Thus, the narrator is unable to distinguish between the illusive image in the tarn and the real form of the house. The "armorial trophies" in a hall are similarly "phantasmagoric"; and in the first version, the influence of the furniture is said to be "phantasmagoric" (M, II, 400, 411). No other word can better describe the indeterminate quality of the tale.

The tension between the image and the perceptual form, or more particularly between art and "reality," reveals itself further in the parallel between Usher's poem and the tale itself, the parallel between Usher's painting of a vault and the actual vault in which Madeline is placed, and the apparently rather contrived parallel between the sounds mentioned in the story of the "Mad Trist" and the actual sounds caused during Madeline's emergence from the vault. The poem makes the identification between Usher and his house

11. G. R. Thompson notes that the narrator would likely see his own face reflected, as well as the reflection of the facelike house. This, then, is the first intimation that the narrator and Usher are doppelgängers. See Thompson, *Poe's Fiction*, 95.

blatantly obvious, although the tale itself establishes a connection between "the vacant eye-like windows" of the house and Usher's eyes, between "minute fungi . . . hanging in a fine tangled web-work from the eaves" and the "wild gossamer texture" of Usher's hair, and between the "leaden-hued" vapor enveloping the house and Usher's "leaden" utterance (M, II, 397, 400, 402).[12] Furthermore, "one unceasing radiation of gloom" emits from Usher and his house (M, II, 405). More importantly, the poem recalls an ideal, arabesque state long departed and replaced by the present chaos. Usher's picture of a vault "with low walls, smooth, white and without interruption or device" and "at an exceeding depth below the surface of earth," but inexplicably illuminated by "a flood of intense rays," would seem to represent the distantly attainable arabesque state (M, II, 406). Appropriately, the vault in which Madeline is placed is similarly "entirely without means of admission for light," being at a "great depth," because she is a projection of that force which is drawing Usher toward the arabesque (M, II, 410). Madeline, Usher's twin, is a projection of Usher's so-called "madness," and the "Mad Trist" literally means the meeting with Mad-eline. The correspondence between the image, the art object, or the dream of arabesque reality and the perceptual form becomes so close that it is finally impossible to distinguish the one from the other by the time the waters of the tarn (the arabesque world) close over the grotesque human state as symbolized by the actual house, after Madeline falls, vampirelike, over Usher.[13]

The house of Usher poised over the tarn is in the same situation as "The City in the Sea," waiting for the lapse from everyday life into arabesque life. Since the house corresponds to the man, the tale is

---

12. Barton Levi St. Armand notes a series of metallic references that correspond exactly to the sequence involved in the alchemical transformation of lead into gold, of the material into the spiritual. See St. Armand, "Usher Unveiled: Poe and the Metaphysic of Gnosticism," *Poe Studies*, V (1972), 1–8. This is a special "Usher" issue.

13. The pictorial nature of the finale, with Madeline dressed in blood-spattered "white robes" poised between "ponderous and ebony jaws" (M, II, 416), suggests a vampiric tooth according to J. O. Bailey, "What Happens in 'The Fall of the House of Usher?' " *American Literature*, XXXV (1964), 463–64. See also Lyle H. Kendall, "The Vampire Motif in 'The Fall of the House of Usher,' " *College English*, XXIV (1963), 450–53.

about Usher's lapse into the arabesque state. Furthermore, if Maurice Beebe is correct in interpreting Usher as God and in applying the cosmology of *Eureka* (and he probably is), the tale is about the collapse into oneness of the universe from its present state of dispersed heterogeneity and deception.[14] There are certainly indications that the House of Usher is the victim of such a deceptive condition. The narrator is met by a "valet of stealthy step" and is "accosted" by the family physician, whose countenance "wore a mingled expression of low cunning and perplexity" (M, II, 400, 401). One of the reasons for not burying Madeline outside is the fear that her body may be exhumed, a fear that the narrator agrees is warranted by "the sinister countenance" of the physician (M, II, 409).

Opposed to these elements of deception are indications that a process of fusion is about to take place. The narrator arrives at a median time, "as the shades of the evening drew on . . . in the autumn of the year" (M, II, 397). Because of "a morbid acuteness of the senses," Usher is able to assert the "sentience of all vegetable things" (M, II, 403, 408). In other words, Usher does not see any real distinction between the animate and the inanimate, or—since the reduplication in the tarn is a factor—between the earthly and the ideal. It is all a matter of awareness and arrangement. In this context, the arabesque furnishings serve to encourage awareness. At one point speaking more accurately than he realizes, the narrator explains, "I endeavoured to believe that much, if not all of what I felt, was due to the bewildering influence of the gloomy furniture of the room—of the dark and tattered draperies, which, tortured into motion by the breath of a rising tempest, swayed fitfully to and fro upon the walls, and rustled uneasily about the decorations of the bed" (M, II, 411). Of course, the whirlwind, which concludes the tale, performs a fusing function.

Whereas Madeline is a projection of that side of Usher which is pulling him toward arabesque reality, the narrator, who has also known Usher since childhood, is a projection of the force that Usher half hopes will keep him in the everyday world. The tale describes

14. Beebe, "The Universe of Roderick Usher," 147–60.

the struggle between the narrator and Madeline for domination of Usher. It is no accident that the vault containing Madeline is "immediately beneath" the narrator's bedroom (M, II, 410). And it is hardly coincidental that, "on the closing in of the evening of my arrival at the house, she succumbed . . . to the prostrating power of the destroyer" (M, II, 404). But in the ensuing pages, she gains strength; and in fleeing from the house, the narrator obscures what amounts to an ejection.

Since both the narrator and Madeline are contrary aspects of Usher's mind, whatever happens should be indirectly attributable to Usher himself. The narrator's journey from nowhere to the house is almost dictated by something like telepathy, "the apparent heart that went with his request" (M, II, 398). "Sympathies of a scarcely intelligible nature had always existed between" Madeline and Usher, and it is with particular reference to Madeline that the force of Usher's mind is apparent (M, II, 410). For example, "while he spoke, the lady Madeline . . . passed slowly through a remote portion of the apartment." Clearly, her materialization depends upon her entrance, at that point, into Usher's consciousness. Consequently, when "for several days ensuing, her name was unmentioned by either Usher or myself," she does not appear (M, II, 404). The reader may assume that she dies when Usher "informed me abruptly that the lady Madeline was no more" (M, II, 409).

The mechanical correspondence between the noises referred to in the "Mad Trist" and their actual occurrence may be explained in similarly psychosomatic terms:

> At the termination of this sentence I started . . . for it appeared to me (although I at once concluded that my excited fancy had deceived me) . . . that, from some very remote portion of the mansion, there came, indistinctly, to my ears, what might have been . . . the echo . . . of the very cracking and ripping sound which Sir Launcelot had so particularly described. (M, II, 414)

This is followed by another sound, "the exact counterpart of what my fancy had already conjured up for the dragon's unnatural shriek as described by the romancer" (M, II, 414). The mere fact that the rationalistic narrator is reading such an unrealistic story is an indi-

196

cation of Madeline's dominance at this point. Furthermore, the fact that it is the narrator's power of suggestion which "creates" the noises, coupled with Usher's designation of him as a "MADMAN!," underlines the narrator's identification with Usher and the completeness of his vanquishment (M, II, 416). The narrator is to be cast in the role of the dragon that Ethelred slays. But all this must be seen as occurring within Usher's mind. Usher is responsible throughout; and for this reason, on three occasions (many elements in the tale appear three times) he is referred to as a "hypochondriac" (M, II, 405, 409, 413).

Not surprisingly, the dichotomy, or tension, in the tale may be finally reduced to Usher (Us/her?)[15] and to the well-known balanced phraseology that describes his countenance:

A cadaverousness of complexion; an eye large, liquid, and luminous beyond comparison; lips somewhat thin and very pallid, but of a surpassingly beautiful curve; a nose of a delicate Hebrew model, but with a breadth of nostril unusual in similar formations; a finely moulded chin, speaking, in its want of prominence, of a want of moral energy; hair of a more than web-like softness and tenuity; these features, with an inordinate expansion above the regions of the temple, made up altogether a countenance not easily to be forgotten. (M, II, 401–402)

Repeatedly, something delicate and spiritual is compensated for by something vulgar or earthly. So the dualism of the house and its reflection in the tarn, the creations of art and the actuality, deception and fusion, Madeline and the narrator—all come home to Usher. Just as Usher is pulled first toward the narrator and then toward Madeline, so the reader experiences a tension between a desire to read the tale in naturalistic terms and a desire to interpret it in supernatural terms. In Usher, this tension has produced a split symbolized by "a barely perceptible fissure" extending down the front of his house (M, II, 400). An "incoherence—an inconsistency," which the narrator notices in his friend's manner, has its counterpart in the appearance of the house, which exhibits "a wild inconsistency

15. Joseph J. Moldenhauer, "Murder as a Fine Art: Basic Connections Between Poe's Aesthetics, Psychology, and Moral Vision," PMLA, LXXXIII (1968), 295.

between its still perfect adaptation of parts, and the crumbling condition of the individual stones" (M, II, 400, 402). But this division is only a mortal condition that the waters of the tarn will heal.

IV

The four arabesques that precede and the four that follow "Ligeia" and "The Fall of the House of Usher" are not as fine as those two stories. "Eleonora" first appeared in the Boston Notion for September 4, 1841, although reprinted from the Gift for 1842. Richard Wilbur has pointed out that everything external to the narrator serves to reflect his state of mind.[16] However, the ultimate reality of the tale is not just psychological. The narrator opens by discussing the condition of his mind:

Men have called me mad; but the question is not yet settled, whether madness is or is not the loftiest intelligence—whether much that is glorious—whether all that is profound—does not spring from disease of thought—from moods of mind exalted at the expense of the general intellect. They who dream by day are cognizant of many things which escape those who dream only by night. In their grey visions they obtain glimpses of eternity, and thrill, in awaking, to find that they have been upon the verge of the great secret. (M, II, 638)

This is the familiar situation "where the confines of the waking world blend with those of the world of dreams" (H, XVI, 88).

Until his twentieth year, the narrator dwells idyllically with his cousin Eleonora in the "Valley of the Many-Colored Grass" (M, II, 639). Encircled by beetling hills, this valley is a dry-land counterpart of the maelstrom. During this period, the narrator is in a state of arabesque harmony. The appearance of the valley, with its river of silence, "brighter than all save the eyes of Eleonora," and its trees whose bark "was smoother than all save the cheeks of Eleonora," apparently reflects Eleonora's condition, or rather the narrator's condition of which she is a projection (M, II, 639, 640). With the advent of

16. Wilbur, Introduction to Poe: Complete Poems, 14–16. See also Sam S. Baskett, "Damsel with a Dulcimer," Modern Language Notes, LXXIII (1958), 332–38; Richard P. Benton, "Platonic Allegory in Poe's 'Eleonora,' " Nineteenth Century Fiction, XXII (1967), 293–98.

passion, art's archenemy, Eleonora becomes ill; and the valley reflects the colors of passion. Distraught, the narrator asks that he be cursed should he ever transfer his love for Eleonora, or his apprehension of the ideal, "to some maiden of the outer and every-day world" (M, II, 642). Following Eleonora's death, the valley undergoes further sympathetic changes; but Eleonora, as promised, rewards the narrator's fidelity by occasional visitations, which (as Wilbur points out) correspond to "fitful recoveries of imaginative power."[17]

However, when the narrator leaves the valley for "a strange city" and marries Ermengarde, it appears that he has broken faith with Eleonora (M, II, 644). Nevertheless, he is not cursed, because by falling in love with the "ethereal . . . seraph . . . the angel Ermengarde," the narrator has succeeded imaginatively in transforming the contours of the everyday world in accordance with his memory of the world of Eleonora (M, II, 644). This is particularly apparent if two passages in the original version, later excised, are taken into account. One passage describes Eleonora; and the other, Ermengarde. Eleonora has "waving auburn hair" (M, II, 641). As for Ermengarde, the narrator glories in "the wavy flow of her auburn tresses" and observes in her countenance "the radical transition from tears to smiles that I had wondered at in the long-lost Eleonora" (M, II, 644). It would appear that Eleonora has been refound. Thus, this tale integrates the setting of poems like "The Lake—To—" and "Romance" with the theme of tales like "Morella" and "Ligeia."

In "The Oval Portrait," originally entitled "Life in Death" in *Graham's Magazine* for April, 1842, it is suggested that art is the means by which a woman of the everyday world might be made representative of an ideal world. The wounded narrator decides to spend the night in a ruined château "of commingled gloom and grandeur" (M, II, 662). By accidentally changing the position of his bedside lamp and altering his perspective, the narrator sees the oval portrait: "The arms, the bosom and even the ends of the radiant hair, melted imperceptibly into the vague yet deep shadow which formed the

17. Wilbur, Introduction to *Poe: Complete Poems*, 15.

back-ground of the whole" (M, II, 664). The portrait appears to be alive, and the narrator assures the reader "that my vision had not deceived me" (M, II, 663). Perhaps to further allay the reader's doubts, when the tale was republished, Poe excised the long opening paragraph describing the narrator's addiction to opium and his now swallowing the drug rather than smoking it. The volume, which describes the château's collection of pictures, informs the narrator that the girl in this particular picture died at the moment the work was completed. The artist has imaginatively transcended the everyday world through the arabesque decoration in the turret of the building: "Its walls were hung with tapestry and bedecked with manifold and multiform armorial trophies, together with an unusually great number of very spirited modern paintings in frames of rich golden arabesque" (M, II, 662). The description of the narrator's situation provides, of course, a kind of open-ended frame for the account of the portrait. This is the first tale in which Poe examines the possibility that the artist, while in the "real" world, might through his art experience arabesque vision.

Prince Prospero, the protagonist of that superbly subtle tale, "The Masque of the Red Death," which first appeared in *Graham's Magazine* for May, 1842, attempts to escape life and to avoid the trauma of death by living in a self-created world of arabesque art.[18] As Joseph Patrick Roppolo points out, the Red Death is not a plague in the usual sense but life itself. Blood, "its Avatar and its seal," is indicative of life (M, II, 670). The seven colored rooms, ranging from the blue room in the east to the black room in the west, represent the seven ages of man. In all the apartments, except the black one, "beat feverishly the heart of life" (M, II, 674). "By deliberate use of the word 'feverishly,' " writes Roppolo, "Poe links life with disease and

18. The masquelike elements in this tale and its connection with Shakespeare's *The Tempest* are explored by Kermit Vanderbilt, "Art and Nature in 'The Masque of the Red Death,' " *Nineteenth Century Fiction*, XXII (1968), 379–91. Besides Shakespeare, the influences of Victor Hugo's *Hernani*, Byron, and Mary Shelley's *The Last Man* are also evident. See Burton R. Pollin, *Discoveries in Poe* (Notre Dame, Ind.: University of Notre Dame Press, 1970), 1–3, 75–90. Pollin's many inquiries into sources indicate the fruitfulness of that particular approach to Poe. But see also Edward William Pitcher, "Horological and Chronological Time in 'Masque of the Red Death,' " *American Transcendental Quarterly*, no. 29 (Winter, 1976), 71–75.

death."[19] Prospero and his followers hope to simulate the arabesque by indulging in a bizarre masquerade, one of the many masquerades in Poe's work: "There were arabesque figures with unsuited limbs and appointments [because of an uneasy arabesque-grotesque confusion]. . . . To and fro in the seven chambers there stalked, in fact, a multitude of dreams. And these—the dreams—writhed in and about, taking hue from the rooms, and causing the wild music of the orchestra to seem as the echo of their steps" (M, II, 673). Periodically, they are halted by the sounds of the ebony clock in the seventh room striking the hour, reminding the revelers of the "external" reality of time, which they are struggling to overcome. The reality of time is hidden by the arrangement of the rooms: "The apartments were so irregularly disposed that the vision embraced but little more than one at a time" (M, II, 671). After the ominous sounds, the fluid movement "to and fro" (the phrase is used four times) continues.

Prospero's desire to slip away from life without dying is also Poe's. For this reason, perhaps, the narrator rejects the view of Prospero's critics, who "have thought him mad" (M, II, 673). Prospero and his followers fail in that they die. However, as Roppolo acutely recognizes, the terrifying figure is not death but, "literally, 'The *Mask* of the Red Death.' " He does not make his first appearance in the black room, as one might expect, but exists with man from the beginning; he is seen by Prospero in the blue room. This figure is, in fact, a creation of man: "Man himself invests death with elements of terror, and he clothes not death but the terror of death in garb of his own making."[20] The reader learns of the hideous figure that "the mask which concealed the visage was made so nearly to resemble the countenance of a stiffened corpse that the closest scrutiny must have had difficulty in detecting the cheat" (M, II, 675). When the revelers catch up with the figure "within the shadow of the ebony clock," they find "the grave-cerements and corpse-like mask . . . untenanted by any tangible form" (M, II, 676). The implication is that

19. Joseph Patrick Roppolo, "Meaning and 'The Masque of the Red Death,' " in Robert Regan (ed.), *Poe: A Collection of Critical Essays* (Englewood Cliffs, N.J.: Prentice-Hall, 1967), 140. This article originally appeared in *Tulane Studies in English*, XIII (1963), 59–69.
20. *Ibid.*, 141, 142.

death is a psychosomatic disease which has its power and occurs only because of man's constricted mental habits and consequent inability to sustain an arabesque existence. It is significant that "the life of the ebony clock went out with that of the last of the gay" (M, II, 677). Time exists within man's mortal consciousness, not outside of it.

However, the victim in "The Pit and the Pendulum," which first appeared in the *Gift for 1843*, does surmount death—like the narrator in "MS Found in a Bottle" and the Norwegian in "A Descent into the Maelström"—by attaining the necessary elasticity of mind. The sensation of dissolving reality is conveyed brilliantly in the long opening paragraph: "The sentence—the dread sentence of death— was the last of distinct accentuation which reached my ears. After that, the sound of the inquisitorial voices seemed merged in one dreamy indeterminate hum." The fatal words, which issue from the white lips of "the black-robed judges," merge with the letters that the narrator is inscribing on paper: "I saw them writhe with a deadly locution" (M, II, 681). The black robes and writhing letters condition the character of the room: "I saw, too, for a few moments of delirious horror, the soft and nearly imperceptible waving of the sable draperies which enwrapped the walls of the apartment" (M, II, 681–82). This blackness is alleviated by the "seven tall candles," which the narrator interprets as angels of charity but which clearly take their color from the judges' white lips and the white paper. Then, the judges and the candles disappear simultaneously, leaving the narrator in "the blackness of darkness" (M, II, 682). It is no wonder that the narrator faints, having lost all conception of a fixed reality.

There are two distinguishable stages, according to the narrator, during the emergence from a faint: the mental, or spiritual, followed by the physical; the sense of the arabesque, followed by the sense of grotesque, "normal" reality. The rest of the tale is devoted to a conflict between these two senses, the one represented by the pit and the possibility it offers of a fortunate fall, the other represented by the consciousness of time, the pendulum.[21] While the arabesque

21. The more sensational interpretation of the symbolic value of the pit and the pendulum as contrary sexual organs originates with Marie Bonaparte, *The Life and Works of Edgar Allan Poe: A Psycho-Analytic Interpretation*, 575–97.

sense predominates, the narrator recalls "indistinctly . . . tall figures" carrying him down and a "hideous dizzyness" (M, II, 683). But the sense of physical reality, or the sense of need for a fixed physical reality, quickly reasserts itself; and the narrator becomes neurotically concerned with establishing the exact dimensions of his chamber. Given the nature of the physical sense, the narrator is constantly deceived in his calculations. After attempting to estimate the perimeter, he recognizes that, because of the "many angles" encountered, he could "form no guess at the shape of the vault" (M, II, 686). Consequently, he begins to walk across the area only to become entangled with his clothing and trip—a second fortunate fall in miniature (he earlier stumbled on the slippery ground). He finds himself overhanging the pit: "Shaking in every limb, I groped my way back to the wall—resolving there to perish rather than risk the terrors of the wells, of which my imagination now pictured many in various positions about the dungeon" (M, II, 687).

But all the narrator's conclusions about the vault are wrong. He finds, "In its size I had been greatly mistaken. . . . I had been deceived, too, in respect to the shape of the enclosure." The angles are niches, and the prison is approximately square. "What I had taken for masonry seemed now to be iron" (M, II, 688). And there is only one pit. Then, the narrator looks up at the ceiling to discover "the painted figure of Time," with what "I supposed to be the pictured image of a huge pendulum" (M, II, 689). In fact, the pendulum is real, razor-sharp, and descending in leisurely arcs upon his now bound body. But ironically and fortuitously, the narrator loses all sense of time. During the excruciating experience, the narrator entertains "a half-formed thought" of hope, the "collected calmness of despair," and "the unformed half of that idea of deliverance"—all familiar to the reader of "MS. Found in a Bottle" and "A Descent into the Maelström" (M, II, 691, 693). The "habitual see-saw" of his one free hand, which keeps the rats from his platter of food, puts the narrator in sympathy with the motion of the pendulum, indeed suggests that the pendulum's motion is his own creation. Immediately, he has an idea, and for once, "Nor had I erred in my calculations" (M, II, 694). After he covers with meat the bandage that restrains him, the rats gnaw him free.

At the same moment, the movement of the pendulum ceases. The narrator attributes the withdrawal of the pendulum, "by some invisible force," to members of the watching Inquisition (M, II, 695). Actually, it is his own increasingly rectified and malleable state of mind that is responsible. To reinforce the lesson, the chamber undergoes a further alteration. The colors of the figures on the walls have assumed a new brilliancy from a surrounding fire outside that forces the narrator toward the center of the room and the pit. This compulsion is made unavoidable by a further change: "And now the change was obviously in the *form*." The walls are closing together: "In an instant the apartment had shifted its form into that of a lozenge. But the alteration stopped not here—I neither hoped nor desired it to stop" (M, II, 696). This last statement is extremely illuminating. The narrator does not want the process to stop precisely *because* it is directing him toward the pit.

This pit, although an object of terror, is also the medium of arabesque release. All the instances of deliverance in the tale are associated with the pit. Although the second fall apparently saves the narrator from the pit, it also provides him with an intimation of arabesque possibilities. The rats, which sever the bandages, "issued from the well" (M, II, 690). And the narrator's final deliverance to the sound of apocalyptic trumpets is accompanied by a fall: "An outstretched arm caught my own as I fell, fainting, into the abyss" (M, II, 697). In symbolic terms, he does fall into the pit, and his deliverance is death. If the rescue is interpreted solely in a literal manner as a last-minute deus ex machina, the tale's conclusion is weak and the reader has been hoaxed. Actually, the rescue is a psychic projection designed to exemplify the narrator's successful and prepared-for lapse into an arabesque state, into the fluid state described in the tale's opening paragraph.[22] The "discordant hum of human voices!" is deliberately reminiscent of the "dreamy inde-

22. The savior's name, General Lasalle (the room), identifies him with the shifting chamber, rather than with the historical general, Comte de Lasalle (1775–1809). The narrator's experiences in the room have encouraged the development of an arabesque elasticity. See Moldenhauer, "Murder as a Fine Art," 296. This reading would seem to be corroborated by the information that "the *general* shape of the prison was square" (italics added; M, II, 688).

terminate hum" of "the inquisitorial voices" (M, II, 681, 697). Thus, the subtlety and fluidity of form and meaning, characteristic of all the arabesques, reaches its climax in "The Pit and the Pendulum," one of the very few tales in which the protagonist successfully manages to lapse from "life."

7

The Ultimate Life

If the afterlife is merely a matter of altered perception, it should be appreciable without the necessity of dying. Acting on this conviction, Poe attempts, in three types of composition—his arabesque landscape pieces, the mesmeric tales, and two metaphysical accounts of the end of the world—to describe its quality. He assumes that, from a supernal point of view, all of nature will exhibit an essential unity. Therefore, to approximate an angelic order of things, it is only necessary to arrange nature artistically; at least, such is the rationale of the landscape pieces. Once this has been established, Poe can confidently write accounts in which supposedly dead people describe their environment. For example, believing in the efficacy of mesmerism as a means of communicating with the dead, he can write a tale in which a "dead" person presents a version of a similarly unified arabesque existence. And in two postapocalyptic pieces, Poe is able to adopt the perspective of the angels looking down on the landscaped universe. The argument is circular; but given the basic assumption, it is quite logical and consistent.

II

In "The Island of the Fay"—first published as a plate article in *Graham's Magazine* for June, 1841 (where it accompanied an engraving by John Sartain based on an original by John Martin), and the first of the landscape pieces—Poe typically begins his preamble about the

206

elevating possibilities of music by correcting a mistranslation and revising a statement by Jean-François Marmontel. He later qualifies an opinion of Jean-Louis Guez de Balzac's. All of this is obviously relevant to Poe's interest in corrected vision, an interest that he believes best served by looking at a natural landscape. The careful observer of nature is able to see things in a larger perspective and to appreciate the universe (to be described in *Eureka*) as "one vast animate and sentient whole" (M, II, 600). The situation of the island has an analogue in "The City in the Sea," and, indeed, an adapted couplet from that poem is applied to the island. As in the case of both "The City in the Sea" and "The Fall of the House of Usher," it is difficult to distinguish between the reality and the image: "So mirror-like was the glassy water, that it was scarcely possible to say at what point upon the slope of the emerald turf its crystal dominion began" (M, II, 602–603). It should be apparent by now that the water represents arabesque reality and the island conventional grotesque reality.

There is, however, a marked difference between the east and the west sides of the island. The distinction is the man-made one between life and death. Poe equivocates this distinction by making the western side, where "everything had motion through the gentle sweepings to and fro of innumerable butterflies," suggestive of arabesque life, while the "sad, solemn, and spectral shapes" of the eastern side "convey ideas of mortal sorrow and untimely death." But because the sun is sinking in the west throughout the piece, the distinction between light and dark becomes increasingly meaningless. So too is the distinction between the island and the water, as witness the activity of the shadows of the trees: "I fancied that each shadow, as the sun descended lower and lower, separated itself sullenly from the trunk that gave it birth, and thus became absorbed by the stream; while other shadows issued momently from the trees, taking the place of their predecessors thus entombed" (M, II, 603). A fay from the west side, circling the island by canoe (maybe just a piece of careening white bark), undergoes a similar process. As the sun declines, the light and her person "grew feebler, and far fainter, and more indistinct," until finally "darkness fell over all things" and everything exists in a state of fusion (M, II, 605). This illumination has all been brought about by the attitude of the narrator, who "mused, with half-shut eyes" (M, II, 604).

The narrator of "Morning on the Wissahiccon" (which accompanied a picture by J. G. Chapman called "Morning") in the *Opal* for 1844, experiences "half-slumberous fancies" similar to those described by the narrator of "The Island of the Fay" (M, III, 865). The one imagines he sees a fay, the other imagines he sees an elk, an animal that he associates with an ideal time of innocence. In fact, the elk proves to be real, thus strengthening the narrator's point that Edens do exist in the New World, that paradise may be regained. If the traveler wishes to appreciate nature at her most beautiful, he must abandon the beaten tracks. The Louisiana valley, for example, is "a realization of the wildest dreams of paradise." But "the real Edens of the land" are even farther afield, like the scenery penetrated by the brook, the Wissahiccon (M, III, 862). It is while floating down its waters that the narrator experiences his vision.

If a natural landscape can stimulate arabesque vision, it is possible that nature, artistically arranged, may do the job even better. Such is the argument of Ellison, architect of "The Landscape Garden," which first appeared in *Snowden's Ladies' Companion* for October, 1842. He is the beneficiary "of *four hundred and fifty millions of dollars*" and the happiest man the narrator knows (M, II, 704). His poetical bent and his love of women, nature, and wealth find expression in the arrangement of an ideal landscape garden that, "in its adaptation to the eyes which were to behold it upon earth," would reveal the same unified beauty as the entire Earth or universe when "viewed *at large* from some remote point in the heavens" (M, II, 707, 709). In other words, the landscape garden should convey to an earthly view the same impression that a heavenly being would receive looking at God's universe. To live within a landscape garden is to experience a sense of the afterlife. As the artistic arranger of nature, Ellison takes on the character of God, and he hopes that the finished product might "convey the sentiment of *spiritual interference*" (M, II, 711). Exterior decoration is analogous to the interior decoration of the Poe rooms. Landscape gardening becomes a

208

means of simulating the arabesque condition, a means of making the afterlife prematurely available. Thus, it is not surprising that Ellison dies young.

In "The Domain of Arnheim," which first appeared in the March, 1847, New York *Columbian Magazine,* the narrator—after retelling "The Landscape Garden"—describes Ellison's accomplishment. Before beginning his description, the narrator hesitates between "detail and generality" but decides on a strategy of fusion "to unite the two in their extremes" (M, III, 1277). The journey by water through the domain of Arnheim encompasses scenes of Blakean integrated perfection, exhibiting "a weird symmetry, a thrilling uniformity, a wizard propriety" (M, III, 1279).[1] Of the flower-carpeted hills, the narrator writes: "As the eye traced upward the myriad-tinted slope, from its sharp junction with the water to its vague termination amid the folds of over-hanging cloud, it became, indeed, difficult not to fancy a panoramic cataract of rubies, sapphires, opals and golden onyxes, rolling silently out of the sky"—a New Jerusalem descending (M, III, 1280). To penetrate further the fused fluidity of the scene, the voyager continues in "a light canoe of ivory, stained with arabesque devices in vivid scarlet, both within and without" (M, III, 1280–81). The journey concludes amidst a "vast amphitheatre" where "there is a dream-like intermingling to the eye of tall slender Eastern trees—bosky shrubberies . . . long intertangled lines of silver streamlets—and, upspringing confusedly from amid all, a mass of semi-Gothic, semi-Saracenic [here as elsewhere the qualification *semi* or *half* implies a process of fusion] architecture . . . seeming the phantom handiwork, conjointly, of the Sylphs, of the Fairies, of the Genii, and of the Gnomes" (M, III, 1283). Clearly, Ellison achieved "the sentiment of *spiritual* interference" (M, II, 711).

A similar amphitheatre is described in "Landor's Cottage: A Pendant to 'The Domain of Arnheim,' " which appeared in the June 9,

1. *Arnheim* is an anagram of *near him,* presumably near God. See Edward William Pitcher, "The Arnheim Trilogy: Cosmic Landscapes in the Shadow of Poe's *Eureka,*" *Canadian Review of American Studies,* VI (1975), 31. This article provides a detailed, generally convincing, allegorical interpretation of the landscape pieces. Pitcher distinguishes between paradise on earth in "The Domain of Arnheim" and a future *Eureka*-type return to unity in "Landor's Cottage" (27–35).

1849, *Flag of Our Union*. Once again, it is hard to distinguish between the image in a lake and the surrounding area: "Its banks, of the emerald grass already described, *rounded*, rather than sloped, off into the clear heaven below; and *so* clear was this heaven, so perfectly, at times, did it reflect all objects above it, that where the true bank ended and where the mimic one commenced, it was a point of no little difficulty to determine" (M, III, 1333). The emphasis on point of view and compass-point specification, important to most of the pieces discussed above, is particularly evident in the description of the cottage. So important is a correct point of view to a correct appreciation that the narrator violates chronology in order to preserve it: "The point of view from which I first saw the valley, was not *altogether*, although it was nearly, the best point from which to survey the house. I will therefore describe it as I afterwards saw it—from a position on the stone wall at the southern extreme of the amphitheatre" (M, III, 1335). The narrator is here verging on the fastidious.[2]

Concerning directions, however, the narrator is decidedly fussy. Everything is given a compass-point identification; for example: "The blank wall of the eastern gable was relieved by stairs (with a balustrade) running diagonally across it—the ascent being from the south. Under cover of the widely projecting eave these steps gave access to a door leading into the garret, or rather loft—for it was lighted only by a single window to the north, and seemed to have been intended as a store-room" (M, III, 1336). Paradoxically, these fixes are so frequent and so specific that they have a dizzying effect on the reader and make it impossible for him to visualize the scene. Rather than render the description static, they tend to encourage the different elements in the scene to drift from their anchorage. Nor are the more usual devices of fluidity and fusion lacking: "The shingles were painted a dull gray; and the happiness with which this neutral tint melted into the vivid green of the tulip-tree leaves that partially overshadowed the cottage, can readily be conceived by an artist" (M, III, 1337). The narrator is invited inside by a woman whom A. H.

2. This passage is also highlighted by Alvin Rosenfield, "Description in Poe's 'Landor's Cottage,' " *Studies in Short Fiction*, IV (1967), 264–66.

Quinn identifies as Mrs. Richmond[3] to discover that the cottage, modeled on Poe's own at Fordham, is ideally furnished along the lines of "The Philosophy of Furniture." But the genius of the scene, both inside and out, is discovered to be Mr. Landor. If paradise is to be regained upon earth, according to Poe, it will be along the lines envisaged by Mr. Ellison and Mr. Landor.

III

In his search for concrete evidence to support his perception of an arabesque dimension, Poe was drawn toward the pseudoscience of mesmerism.[4] Three pieces—"A Tale of the Ragged Mountains," "Mesmeric Revelation," and "The Facts in the Case of M. Valdemar" —reflect this interest. In these tales, Poe used the findings of Mesmer to indicate that a man may exist prior to his birth and after his death. In "A Tale of the Ragged Mountains," first published in *Godey's Lady's Book* for April, 1844, Doctor Templeton, a mesmerist, seeks to regain contact with a friend named Oldeb, who died during an insurrection in India.[5] He engineers a professional association with a Mr. Augustus Bedloe, who bears an uncanny resemblance to the departed Oldeb. Such is the rapport between Dr. Templeton and Bedloe that the doctor is able to place his subject in a trance "almost instantaneously, by the mere volition of the operator, even when the invalid was unaware of his presence" (M, III, 941).

Presumably, the strange vision paralleling the circumstances of Oldeb's death, which Bedloe experiences while walking among the Ragged Mountains, is directed by Dr. Templeton, who reveals "that at the very period in which you fancied these things amid the hills, I was engaged in detailing them upon paper here at home" (M, III,

3. Arthur Hobson Quinn, *Edgar Allan Poe: A Critical Biography* (New York: Appleton-Century-Crofts, 1941), 587–88.
4. In an important article, Doris V. Falk distinguishes between mesmerism, or animal magnetism, and hypnotism. Mesmerism depends upon a unifying physical fluid similar to electricity, which is presumed to pervade the universe. Thus the universe of the mesmeric tales is consistent with the universe of *Eureka*. See Falk, "Poe and the Power of Animal Magnetism," *PMLA*, LXXXIV (1969), 536–46.
5. In describing this insurrection, Poe plagiarizes from Thomas Macaulay's October, 1841, review of G. R. Glieg (ed.), *Memoirs of the Life of the Right Hon. Warren Hastings*. The name Bedloe occurs in the same source. See Burton R. Pollin, *Discoveries in Poe* (Notre Dame, Ind.: University of Notre Dame Press, 1970), 25–26.

949). Apparently, Bedloe undergoes a mesmerically induced hallucination, which Templeton misunderstands as metempsychosis.[6] But this does not fully dissipate the difficulties of the tale. First of all, there is the matter of Mr. Bedloe's zombielike appearance and indeterminate age: "He certainly *seemed* young—and he made a point of speaking about his youth—yet there were moments when I should have had little trouble in imagining him a hundred years of age" (M, III, 940). Second, Bedloe without the final e and reversed reads Oldeb. Third, Bedloe finally dies in a manner presaged by Oldeb's death. Oldeb was struck in the right temple by a poisonous black arrow, made like "the writhing creese of the Malay . . . to imitate the body of a creeping serpent" (M, III, 947). Bedloe dies as a result of the apparently careless medication of Dr. Templeton. Accidentally, among the leeches that Templeton applies to Bedloe's forehead was a "poisonous sangsue," which is described as black and snakelike and which attaches itself to Bedloe's right temple (M, III, 950).[7]

It must be accepted that Bedloe is a resurrected Oldeb.[8] The Usher-like incongruities in his description, his creative imagination, and his addiction to morphine would suggest that he possesses an arabesque awareness. When he reexperiences his Indian death, it is a median time "during the strange *interregnum* of the seasons which in America is termed the Indian Summer" (M, III, 942). (A similarly hazy Indian summer's day is the occasion of the vision described in "Landor's Cottage.") Actually, Oldeb himself exists in a kind of Indian summer. The fog, the dazzling, mobile, and exotic city of Bedloe's vision, and the "sense of elasticity and of light" consequent upon death are further indications of an arabesque condition (M, III, 948). But there are still too many questions, ragged ends, remaining for a reader fully to disperse the interpretive fog surrounding this

6. This is Sidney E. Lind's argument in "Poe and Mesmerism," *PMLA*, LXII (1947), 1077–94.

7. It may be that Templeton (a medical leech), horrified by Oldeb's "return," deliberately murders Bedloe. See G. R. Thompson, *Poe's Fiction: Romantic Irony in the Gothic Tales* (Madison: University of Wisconsin Press, 1973), 150–51. *Sangsue*, it should be noted, is simply the French word for *leech*. See Pollin, *Discoveries in Poe*, 27–28.

8. Doris V. Falk comes to this conclusion in "Poe and the Power of Animal Magnetism," 540–43.

story.[9] The name Templeton would seem to connect with Bedloe's "right temple" and to imply that the doctor is responsible for enabling Oldeb to surmount death (M, III, 950). Maybe the doctor is to blame for detaining Oldeb from fully entering the arabesque state, an experiment to be attempted in the two following mesmeric tales.

"Mesmeric Revelation," a colloquy occurring between a sleep-walker and the narrator-mesmerist, is basically a vehicle for the cosmological theory later amplified in *Eureka* (M, III, 1030). It first appeared in the August, 1844, *Columbian Magazine*. Trickily, the narrator begins by ridiculing those who doubt the ability of the mesmerist to place his subject in a deathlike state. Mr. Vankirk, the subject in this case, claims that only while under the mesmeric influence is he intellectually convinced of the soul's immortality, because in that condition "there has been a certain deepening of the feeling, until it has come so nearly to resemble the acquiescence of reason, that I find it difficult to distinguish between the two" (M, III, 1031). The narrator questions Vankirk, after putting him in a trance that presumably extends beyond the point of his death. Thus the reader is invited to give Vankirk's revelations of Poe's theory the same credence that the mesmeric power demands.

In his deathlike state, Vankirk reveals that God is unparticled matter and that "all created things are but the thoughts of God" (M, III, 1036). (These ideas are also found respectively in *Eureka* and "The Power of Words.") There is no such thing as spirit: "When we flatter ourselves that we have formed its conception, we have merely deceived our understanding by the consideration of infinitely rarefied matter" (M, III, 1035). He goes on to distinguish between the rudimental and "the ultimate life," or man "individualized," and man as God, "divested of corporate investiture" (M, III, 1036, 1037). "To rudimental beings," Mr. Vankirk explains in a Blakean analogy, "organs are the cages necessary to confine them until fledged" (M, III, 1038). People have different perceptions depending upon which

9. There are, for example, questions regarding the existence of ambiguous parallels with Charles Brockden Brown's *Edgar Huntly*. These parallels are taken seriously in Boyd Carter, "Poe's Debt to Charles Brockden Brown," *Prairie Schooner*, XXVII (1935), 190–96. A burlesque intent is sensed in Thompson, *Poe's Fiction*, 151–52.

condition they are in: "There are many things on the Earth, which would be nihility to the inhabitants of Venus—many things visible and tangible in Venus, which we could not be brought to appreciate as existing at all" (M, III, 1039). It is this assumption that forms the basis of Poe's art.

Vankirk suffers from phthisis, as does the mesmeric subject in "The Facts in the Case of M. Valdemar," first published in the New York *American Review: A Whig Journal* for December, 1845. In this piece, as seemingly in "A Tale of the Ragged Mountains," mesmerism is used to retard absolute death. During the period of almost seven months between Mr. Valdemar's death and his putrefaction, the subject is able to speak in a voice that impresses the narrator synesthetically "as gelatinous or glutinous matters impress the sense of touch" (M, III, 1240).[10] When the piece was reprinted in England, it was taken as fact; and it has been suggested that Poe intended a hoax, as he himself later twice insisted (*Letters*, II, 337, 349). However, although the event did not occur, there can be little doubt that Poe believed in such a possibility.

IV

This chapter concludes, as did Chapter 4, with two more of Poe's six metaphysical pieces. The chronological pairing of "Shadow—A Parable" and "Silence—A Fable," of "The Conversation of Eiros and Charmion" and "The Colloquy of Monos and Una," and of "The Power of Words" and *Eureka* represents the simplest method of gauging the stages in Poe's philosophic development. About "The Conversation of Eiros and Charmion," which first appeared in *Burton's Gentleman's Magazine* for December, 1839, there is not a great deal to be said.[11] Eiros is telling Charmion (the names are those of

10. The realm from which Valdemar speaks is implied by his very name. As Daniel Hoffman notes, it may be translated as "*valley-of-sea*" and connected with Poe's symbolic maelstrom. See Daniel Hoffman, *Poe Poe Poe Poe Poe Poe Poe* (New York: Doubleday, 1972), 166–67. The same point is made in Roland Barthes, "Textual Analysis of a Tale by Edgar Poe," trans. Donald G. Marshall, *Poe Studies*, X (1977), 4. The French original appears in Claude Charbrol (ed.), *Sémiotique narrative et textuelle* (Paris: Librairie Larousse, 1973), 29–54.

11. Most of what needs to be said about the angelic dialogues has been well stated by Allen Tate, "The Angelic Imagination: Poe and the Power of Words," *Kenyon Review*, XIV (1952), 455–75.

Cleopatra's faithful handmaidens) about the destruction of the world and man's ability to deceive himself. Everybody believed the savant's assertion that no comet could cause the end of the world, an assertion backed in Harrison's edition by Professor W. LeConte Stevens (H, IV, 276–77). However, human consciousness in this regard and others is to be expanded, as presaged by the development of a universal and "unusual elasticity of frame and vivacity of mind," coupled with the "wild luxuriance of foliage." Meanwhile, the comet had taken "the character of a gigantic mantle of rare flame, extending from horizon to horizon" (M, II, 460). This phenomenon, plus the moment of calm, is analogous to precataclysmic events in "MS. Found in a Bottle" and "A Descent into the Maelström." The moment of fiery apocalypse occurs when the comet robs Earth's atmosphere of nitrogen.

Sensations are of prime importance, according to the editor in "How to Write a Blackwood Article." The sensations accompanying the moment of apocalypse are detailed in "The Colloquy of Monos and Una," which first appeared in Graham's Magazine for August, 1841. Like Eiros and Charmion, Monos and Una, as their names imply, have realized the unified state—which is akin to Al Aaraaf, judging from the "prototypes" of Earth flowers (M, II, 613). Lovers on Earth, they are together again one century after their respective deaths. (Perhaps this is the time that elapsed between their demise and the final apocalypse described by Eiros.) Because Una watched Monos die, she asks him to describe what happened when "the fever" of life abandoned him (M, II, 609).

Monos begins by linking Earth's destruction with man's misappropriation of his reason, finding "in the mystic parable that tells of the tree of knowledge, and of its forbidden fruit, death-producing, a distinct intimation that knowledge was not meet for man in the infant condition of his soul" (M, II, 609). He speaks of "the Art-scarred surface of the Earth" with "its rectangular obscenities" (M, II, 611–12). Presumably, he is referring to the scientific "Arts," which "arose supreme, and, once enthroned, cast chains upon the intellect which had elevated them to power." Like Blake's Urizen, man "grew infected with system, and with abstraction." All evil, but particularly man's blasphemous attempts at establishing a system of democracy, "sprang necessarily from the leading evil, Knowledge" (M, II, 611). After more raillery at "the harsh mathematical reason of the schools," Monos concludes, "Prematurely induced by intemperance of knowledge, the old age of the world drew on" (M, II, 612). This, of course, is all consistent with Poe's belief that the rudimental state is one of self-induced deception.

In this condition, Una mistook the "dreamy delirium" of Monos for pain, while Monos "longed but was impotent to undeceive" her (M, II, 612). However, Monos is now able to describe how all his senses underwent alteration: "The senses were unusually active, although eccentrically so—assuming often each other's functions at random. The taste and the smell were inextricably confounded, and became one sentiment, abnormal and intense" (M, II, 612–13). Light and dark are appreciated as sound. All the senses, but particularly those of hearing and touch, "were purely sensual" (M, II, 613). With "extinct reason," Monos apprehended the shapes of life as grotesque ghouls: "Their images impressed me with the idea of shrieks, groans, and other dismal expressions of terror, or horror, or of wo" (M, II, 613, 614). To his corrected senses, the oppression of night "was palpable" (M, II, 614). "And now, from the wreck and chaos of the usual senses, there appeared to have risen within me a sixth, all perfect," which he designates a "sentiment of *duration*" and by means of which he is able to recognize the irregularities of human time (M, II, 614, 615). With the passage of time, "the idea of entity was becoming merged in that of *place*" (M, II, 616). He becomes at one with his surroundings.

Monos describes the transition from the rudimental to the ultimate life in terms of corrected perception. The conventional world is an illusion predicated by the separation of the senses and the distinguishing propensity of man's reason. The perception of an arabesque world depends upon the fusion of the senses and the obliteration of reason. Inevitably, the result is disappointing; but no religious system has succeeded in describing heaven in any terms other than an ecstatic, but essentially bovine, torpor. It should be stressed, however, that the condition which Poe describes or assumes in the ten pieces discussed above does have the advantage,

216

like the nirvana of Indian mysticism, of being humanly attainable.[12] Heaven is a matter of altered perspective and not above, or beyond, Earth. Consequently, Earth and Al Aaraaf are not physically distant; and the distance traveled by Hans Pfaal between Earth and a land of the "dead," apparently the moon, is ultimately not through space.

The three final chapters, however, will be concerned with developments in, or contrary aspects of, Poe's thinking that significantly modify his philosophical position as described up to this point. The ambiguous concept of *intuition* takes on the positive role of the imagination and muddies what has appeared to be a clear distinction between reason and imagination. It becomes increasingly relevant that, in fact, reason is not exclusively negative. If Poe adopted a split attitude toward reason, it also seems likely that he developed a twofold notion of the unified state. In one sense it is omnipresent; and in another, elaborated in *Eureka*, it is regarded as, in the fullest degree, only cyclically available.

12. Richard Wilbur notes of the phrase "bottomless vale" in "Ulalume" that "Poe's strategy here is analogous to that of the Zen Buddhist who contemplates a logical contradiction in hopes of short-circuiting the intellect and so inviting a mystic illumination." See Wilbur, Introduction to *Poe: Complete Poems* (New York: Dell, 1959), 36. See also, in this connection, D. Ramakrishna, "Poe's *Eureka* and Hindu Philosophy," *Emerson Society Quarterly*, no. 47 (1967), 28–32.

Part Three

INTUITION

8

The Powers of Causality

Whether or not Poe can be called a schizophrenic, a good deal of evidence exists to suggest that he was a deeply divided personality. John R. Thompson, in an obituary that appeared in the *Southern Literary Messenger* for November, 1849, testified: "It is remarkable ... that a mind so prone to unrestrained imaginings should be capable of analytic investigation or studious research. Yet few excelled Mr. Poe in power of analysis or patient application. Such are the contradictions of the human intellect. He was an impersonated antithesis" (H, I, 395). Baudelaire, referring to the same conflict, said of Poe: "He might be called an antithesis come to life." As indicated previously, the belief that man's reason clouds his perception is fundamental to Poe's philosophy. But increasingly, Poe recognized and utilized the very intellectual power that he himself possessed and that he professed to despise. Although A. H. Quinn, perhaps fancifully, finds the duality in Poe's nature "reflected most concretely in his countenance," there can be no doubt that he was plagued all his life by a sense of inner contradiction.[1] At the same time, this conflict between the call of imagination and the demands of reason provides strong evidence for locating Poe squarely in the traditional mainstream of American literature. Generally speak-

1. Lois Hyslop and Francis E. Hyslop, Jr. (eds.), *Baudelaire on Poe* (Philadelphia: Bald Eagle Press, 1952), 66; Arthur Hobson Quinn, *Edgar Allan Poe: A Critical Biography* (New York: Appleton-Century-Crofts, 1941), 693.

ing, the preeminent American writers display a tension in their work between the transcendental and the speculative on the one hand and the materialistic and the pragmatic on the other. Poe appears to be a fitting representative of a schizophrenic American condition, although on balance Poe belongs primarily with the Transcendentalists.

To turn from the general to the specific, in examining the observable character of Poe's analytic activities, it will become ironically apparent that Poe's own practice confirms most of his own strictures about man's reason. Reason, Poe claims, is subject to idiopathic limitation. Likewise, many of Poe's analytic exercises, if not wrong outright, are severely limited by personal bias. Furthermore, Poe's intellectualism often takes the form of rationalization and camouflage. Poe frequently uses his reason to deceive others and, unwittingly, himself.

II

More often than not, the cranky gimcrack nature of the subjects Poe submitted to his analytical intellect are a measure of his reasoning ability. His interest in cryptography and the pseudosciences of autography, phrenology, and mesmerism—at least from today's perspective—seem to merit him a sideshow booth in some Barnum and Bailey circus. In spite of the fact that such interests were the common eccentricities of the age, suggestions of the tawdry and the freakish, which have always clung to Poe, are not without some foundation in fact.[2] It is, then, fitting that Poe's first sustained ratiocinative exercise, "Maelzel's Chess-Player," which appeared in the Southern Literary Messenger for April, 1836, should be devoted to explaining what was essentially a famous contemporary conjuring act. The challenge of revealing a deception always intrigued Poe; and in this case, he was concerned with demonstrating that the Automaton Chess-Player, invented by Baron Kempelen and later owned by Mr. Maelzel, was not a machine but depended upon the

2. For example, see N. Vachel Lindsay's poem, "The Wizard in the Street," reprinted in Eric W. Carlson (ed.), The Recognition of Edgar Allan Poe (Ann Arbor: University of Michigan Press, 1966), 101–102; N. Bryllion Fagin, The Histrionic Mr. Poe (Baltimore, Md.: Johns Hopkins University Press, 1949).

agency of someone concealed within the box on which the chessboard rested.

Poe's exposition, a classic of its kind, divides readily into five parts. In the first part, he describes similar automata, including the "duck of Vaucanson," which "was so perfect an imitation of the living animal that all the spectators were deceived" (H, XIV, 8). He then gives the history and a detailed description of the Automaton Chess-Player, followed by an account of the various theories adduced to explain the machine's operations (concealed dwarf, thin boy, etc.), all of which are contemptuously rejected. In the fourth part Poe reveals his own explanation; and in the fifth, he lists seventeen points of observation—some of a spurious logicality—which led him to his conclusions. Unfortunately, as W. K. Wimsatt, Jr., has conclusively demonstrated, the bulk of the deception revealed in this "exposure" is on Poe's part. Although Poe states that "nothing has been written on this topic which can be considered as decisive" and refers disparagingly to the analysis of the Automaton Chess-Player by Sir David Brewster in his *Letters on Natural Magic,* almost everything that is valid in his explanation is indebted to Brewster's study (H, XIV, 6). And although, in a footnote, Poe rejects as preposterous Brewster's notion that the bottom drawer was a false one, such does appear to have been the case. Furthermore, the greater part of Poe's paper is devoted to proving that the Automaton Chess-Player cannot be a pure machine, although most of the previous commentators had taken this for granted. By the ingenious use of flannel in proving the obvious, Poe seems to indicate that his arguments in this area are of more importance than the explanation of how the man was actually concealed inside the machine. As Wimsatt puts it, "What is but the superstructure of Brewster's account is made to seem the foundation—while the real foundation Poe has shifted into his own essay without acknowledgement."[3]

Poe's basic intellectual showmanship is also evident in his cryptographic interest, already touched on in Chapter 2. In this case, however, his dishonesty takes the form of business acumen. By chal-

3. W. K. Wimsatt, Jr., "Poe and the Chess Automaton," *American Literature,* XI (1939), 150.

lenging the readers of the Philadelphia *Alexander's Weekly Messen-ger*, in December, 1839, that he could crack any cipher which they might submit, Poe hit upon an effective advertising angle—one that remained in use until April of the following year. In a series of articles for *Graham's Magazine* on "Secret Writing," beginning in July, 1841, and ending in December, 1841, Poe exhausted the subject. The account that Poe gave of the various types of cipher and of his own success in breaking those submitted to *Alexander's* makes very impressive reading—for the layman. Poe emerges as a mental giant. Of the one hundred cryptograms received, he solved all but one and proved that that one was insoluble. Perhaps with a hope of repeating the phenomenon, Poe lodged a similar challenge in a book review in *Graham's* for April, 1841; but he received only one reply. The loss of interest may reflect the fact, demonstrated by William F. Friedman, that Poe's cryptographic knowledge was amateurish and that he deliberately overemphasized the difficulties involved in the solution of those cryptograms submitted to him. Furthermore, it has been pointed out that the cipher described in "The Gold-Bug" contains numerous errors.[4] As in the case of the Automaton Chess-Player, Poe, attracted by something inherently deceptive, practices deceptions of his own upon his readers. Nevertheless, the broader base on which his interest in cryptography rests is apparent in the statement that "the soul is a cipher, in the sense of a cryptograph" (H, XV, 81). Poe's interest in cryptography is indicative of his basic assumptions concerning the nature of reality.

Also in 1841, Poe wrote a series of articles on autography. He toyed with autography, along with phrenology, as an infallible analytic key to character. Much earlier, in February, 1836, in the *Southern Literary Messenger*, Poe used the signatures of thirty-eight people who had replied to a bogus letter as a rather dreary humorous index to the characters of the signatories. In November, 1841, Poe took up the subject again in "A Chapter on Autography," proposing to treat it seriously on the grounds that "a strong analogy does gener-

4. William F. Friedman, "Edgar Allan Poe, Cryptographer," *American Literature*, VIII (1936), 266–80; on "The Gold-Bug," see W. K. Wimsatt, Jr., "What Poe Knew About Cryptography," *PMLA*, LVIII (1943), 754–79; J. Woodrow Hassell, Jr., "The Problem of Realism in 'The Gold Bug,' " *American Literature*, XXV (1953), 182–86.

ally and naturally exist between every man's chirography and character" (H, XV, 178). The task of "analysing" one hundred signatures of "the most noted among the living literati of the country" occupied three issues of Graham's Magazine (H, XV, 179). Like the cipher challenge, this concern with calligraphy was largely a journalistic device, and Poe has no claim to be considered an expert on the subject. Nevertheless, it is an indication that his analytic intelligence was of the kind to be attracted by simple, unitary answers to problems.

More weight should be attached to Poe's interest in phrenology. In that series of portraits, "The Literati of New York City," which appeared in issues of Godey's Lady's Book from May to October, 1846, Poe invariably takes time to consider the dimensions and proportions of his subjects' foreheads, usually to find them disappointing. There is no definite indication of any concern with the subject until March, 1836, when Poe wrote in a review of Mrs. L. Miles's Phrenology and The Moral Influence of Phrenology that "phrenology is no longer to be laughed at" (H, VIII, 252). In a review of Robert Walsh's Didactics the same year, Poe objects to that author's ridicule of the subject. Edward Hungerford points out that phrenological terms, like the organs of causality and ideality, inform Poe's criticism and that a number of tales—"Lionizing," "Diddling," "The Business Man," and "Some Words with a Mummy"—involve satire on certain phrenological categories. For example, in "Diddling" Poe is burlesquing the organ of constructiveness. Phrenology itself is not attacked, although it is possible that Poe became disenchanted with the system as a master science.[5] Nevertheless, because phrenological terminology permeates Poe's thinking, a phrenological category is used as the title for this chapter.

III

One of Poe's best-known exercises in detection, and a convenient point of transition from the hocus-pocus examined above to the crit-

5. Edward Hungerford, "Poe and Phrenology," American Literature, II (1930), 209–31: on Poe's disenchantment, see Marvin Laser, "The Growth and Structure of Poe's Concept of Beauty," Journal of English Literary History, XV (1948), 72–75.

ical expression of Poe's analytic intellect, is his essay on *Barnaby Rudge*, which appeared in *Graham's Magazine* for February, 1842. In this essay, Poe refers to an original note in the Philadelphia *Saturday Evening Post* for May, 1841, in which, after reading an early portion of Charles Dickens' book, he was able to prophesy that Rudge was the murderer. But this hit and Poe's own trumpeting distract attention from the four inaccurate predictions in the review. Poe was mistaken in believing Geoffrey Haredale to be involved in his brother's murder and in claiming that Barnaby, or Joe Willett, would help bring about his father's arrest. Furthermore, although there is some doubt, Poe was probably wrong in suspecting "an analogical resemblance" between Grip and Barnaby and in supposing that the croaks of the raven would be heard *"prophetically"* (H, XI, 63). More appositely, Grip is prophetic of Poe's "The Raven." As Gerald G. Grubb points out, one hit out of five is not very accurate shooting.[6]

More heinous, in referring to the earlier note, Poe took advantage of its nonavailability to most of his readers in stating that "the secret was distinctly understood immediately upon the perusal of the story of Solomon Daisy, which occurs at the seventh page of this volume of three hundred and twenty-three" (H, XI, 52). He claimed that, when he first presented the solution, the serialization of *Barnaby Rudge* had only just begun, whereas in that first note, he informed the reader that he had Parts I, II, and III, or eleven chapters (possibly thirteen), before him. Furthermore, Poe's claim that he received a congratulatory letter from Dickens is extremely unlikely. Since this is the case, it is ironic that he should criticize Dickens for distracting the reader's attention from the main line of the plot by including an account of the Gordon Riots and for committing "the error of *exaggerating anticipation*" (H, XI, 57). Poe's own review contains examples of analogous smoke-screen devices. Poe even complained that, where Dickens strayed from Poe's prognostications, he erred artistically. It is not surprising that the relationship between Poe and Dickens finally proved abortive.

6. Gerald G. Grubb, "The Personal and Literary Relationships of Dickens and Poe," *Nineteenth Century Fiction*, V (1950), 10; see also W. Robertson Nicoll, *Dickens' Own Story: Side-Lights on His Life and Personality* (London: Chapman & Hall, 1923).

In spite of his understanding that truth can be many-sided, as a literary detective Poe displayed an obstinate bias, particularly in the identification of plagiarism. However, as a literary critic he was generally fair, notwithstanding Griswold's estimate that "he was more remarkable as a dissector of sentences than as a commentator of ideas" (H, I, 359). During his lifetime, Poe was, in fact, best known as a critic. In an article on the subject of literary criticism in *Graham's Magazine* for January, 1842, Poe speaks of "the importance of the science (shall we so term it?)" and protests against the "frantic spirit of *generalization*" (H, XI, 1, 6). He follows up with a definition that is recognizably New Critical in spirit: "Following the highest authority, we would wish, in a word, to limit literary criticism to comment upon *Art*. . . . With the opinions of the work, considered otherwise than in their relation to the work itself, the critic has really nothing to do" (H, XI, 7). Generally Poe's reviews follow this precept. Characteristically, in the case of a novel, Poe begins with a thorough rehearsal of the plot and then balances the technical virtues of the work against the technical blunders or inelegancies before making a value judgment. A lack of balance more often occurs between the paltry nature of the art product and the intelligence and sophistication of the review, whether Poe is exposing a sophistry or delivering a judgment. Although Poe had a reputation as a hatchet man during his lifetime, he praised more often than he blamed. Indeed, Poe might be blamed for praising too extravagantly, particularly in the case of certain poetesses where Poe's usual discrimination seems to have deserted him entirely. But on the whole James Russell Lowell's evaluation is accurate: "Mr. Poe is at once the most discriminating, philosophical, and fearless critic upon imaginative works who has written in America" (H, I, 369).[7]

In turning from Poe's practical criticism to his critical theory, al-

7. On the subject of Poe's criticism, see Edd Winfield Parks, *Edgar Allan Poe as Literary Critic* (Athens: University of Georgia Press, 1964); and what is the best such study to date, Robert D. Jacobs, *Poe: Journalist and Critic* (Baton Rouge: Louisiana State University Press, 1969). For particular biases, see George Snell, "First of the New Critics," *Quarterly Review of Literature*, II (1945), 333–40; Richard Cary, "Poe and the Literary Ladies," *Texas Studies in Literature and Language*, LXXXII (1967), 91–101.

though the two activities are intimately connected, the reader turns from a basic objectivity to a basic subjectivity. In his theories about the purpose of literature and his prescriptions for poetry and prose, Poe displays a marked idiopathic tendency to turn his personal limitations into universal principles. Although such a development is to be expected in the work of most writer-critics, Poe's theory is overly exclusive. (It is significant in this regard and in view of the common assumption that Poe is a writer of horror stories that his critical theory has virtually nothing to say about the nature and techniques of the horror genre.) His emphasis on unity leads him, indirectly, to condemn narrative techniques other than first person. In a review of Joseph H. Ingraham's *Lafitte: The Pirate of the Gulf*, Poe disapproves of the changing points of view adopted: "As a general rule it may be safely assumed, that the most simple, is the best, method of narration" (H, IX, 113). And in the following review concerning James S. French's *Elkwatawa; or the Prophet of the West*, the author is criticized for falling into the "mannerisms of Sir Walter Scott," namely "the bringing up of his narrative," with the result "that Mr. French's readers are kept in a constant state of chronological hornpipe" (H, IX, 123–24). Very few of Poe's fictions, it will be recalled, make use of an omniscient narrator. As Emerson R. Marks points out, Poe is blind to the aesthetic value of a complex whole and tends to throw out all poetry that is not lyrical in the interests of a rigid consistency.[8]

However, the theory is not without its own inconsistencies. At one point, Poe eradicates the Coleridgean distinction between fancy and imagination as being "without a difference; without even a difference of degree. The fancy as nearly creates as the imagination; and neither creates in any respect. All novel conceptions are merely unusual combinations. The mind of man can *imagine* nothing which has not really existed" (H, X, 61–62). But in practice, Poe does distinguish between fancy and imagination and writes, in a footnote to the Drake-Halleck review: "Imagination is, possibly in man, a lesser degree of the creative power in God" (H, VIII, 283). *The Culprit Fay*

8. Emerson R. Marks, "Poe as Literary Theorist: A Reappraisal," *American Literature*, XXXIII (1961), 296–97.

is described as fanciful but not imaginative and therefore attributed to "the faculty of Comparison" (H, VIII, 295). Elsewhere, allegory is banished on the grounds of its "appealing only to our faculties of comparison, without even a remote interest for our reason, or for our fancy" (H, X, 130). Is the fancy connected with the faculty of comparison or not? This discussion will not go deeply into the knotty question of the consistency of Poe's criticism. The subject demands a rigorous book-length study, and much depends upon definition of terms.[9]

At the same time, it should be observed that certain interpreters of Poe's critical theory appear to have manufactured minor inconsistencies. George Kelly, for example, believes that Poe confuses *taste* with *ideality* in using the words as synonyms. "The probable reason for Poe's dual terminology," writes Kelly, "lies in his initial interest in phrenology and his subsequent cooling off towards it," ideality being the phrenological term. But Poe uses ideality as a synonym for beauty, not for taste. Taste, that aspect of the mind mediating between the intellect and the moral sense (which may be termed the *faculty of* ideality), is able to appreciate ideality, or beauty. However, Kelly does effectively answer an objection of Norman Foerster, who blames Poe's "literalness" and "dependence on 'mere logic' " for his "conclusion that of all topics death is the most melancholy, and that death is most melancholy when it is the death of a beautiful woman." Kelly recognizes that the death of a beautiful woman is not among Poe's poetic principles. The pertinent general principle is the association of beauty with melancholy because of the gap between man's aspirations toward supernal beauty and his inability to realize those aspirations. The death of a beautiful woman is

9. Such a study might profitably draw on J. Lasley Dameron and Louis C. Stagg, *An Index to Poe's Critical Vocabulary* (Hartford, Conn.: Transcendental Books, 1966). Jacobs provides the following helpful overview: "Poe's reviews during the first five months of 1842 illustrate as clearly as do 'The Philosophy of Composition' and 'The Poetic Principle' an apparent divergence between his attitude as a literary critic and his attitude as a romantic poet. As a literary critic he attempted to use science and reason in his proofs. As a romantic poet he found value in the experience of a transcendent visionary beauty. When these two orientations conflicted, his theoretical statements sometimes became obscure and even contradictory, as he attempted to accommodate the vision of beauty to a practical methodology." See Jacobs, *Poe: Journalist and Critic*, 296.

merely emblematic of this tragic awareness of beauty. More specifically, "the death . . . of a beautiful woman is, unquestionably, the most poetic topic in the world" for Poe because in death the idea of beauty embodied in the woman is free of the imprisoning realm of temporal corruption (H, XIV, 201).[10]

But Norman Foerster and George Kelly do agree in condemning Poe's linkage of beauty and indefiniteness as a sophistry. They point out that, although the infinite is indefinite, it does not follow that the indefinite is also infinite and spiritual.[11] Poe's strategy of fusion would seem to imply that he does make this logical blunder. In a review of Elizabeth Barrett's *The Dream of Exile*, Poe states in relation to "the cant of the transcendentalists" that "what is worth thinking is distinctly thought: what is distinctly thought, can and should be distinctly expressed, or should not be expressed at all" (H, XII, 5, 6). However, he makes an exception of the case "where the design is to convey the fantastic—not the obscure. To give the idea of the latter we need, as in general, the most precise and definite terms, and those who employ other terms but confound obscurity of expression with the expression of obscurity" (H, XII, 6). In an earlier review, Poe accused Macaulay of "confounding obscurity of expression with the expression of obscurity" (H, X, 156). Although in practice Poe might be guilty of the same confusion, theoretically he was aware of the distinction that Kelly and Foerster believe they are revealing.

A more complicated matter is the axiomatic divorce that Poe appears to make between truth and beauty, with only the latter being the province of poetry, and his calling *Eureka* a prose poem embodying the Keatsian revelation that beauty and truth are one. It is tempting to give credence to Poe's later statements, rather than his earlier pronouncements and to pay testimony to the advancing wisdom of age. But the contradiction disappears if one supposes that he is using terms clumsily and means to distinguish between two kinds of truth. The kind of truth to be disassociated from poetry would

10. George Kelly, "Poe's Theory of Beauty," *American Literature*, XXVII (1956), 529, 532–33; Norman Foerster, *American Criticism: A Study in Literary Theory from Poe to the Present* (Boston: Houghton Mifflin, 1928), 44. See also Charles C. Walcutt, "The Logic of Poe," *College English*, II (1941), 438–44.

11. Foerster, *American Criticism*, 39; Kelly, "Poe's Theory of Beauty," 533–34.

come under the heading of the didactic, which Poe condemns, particularly in "The Letter to B———." This everyday truth, or what Patrick Quinn calls "the truth of logic and fact," is something quite apart from "the truth of insight and imagination," which a successful poem exhibits by definition.[12] Nevertheless, it is true that Poe himself does not directly make this distinction.

Although Poe overvalued the power of his analytic intellect, some critics are in danger of seriously undervaluing it. The basis of Poe's critical theory is not original, in spite of his emphasis on originality. (He drew on Aristotle and the Neoplatonists, Samuel Taylor Coleridge, August Wilhelm and Friedrich Schlegel, and perhaps Percy Bysshe Shelley.[13]) But Poe did assemble a number of important and consistent insights concerning the nature of artistic imitation, the need for a poem to be organic and dispassionate, and the role of the intellect in the creative process. Poe, using phrenological terminology, declares: "We do not hesitate to say that a man highly endowed with the powers of Causality—that is to say, a man of metaphysical acumen—will, even with a very deficient share of Ideality, compose a finer poem . . . than one who, without such metaphysical acumen, shall be gifted, in the most extraordinary degree, with the faculty of Ideality." As an example, Poe singles out Coleridge, whose head "gave no great phrenological tokens of Ideality, while the organs of Causality and Comparison were most singularly developed" (H, VIII, 284–85). In seeing that a poem is a combined production of the intellect and the imagination, Poe appears to reconcile what elsewhere is presented as an antagonistic relationship. Two-thirds of the question "What is Poetry?" belong to mathematics, Poe suggests in his "Marginalia" (H, XVI, 111).

12. Patrick F. Quinn, "Four Views of Edgar Poe," *Jahrbuch fur Amerikastudien*, V (1960), 140.
13. Margaret Alterton, *Origins of Poe's Critical Theory* (Iowa City: University of Iowa Press, 1925); Floyd Stovall, "Poe's Debt to Coleridge," *University of Texas Studies in English*, X (1930), 120–27, reprinted in Stovall, *Edgar Poe the Poet: Essays New and Old on the Man and His Work* (Charlottesville: University of Virginia Press, 1969), 126–74; Laser, "The Growth and Structure of Poe's Concept of Beauty," 69–84; Albert J. Lubbell, "Poe and A. W. Schlegel," *Journal of English and Germanic Philology*, LII (1953), 1–12; "The Influence of Shelley on Poe," in Julia Powers, *Shelley in America in the Nineteenth Century* (Lincoln: University of Nebraska Press, 1964), 99–117.

Indeed, the mathematical precision of Poe's art drew the admiration of Paul Valéry and Charles Baudelaire. Baudelaire wrote, "It could be said that he seeks to apply to literature the processes of philosophy, and to philosophy the methods of algebra."[14]

Of obvious relevance here is "The Philosophy of Composition," which appeared in *Graham's Magazine* for April, 1846. In this work Poe maintains, apropos "The Raven," that "it is my design to render it manifest that no one point in its composition is referable to accident or intuition—that the work proceeded, step by step, to its completion with the precision and rigid consequence of a mathematical problem" (H, XIV, 195). A number of critics have argued that this essay is a hoax and that, in revealing "the wheels and pinions" at work during the composition of "The Raven," Poe is deceiving his readers in much the same way as the "wheels, pinions, levers, and other machinery" within the Automaton Chess-Player deceive the public (H, XIV, 14, 195).[15] Although the Automaton Chess-Player was not a pure machine, it is also true that the artist does not create by magic. Furthermore, before writing "The Philosophy of Composition," Poe had entertained this idea of the orderly progression of literary composition. In "A Chapter of Suggestions" in the 1845 *Opal* is the following: "An excellent magazine paper might be written upon the subject of the progressive steps by which any great work of art—especially of literary art—attained completion" (H, XIV, 188). In the "Marginalia" he writes, "It is the curse of a certain order of mind, that it can never rest satisfied with the consciousness of its ability to do a thing. Still less is it content with doing it. It must both know and show how it was done" (H, XVI, 40). These progressive steps leading to "The Philosophy of Composition" would seem to imply that Poe's intention was genuine. On the other hand, the argument of "The Philosophy of Composition" is characteristically false insofar

14. Hyslop and Hyslop, *Baudelaire on Poe*, 80.
15. For example, Joseph Wood Krutch, *Edgar Allan Poe: A Study in Genius* (New York: Alfred A. Knopf, 1926), sees the work as defensive rationalization (98, 115, 118). See also Joseph Chiari, *"Symbolisme" from Poe to Mallarmé* (London: Rockliff, 1956), 108; Thomas Ollive Mabbott (ed.), *Collected Works of Edgar Allan Poe* (6 vols. projected; Cambridge, Mass.: Belknap Press of Harvard University Press, 1969–), I, 335, 560.

as Poe does not acknowledge any debt to the conception of Grip in *Barnaby Rudge*, although the article opens with a misquotation from one of Dickens' letters to Poe "now lying before me, alluding to an examination I once made of the mechanism of 'Barnaby Rudge' " (H, XIV, 193).[16] Presumably, Poe did not have the letter before him; and in recalling the devious practice of Poe in relation to *Barnaby Rudge*, it is hard not to be suspicious about "The Philosophy of Composition."

IV

Poe was certainly a conscious artist. Perhaps he was an overly conscious artist. At least he recognizes the danger in a late "Marginalia" entry:

> To see distinctly the machinery—the wheels and pinions—of any work of Art is, unquestionably, of itself, a pleasure, but one which we are able to enjoy only just in proportion as we do *not* enjoy the legitimate effect designed by the artist:—and, in fact, it too often happens that to reflect analytically upon Art, is to reflect after the fashion of the mirrors in the temple of Smyrna, which represents the fairest images as deformed. (H, XVI, 170)

Elsewhere Poe quotes a reviewer who does make such a criticism: "The ill-boding 'Raven,' which you meet at the threshold of his edifice, is a fit warning of the hospitality you will find inside. . . . Edgar Poe does not write for Humanity; he has more of the art than the soul of poetry" (H, XIII, 29–30). There is some truth in this stricture, and it is significant that Poe's contemptuous answer is extremely poor. The reviewer refers particularly to Poe's "critical study of the matter of versification" in "The Rationale of Verse," which appeared in the *Pioneer* for March, 1843 (H, XIII, 29). Here Poe's reason oversteps its bounds. Poe's argument rests on the assumption that the measure of English verse, like Latin verse, is basically quantitative and not accentual. Unfortunately, such is not the case. Gay Wilson Allen attributes Poe's mistake to his conviction that poetry is "an inferior or less capable music."[17] Consequently,

16. Grubb, "The Personal and Literary Relationships of Dickens and Poe," 212–14.

17. Gay Wilson Allen, *American Prosody* (New York: American Book Co., 1935), 58.

unless one wants to mount a case for irony, Poe apparently erects a beautifully logical structure on a foundation of error, although he claims to be displacing error. He points out that the topic is characterized by "inaccuracy, confusion, misconception, misrepresentation, mystification, and downright ignorance on all sides" (H, XIV, 209). And the same is still true in spite of Poe's efforts. The scholars, Poe argues, have failed because they were bound by authority and because there were too many of them. Accordingly and characteristically, Poe begins by sweeping aside all previous thought on the matter since "there is not one point of the definition in question which does not involve an error" (H, XIV, 216). Previous definitions are inadequate because they are limited to English verse. Poe, on the other hand, is concerned with verse in the widest understanding of that term.

Because everything is to be understood as relating to a principle of unity, "Ex una disce omnia," Poe maintains that the appreciation of quantity is universal: "To melody and to harmony the Greeks hearkened with ears precisely similar to those which we employ for similar purposes at present" (H, XIV, 217). Then follows the golden rule: "Verse originates in the human enjoyment of equality, fitness" (H, XIV, 218). In view of the sophisticated methodolgy to come, it is surprising that Poe should declare of verse that "its rigidly simple character not even Science—not even Pedantry can greatly pervert" (H, XIV, 220). Poe's principle of equality leads him to criticize Coleridge's method of scansion and to propose a new system based on the length of time it takes to pronounce a particular syllable. In order to achieve a quantitative equality, he invents the notion of bastard feet and the concept of the caesura as a variable foot. The phyrric foot is dismissed as "a mere chimera bred in the mad fancy of a pedant" (H, XIV, 241). The spondee is discovered to be the basis of most ancient rhythms, although it is impossible to write English hexameters on the model of the Greek and write poetry, as Longfellow and others attempted to do. Because the French enunciate uniformly, they "have no verse worth the name"—if Poe's theory is to hold (H, XIV, 261).

In the interests of variation, equivalent feet are interchangeable, provided that the distinctive rhythm remains dominant, otherwise "the ear becomes at once balked by the *bouleversement* of the rhythm" (H, XIV, 235). But the *bouleversement* that Poe proposes, in so "sudden and radical an alteration of the conventionalities to which the reader has been accustomed," is quite justified (H, XIV, 248). Due to the efficiency of his new system, Poe is able to scan the hitherto unscannable lines of Byron's "Bride of Abydos," reveal the rhythm of Latin verse, and write "a truly Greek hexameter" in English. Along the way, Poe quotes from "a boyish poem" of his own— "Al Aaraaf"—as an example of his theories (H, XIV, 235). Presumably, Poe wrote his poetry in accordance with his theory, although Gay Wilson Allen believes that no natural reading could be consistent with the theory. Either Poe is literally the artist of the impossible, or there is some truth in his rationale. In fact, a number of scholars do accept that English verse is to some small extent quantitative.[18] Nevertheless, the insistence that English verse is totally quantitative in "The Rationale of Verse" does show Poe constricted by his own reason.

George Kelly believes that, in stressing equality, Poe is moving toward a new theory of beauty which is quite different from the theory that equates the indefinite and the beautiful. Poe embodies this secondary theory of symmetry in *Eureka*.[19] Kelly is probably manufacturing difficulties here and confounding technique with content in assuming that Poe confuses obscurity of expression with the expression of obscurity—the very thing for which he previously criticized Poe. The theory of equality, or symmetry, is in no way inconsistent with the expression of the indefinite. Furthermore, the concept of equality occurs in Poe's early critical writings. In January, 1837, reviewing the work of William Cullen Bryant, Poe justifies "excesses of measure" as employed "with reference to the proper

18. *Ibid.*, 58–59. "Neither Saintsbury nor Oliver Wendell Holmes despised Poe's notions," according to Edward Wagenknecht, *Edgar Allan Poe: The Man Behind the Legend* (New York: Oxford University Press, 1963), 153.

19. Kelly, "Poe's Theory of Beauty," 535–36. *Eureka* and "The Rationale of Verse" are also connected in Alterton, *Origins of Poe's Critical Theory*, 171–73.

equalization, or *balancing,* if we may so term it, of time, *throughout an entire sentence"* (H, IX, 272). Writing in December, 1839, Poe refers to the "mathematical recognition of *equality* which seems to be *the root of all Beauty"* in the same paragraph which contains the statement "that the *sentimental* pleasure derivable from music, is nearly in the ratio of its indefinitiveness" (H, X, 41, 42).

If Kelly is wrong in distinguishing two theories of beauty, he is certainly correct in linking "The Rationale of Verse" with *Eureka.* There is the same pretension verging on paranoia in both works, the same professed infallibility, and perhaps a similar irony. The apparent materialism of Poe's later critical theory may be attributed to an increasing concern with technique rather than content; and in the mechanistic universe posited by *Eureka,*[20] Poe equates a scientific cosmology with aesthetic principles. In both "The Rationale of Verse" and *Eureka,* Poe is concerned with arrogantly displacing previous modes of thought; and in both works he uses an introductory analogy. In "The Rationale of Verse," the reader is asked to examine the sides of a revolving crystal. In *Eureka,* the reader is invited to perform a gyration on the heel "on the summit of Aetna" (H, XVI, 186). At the same time, there is a parallel between the principle of "Uniformity," with its necessary consequence of "Variety" as "the principle's natural safeguard from self-destruction by excess of self" in "The Rationale of Verse" (H, XIV, 220), and the balancing forces of attraction and repulsion necessary to maintain the stable universe of *Eureka.* Similarly, Poe's theory about the development of verse from the simple spondee to more complicated forms parallels the development of the universe from unity to multiformity. Furthermore, in talking about the dangers of "the *bouleversement* of the rhythm," it is hard not to recall the *bouleversement* of Hans Pfaal and not to equate both situations with that glorious moment, hypothesized in *Eureka,* when the universe begins its collapse into unity (H, XIV, 235).

Internally, then, Poe's thought displays a remarkable if tautological consistency. Although it does not always agree with the em-

20. On the mechanistic universe of *Eureka,* see Edward H. Davidson, *Poe: A Critical Study* (Cambridge, Mass.: Harvard University Press, 1957), 227–32.

pirical facts, directly or indirectly it bolsters Poe's basic philosophy. At one moment, Poe uses his analytic faculty to reveal deception (for example, the essay on Maelzel's Chess-Player). At the next moment, often in relation to the same subject, he is using it to deceive others (particularly in the pieces on cryptography and *Barnaby Rudge*). But in betraying his preference for unitary keys, Poe unwittingly reveals the idiopathic limitations of his analytic faculty. Yet there is always room for doubt. Just as, in reading "Maelzel's Chess-Player," it is difficult to distinguish between Poe the revealer of deception and Poe the perpetrator of deception, so in reading "The Rationale of Verse," it is difficult to distinguish between Poe the victim of deception and Poe the visionary or intuitive perceiver of truth.

9

Tales of Ratiocination

It is possible to read the tales of ratiocination as demonstrations of Poe's growing conviction that reason is as necessary as imagination for productions of supreme genius. According to a statement made in the "Letter to B——," printed as a preface to the 1831 edition of *Poems*, Poe envisaged an opposition between the imaginative and reasoning faculties, imagination being the only avenue to a perception of ideality and reason being largely responsible for man's state of deception. Because of his mistrust of reason, Poe saw the overall effect, rather than the struggle for and attainment of truth, as the object of art. But he found himself in the uncomfortable position of possessing to a large degree the logical ability that he professed to despise. This, plus a consciousness of his own necessarily reasoned artistic practice, led him by 1835 to incorporate the workings of the analytical faculty into his conception of the artistic process.[1] This new synthesis allowed Poe to describe poetry as the means by which "thought is logicalized" and to admit the possibility of a "species of composition" in which the expression of truth might have its place: "Truth is often, and in very great degree, the aim of the tale. Some of the finest tales are tales of ratiocination. Thus the field of this species of composition, if not in so elevated a region on the mountain of Mind, is a table-land of far vaster extent

1. Edd Winfield Parks, *Edgar Allan Poe as Literary Critic* (Athens: University of Georgia Press, 1964), 3.

238

than the domain of the mere poem" (H, XI, 109; H, XVI, 88). Hence, Poe's own tales of ratiocination and most of the current clichés of the detective novel. That Poe should have fathered this genre is not really so surprising. An awareness of deception presupposes a detective ability.

The conclusion that reason and imagination must work as one finds occasional utterance in Poe's critical writings. Pure allegory is condemned as "appealing only to our faculties of comparison, without even a remote interest for our reason" (H, X, 130). In 1842, Poe rationalizes the synthesis by maintaining that "the end of instruction should be pleasure," and pleasure is the end of poetry (H, XI, 12). In the same year, Poe refutes the mistaken belief that Americans are unpoetical:

The mistake is but a portion, or corollary, of the old dogma, that the calculating faculties are at war with the ideal; while, in fact, it may be demonstrated that the two divisions of mental power are never to be found in perfection apart. The highest order of the imaginative intellect is always preeminently mathematical; and the converse. . . . Our necessities have been mistaken for our propensities. (H, XI, 148)

As if by way of demonstration, the word distinct, which often has pejorative associations in Poe's earlier work, is used repeatedly and positively in the remainder of the review—"a more distinct view," "a distinct impression"—and Poe stresses the need to "separate in the mind's eye" (H, XI, 150, 152, 156). Discussing American drama, he recalls that " 'wherever Reason predominates we advance; where mere Feeling or Taste is the guide, we remain as we are.' We wish now to suggest that, by the engrafting of Reason upon Feeling and Taste, we shall be able, and thus alone shall be able, to force the modern Drama into the production of any profitable fruit" (H, XIII, 35–36). Perhaps an index of Poe's commitment to reason might be gauged by a statistical study of his increasing use of the word ratio. This single word is especially suggestive of the prejudices of Poe's mind, reflecting as it does his emphasis on putting things in proportion and his desire to see relationships between things in the interest of formulating an intellectually satisfying construct of a universal unity. As a ratiocinator, Dupin performs both these functions.

To rationalize the rapprochement of reason and truth, Poe is obliged to propose two kinds of reason and two kinds of truth. The lesser reason is that exemplified by the prefect who repeatedly calls on Dupin's aid. The factual truths that his plodding methods unearth contribute to the web of deception in which the majority of men are bound. During "the seven or eight leaden-footed hours" of the prefect's discourse in "The Mystery of Marie Rogêt," Dupin sleeps behind green glasses (M, III, 728). (Compare these glasses with the tinted window of the stranger's arabesque room in "The Assignation.") Dupin's kind of reason is akin to imagination and reveals the truth that is beauty. In the preamble to "The Murders in the Rue Morgue," which first appeared in Graham's Magazine for April, 1841, the narrator points out that "the analytical power should not be confounded with simple ingenuity" (M, II, 530). Apparently, the difference between chess and draughts is that the former requires only the common ability to "remember distinctly"; but with draughts, as with whist (and the marble game of "even and odd"), the "skill of the analyst is evinced" (M, II, 529, 530). It must be admitted, however, that the implication that draughts is a tougher game than chess contains more than a whiff of irony. Presumably, the analytic faculty is enhanced by a willingness to lose one's bearings.

The skill of the analyst, it is asserted, rests largely on his powers of identification. As expressed in connection with the schoolboy champion of "even and odd" in "The Purloined Letter": "It is merely . . . an identification of the reasoner's intellect with that of his opponent" (M, III, 984).[2] Although "the Chevalier's analytical abilities acquired for him the credit of intuition," the "apparently intuitive perception" of the analyst is based on logic (M, II, 530; M, III, 724). Poe is not yet about to palm off reason as imagination under the new

2. As a demonstration of this ability, Dupin reconstructs his companion's train of thought leading to the reflection concerning an actor, "He is a very little fellow, that's true, and would do better for the Théâtre des Variétés" (M, II, 534). This episode also reveals an aspect of Dupin's own mind, his interest in the plays of Crébillon. The actor, referred to in "The Murders in the Rue Morgue," was in Xerxes (1714), a tragedy of Crébillon; and "The Purloined Letter" concludes with a quotation from Crébillon's Atrée et Thyeste (1707).

name of intuition, as he sometimes seems to be doing in *Eureka*. The analyst, as seen in the preceding chapter, "is fond of enigmas, of conundrums, of hieroglyphics; exhibiting in his solutions of each a degree of *acumen* which appears to the ordinary apprehension preternatural. His results, brought about by the very soul and essence of method, have, in truth, the whole air of intuition"—but not, it would seem, the reality (M, II, 528). In the tales of ratiocination, the method of identification implies—and the implication is born out—that Dupin, in a very real sense, is both victim and criminal.

According to the narrator, "the faculty of re-solution is possibly much invigorated by mathematical study," particularly the study of the calculus of probabilities: "Now this Calculus is, in its essence, purely mathematical; and thus we have the anomaly of the most rigidly exact in science applied to the shadow and spirituality of the most intangible in speculation" (M, II, 528; M, III, 724). In "The Murders in the Rue Morgue," Le Bon is arrested because the police do not understand the calculus: "Coincidences, in general, are great stumbling-blocks in the way of that class of thinkers who have been educated to know nothing of the theory of probabilities—that theory to which the most glorious objects of human research are indebted for the most glorious of illustration" (M, II, 556). Coincidences should not be attributed to any supernatural intervention, as "the insanity of logic" would often have it. Dupin affirms, "in my own heart there dwells no faith in praeter-nature" (M, III, 772). An omniscient God would have no need to modify his laws.

In order to reason scientifically, it is necessary to put matters in their widest possible context:

Not the least usual error, in investigations such as this, is the limiting of inquiry to the immediate, with total disregard of the collateral or circumstantial events. It is the mal-practice of the courts to confine evidence and discussion to the bounds of apparent relevancy. Yet experience has shown, and a true philosophy will always show, that a vast, perhaps the larger portion of truth, arises from the seemingly irrelevant. It is through the spirit of this principle, if not precisely through its letter, that modern science has resolved to *calculate upon the unforeseen*. (M, III, 751–52)

Thus, in the case of "The Murders in the Rue Morgue," "this mystery is considered insoluble, for the very reason which should cause it to be regarded as easy of solution—I mean for the *outré* quality of its features" (M, II, 547). The police confound "the unusual with the abstruse" (M, II, 547–48). In "The Purloined Letter," the prefect is unsuccessful because he acts in accordance with "one principle or set of principles of search, which are based upon the one set of notions regarding human ingenuity, to which the Prefect, in the long routine of his duty has been accustomed" (M, III, 985). His resources are a "sort of Procrustean bed, to which he forcibly adapts his designs" (M, III, 984).

However, analytic ability is not simply a mathematical ability. The art of analysis is important to the poetic imagination, and the difference between mere ingenuity and the analytic ability is comparable to the distinction between the fancy and the imagination: "It will be found, in fact, that the ingenious are always fanciful, and the *truly* imaginative never otherwise than analytic" (M, II, 531). Thus, Dupin the analyst is actually Dupin the artist. The identification of the analytic intellect and the imagination is stated most plainly in the opening paragraph (excised in the final 1845 version) of "The Murders in the Rue Morgue." Poe proposes "an organ of *analysis*" that "may be a constituent of ideality," on the grounds that "the processes of invention or creation are strictly akin with the processes of resolution—the former being nearly, if not absolutely, the latter conversed" (M, II, 527).

Poe indicates dramatically that the Dupin combination of analytic and imaginative ability is not inconsistent with his earlier admiration for the unhindered imagination by making him a Parisian version of Usher (Parisian, perhaps, because ratiocination is often assumed to be a peculiarly French talent and because of the detection passage in Voltaire's *Zadig*[3]). Indeed, the narrator speaks of the "depicting of character"—Dupin's character—as his "design" in "The Murders in the Rue Morgue" (M, III, 724). As Dupin's companion,

3. Mozelle S. Allen, "Poe's Debt to Voltaire," *University of Texas Studies in English*, XV (1925), 63–75. Poe may also have been influenced by reading "Unpublished Passages in the Life of Vidocq, the French Minister of Police" (*Burton's Gentleman's Magazine*, September–December, 1838). The first of these "passages" contains a heroine named Marie Dupin. Arthur Hobson Quinn, *Edgar Allan Poe: A Critical Biography* (New York: Appleton-Century-Crofts, 1941), 310–11.

the narrator is entranced "by the wild fervour, and the vivid fresh-ness of his imagination." Their residence, "a time-eaten and gro-tesque mansion, long deserted through superstitions into which we did not inquire, and tottering to its fall," but suited to "the rather fantastic gloom of our common temper," is clearly a Gallic variation of Usher's house. Dupin and his companion would have been re-garded by the outside word "as madmen" (M, II, 532). Dupin favors darkness, and during the day he would "counterfeit" night by clos-ing all the shutters so that they might engage "in dreams" (M, II, 533). When the prefect arrives to tell Dupin and his friend of the pur-loined letter, he finds them "sitting in the dark" (M, III, 975). After the Rue Morgue affair, the narrator explains, "We gave the Future to the winds, and slumbered tranquilly in the Present, weaving the dull world around us into dreams" (M, III, 724). Dupin's character, the *raison d'être* of the tales of ratiocination, exhibits the potent combi-nation of intellect and imagination, making him a viable Usher.

II

Usually, Dupin expects considerable financial remuneration for his labor; but in the case of the Rue Morgue murders, he gets no reward and explains that he is motivated by the desire for "amusement . . . and, besides, Le Bon ["the good" man initially suspected of the mur-ders] once rendered me a service for which I am not ungrateful" (M, II, 546). But this is merely a pretext. Actually, Dupin is interested be-cause he sees himself as the murdered victim. The relationship be-tween Dupin and his comrade is very similar to that between Madame L'Espanaye and her daughter, Mademoiselle Camille L'Espanaye. The narrator says of his relationship with Dupin, "We existed within ourselves alone" (M, II, 532). The same might be said of the mother and daughter: "No one was spoken of as frequenting the house. It was not known whether there were any living con-nexions of Madame L. and her daughter. The shutters of the front windows were seldom opened. Those in the rear were always closed, with the exception of the large back room, fourth story." (Much later the reader learns that Dupin's house also has four floors.) Like Dupin and his friend, they apparently prefer to live in the dark. But more important is the belief that "Madame L. told fortunes for a living" (M, II, 539). Dupin's own abilty might seem, to an uninitiate, like clairvoyance. Thus, Dupin sees his own death mirrored in that of Madame L.

Blood and gore to the contrary, the death of the couple is to be attributed to their having achieved the arabesque state. For this reason Dupin repeatedly refers to the *"excessively outré"* nature of the case, "the almost praeternatural character" of the murderer (M, II, 555, 557). To solve the matter, Dupin recommends the stance of the half-closed eye, the perspective that allows for the perception of the arabesque:

To look at a star by glances—to view it in a sidelong way, by turning toward it the exterior portions of the *retina* (more susceptible of feeble impressions of light than the interior), is to behold the star distinctly—is to have the best appreciation of its lustre—a lustre which grows dim just in proportion as we turn our vision *fully* upon it. A greater number of rays actually fall upon the eye in the latter case, but, in the former, there is the more refined capacity for comprehension. By undue profundity we perplex and enfeeble thought; and it is possible to make even Venus herself vanish from the firmament by a scrutiny too sustained, too concentrated, or too direct. (M, II, 545–46)

The attainment of the arabesque, however, necessarily involves the destruction of the material world and "death," in this case the "murder" of Madame L. and her daughter. As the matter is explained to him, the narrator states, "A vague and half-formed conception of the meaning of Dupin flitted over my mind" (M, II, 555).

On a literal level, the murder was committed by an orangutan that had escaped from its owner, a Maltese sailor. But the combination of the irrational, as represented by the animal, and the sea, associated with the sailor, indicates that Poe is invoking arabesque qualities. From his own experience, Dupin realizes that the L'Espanayes have destroyed the world of conventional reason in favor of an arabesque existence. The real victim, or loser, is that representative of conventional reason, the prefect of police. His "hermetically sealed" perceptions create a closed world, as symbolized by the scene of the crime, which admits of no apparent entrance or exit (M, II, 558). Consequently, after the narrator describes the death of Madame L. and how the animal "nearly severed her head from her body," Dupin says of the prefect's wisdom, "It is all head and no body, like the pictures of the Goddess Laverna" (M, II, 567, 568). Since it is Dupin who defeats the prefect, in a sense it is Dupin who is the murderer. The entire submerged pattern of action takes place within his own person.[4] By identifying with the victims and the murderer, Dupin displaces conventional reason and conventional truth in order to establish his own superior reason and arabesque truth. Dupin is a surrogate of the artist, and the theme behind "The Murders in the Rue Morgue" is a variation of the Usher theme—the paradigm of reality readjustment—with the difference that a specially exalted reason is now incorporated into Poe's scheme. At this submerged level, the three Dupin stories display exactly the same movement.

It is ironic that the best demonstration of Poe's thesis that the reasoning faculty and the imaginative faculty work most effectively in conjunction is provided (by default) in his poorest tale of ratiocination, "The Mystery of Marie Rogêt," which first appeared in Snowden's Ladies' Companion for November and December, 1842, and February, 1843. As is well known, the case actually concerned a New Yorker named Mary Cecilia Rogers, the mystery of whose death is today not completely solved.[5] Poe used the event as an exercise for his analytic abilities, putting the case in the hands of Dupin, Frenchifying the names, and giving the story a Parisian setting. "The Mystery of Marie Rogêt" is the only genuine tale of ratiocination, since Poe did not have to first imagine the events; he got the facts from newspaper accounts. In other words, the tale called primarily on Poe's powers of ratiocination and not, to an equal extent, on his powers of imagination. Since "The Myśtery of Marie Rogêt" is the least

4. For a similar allegorical interpretation, see "The Poe Mystery Case," in Richard Wilbur, Responses: Prose Pieces, 1953–1976 (New York: Harcourt Brace Jovanovich, 1976), 133–37.

5. See in this regard: W. K. Wimsatt, Jr., "Poe and the Mystery of Mary Rogers," PMLA, LV (1941), 230–58; W. K. Wimsatt, Jr., "Mary Rogers, John Anderson, and Others," American Literature, XXI (1950), 482–84; Samuel C. Worthem, "A Strange Aftermath of the Mystery of 'Marie Rogêt,'" Proceedings of the New Jersey Historical Society, LX (1942), 116–23; Samuel C. Worthem, "Poe and the Beautiful Cigar Girl," American Literature, XX (1948), 305–12.

gripping imaginatively of the ratiocinative tales and since Poe's analysis is at its most inconsistent in this tale, it follows indirectly that the combination of reason and imagination is necessary for the practicing artist.

In "The Murders in the Rue Morgue," the crime is considered difficult to solve because of its *outré* quality. In the case of Marie Rogêt, the crime is described as "atrocious" but *"ordinary"*; and "the mystery has been considered easy, when, for this reason, it should have been considered difficult, of solution" (M, III, 736). As in "The Murders in the Rue Morgue," Dupin proceeds by disproving the newspaper accounts, products of inferior reason written "to create a sensation," and by substituting his own supposedly analytical account (M, III, 738). Once again a mother and daughter are involved, but it is the death of the daughter that occasions the case. At the same time, the mother's premonition "that she should never see Marie again" recalls something of Madame L'Espanaye's clairvoyance (M, III, 729). Poe believed that the most poetically affecting subject, and therefore the one most likely to stimulate a vision of arabesque reality, was the death of a beautiful girl. Hence, his interest and Dupin's. Again, as in the case of "The Murders in the Rue Morgue," Dupin's interest is justified when the murder turns out to have a connection with the sea. Dupin concludes that the murderer is a sailor, a naval officer. This solution is, of course, dictated essentially by the underlying action pointing to Poe's conviction that reasoning is as important as imagination in the appreciation of the arabesque condition. The murderer must evoke an arabesque quality.

Unfortunately, the reasoning that Dupin uses to arrive at this conclusion is often incredibly (or perhaps ironically) specious. Poe makes glaring errors in "The Gold-Bug" and "The Purloined Letter," but in those cases the imaginative pull of the story is sufficient to ensure that such mistakes are not harmful.[6] This is not always the case in "The Mystery of Marie Rogêt"; for example, Dupin's laborious demonstration, with reference "to the highly artificial arrangement

6. For example, in "The Purloined Letter," Dupin claims to be able to see both sides of the letter without removing it from a rack against the wall.

of the articles," that the torn clothes found in the thicket were a plant: "Here is just such an arrangement as would *naturally* be made by a not-over-acute person wishing to dispose the articles *naturally*" (M, III, 761–62). However, Dupin later concludes that the thicket was the scene of the crime, on the assumption that the murder was not the work of a gang but of an individual. The reader is now asked to accept that the supposedly artificial arrangement of the clothes was natural after all.

Dupin emphasizes the calculus of probabilities, but in this tale he makes highly illogical use of it. He argues that popular opinion, "manifesting itself in a strictly spontaneous manner" with "no palpable traces of *suggestion*," is "analogous with that *intuition* which is the idiosyncrasy of the individual man of genius" (M, III, 757). Consequently, Dupin dismisses the public belief that Marie Rogêt was murdered by a gang of ruffians because a newspaper report concerning a second girl murdered at about the same time and place by a gang of ruffians suggested the connection. Dupin reasons:

But, in fact, the one atrocity, known to be so committed, is, if any thing, evidence that the other, committed at a time nearly coincident, was *not* so committed. It would have been a miracle indeed, if, while a gang of ruffians were perpetrating, at a given locality, a most unheard-of wrong, there should have been another similar gang, in a similar locality, in the same city, under the same circumstances, with the same means and appliances, engaged in a wrong of precisely the same aspect, at precisely the same period of time! (M, III, 757)

Unaccountably, Dupin fogs the issue by assuming the existence of two gangs, whereas it is extremely likely, as the public believes, that one gang might have committed two similar murders at about the same time. Dupin argues that the obvious and wrong connection has been made between two murders and the less obvious and more fruitful connection between two disappearances forgotten, although this latter coincidence was also reported in the paper to misguide public opinion!

A final example of similar confusion or, perhaps it should be allowed, conscious irony on Poe's part—somehow the lapses in the logic are too obvious to be accidental—occurs at the tale's conclusion. To protect himself from the possibility that Mary Cecilia

Rogers died in a manner differing from that of Marie Rogêt, the narrator—contrary to his assertion in an opening explanatory footnote that his solution to Marie Rogêt's murder be applied to Mary Rogers'—states that an exact parallel between the two cases is extremely unlikely: "Nothing, for example, is more difficult than to convince the merely general reader that the fact of sixes having been thrown twice in succession by a player at dice, is sufficient cause for betting the largest odds that sixes will not be thrown in the third attempt. A suggestion to this effect is usually rejected by the intellect at once" (M, III, 773). Surely Poe has this the wrong way round? The "merely general reader" would be increasingly amazed at the recurrence of sixes. But Poe's admission of fallibility is fortunate. It appears almost certain that Mary Rogers died as the result of an abortion.[7] The "man of the dark complexion," whom Dupin identifies as the guilty officer, was guilty only if he was also the abortionist (M, III, 770).

III

Poe's prizewinning story "The Gold-Bug," which first appeared in the Dollar Newspaper for June 21 and 28, 1843, contains many slips, as pointed out by Woodrow J. Hassell; but they simply do not matter, thanks to the tale's imaginative momentum. As Hassell concludes, it is a product of the skillful fusion of the poet and the reasoner. In this tale, Poe is making artistic capital out of the cryptographic ability he prized so jealously. Now the reward is not a year's subscription to Graham's Magazine and the Saturday Evening Post but Captain Kidd's treasure. Legrand, the protagonist, even uses the same slogan that Poe used: "It may well be doubted whether human ingenuity can construct an enigma of the kind which human ingenuity may not, by proper application, resolve" (M, III, 837). Poe claims in Graham's Magazine, "Human ingenuity cannot concoct a cipher which human ingenuity cannot resolve" (H, XIV, 116). The treasure, like the money that Dupin insisted on and received for his services, may

7. John Walsh has discovered that Poe revised the tale as it was being serialized because the revelation of new facts threatened to prove his original hypothesis incorrect. See Walsh, Poe the Detective: The Curious Circumstances Behind "The Mystery of Marie Rogêt" (New Brunswick, N.J.: Rutgers University Press, 1968).

be interpreted as the reward of arabesque vision afforded to the analytic imagination.[8]

As for the gold-bug, it should be apparent that, just as Captain Kidd used "a kind of punning or hieroglyphical signature," so Poe's title contains a pun (M, III, 833). The gold-bug refers first of all to the insect and second to an obsession for riches. Jupiter, Legrand's Negro servant, is correct in saying that his master is "berry sick" (M, III, 811). He elaborates: "De bug—I'm berry sartain dat Massa Will bin bit somewhere bout de head by dat goole-bug.... What make him dream bout de goole so much, if taint cause he bit by de goole-bug?" (M, III, 812, 813). Legrand appears so deranged to Jupiter that the servant finds his relationship with his master reversed and, playing the godlike role suggested by his name, feels the need to chastise him with a stick. However, Legrand also points to the insect's symbolic role when he talks about "views of Fate and of the bug—" (M, III, 825). The narrator, too, confesses to being bitten by the bug: "I had become most unaccountably interested—nay, even excited" (M, III, 825).

From one point of view, a desire for wealth may be an ugly thing, as unpleasant as an insect; but on a submerged level, Poe once again is pointing out that the attainment of arabesque riches implies the murder of the everyday world. It transpires that murder has been committed in connection with the gold.

The weight of the bug and its association with a skull are intended to draw attention to the pain and possible danger accompanying greed and arabesque ambition. Jupiter is afraid that the bough he is climbing will break under the combination of his own weight and that of the beetle. Indeed, it becomes apparent at the end

---

8. J. Woodrow Hassell, Jr., "The Problem of Realism in 'The Gold Bug,' " *American Literature*, XXV (1954), 179–92. In an excellent analysis, John F. Lynen recognizes that the treasure represents an all-inclusive reality. Thus, the slave-god paradox and other "instances of the merging of apparent opposites indicate that process of simplification by which diverse kinds of value are united in the ambiguous gold." See Lynen, *The Design of the Present* (New Haven, Conn.: Yale University Press, 1969), 245. Further corroboration is provided by another critic's ingenious explication of a consistent alchemical symbolism in the tale. See Barton Levi St. Armand, "Poe's Sober Mystification: The Uses of Alchemy in 'The Gold-Bug,' " *Poe Studies*, IV (1971), 1–7.

of the tale that greed has led to death. There are two skeletons in the hole containing the treasure. Legrand explains:

It is clear that Kidd—if Kidd indeed secreted this treasure, which I doubt not —it is clear that he must have had assistance in the labor. But, the worst of this labor concluded, he may have thought it expedient to remove all participants in his secret. Perhaps a couple of blows with a mattock were sufficient, while his coadjutors were busy in the pit; perhaps it required a dozen—who shall tell? (M, III, 844)

The final lines of a Poe tale are frequently revealing. Unwittingly and indirectly, Legrand has here convicted himself of "murder." At this point, an acute reader should recall Legrand's threat to Jupiter if he dropped the beetle, "I'll break your neck," and his earlier threat that, if Jupiter did not climb up the tree, "I shall be under the necessity of breaking your head with this shovel" (M, III, 818, 820).

"The Gold-Bug" is actually just as much a crime story as any of the Dupin tales. In each case, the crime represents that necessary disturbance of everyday reality which allows the perception of arabesque reality. However, "The Gold-Bug"—one of Poe's finest tales —is not a detective story in the strictest sense because "every shred of the evidence on which Legrand's brilliant deductions are based is withheld from the reader until *after* the solution is disclosed."[9] Similarly, "Thou Art the Man," which was published in *Godey's Lady's Book* for November, 1844, and seems to be almost a parody of Poe's ratiocinative tales, does not play fair because the information that the bullet passed *through* the horse is withheld. Neither is the narrator honest concerning "Old Charley" Goodfellow's threat upon being knocked down by Mr. Pennifeather: "He arose from the blow, adjusted his clothes, and made no attempt at retaliation at all— merely muttering a few words about 'taking summary vengeance at the first convenient opportunity,'—a natural and very justifiable ebullition of anger, which meant nothing, however, and, beyond doubt, was no sooner given vent to than forgotten" (M, III, 1048). At the conclusion of the tale, the narrator reveals, "I was present when Mr. Pennifeather had struck him, and the fiendish expression which

9. Howard Haycraft, *Murder for Pleasure* (New York: Appleton-Century-Crofts, 1941), 9.

then arose upon his countenance, although momentary, assured me that his threat of vengeance would, if possible, be rigidly fulfilled" (M, III, 1058).

Nevertheless, "Thou Art the Man" does have its logical place in the chronological development of Poe's ratiocinative tales. When Old Charley speaks of "disinterring the treasure," opening the box, he is anticipating the discovery that the box contains a corpse; but he is also recalling the action of "The Gold-Bug" (M, III, 1056). The similarity cannot be pursued. If "The Gold-Bug" is one of Poe's best tales, "Thou Art the Man," although a forerunner of the "murder-in-a-small-town" theme, is among his least interesting productions. Balancing the look back to the previous ratiocinative tale is a look forward to the next. The employment of the "least-likely-person" theme in "Thou Art the Man" anticipates the "overlooked-obvious" theme in "The Purloined Letter."

More relevant to the development being traced in this chapter is the progressively narrowing gap between the innocent ratiocinator and the criminal. In "The Murders in the Rue Morgue" and "The Mystery of Marie Rogêt," Dupin's connection with the crime is indirect. In "The Gold-Bug," Legrand is connected specifically with piratical violence. In "Thou Art the Man," innocence and guilt are made to change places. Good Old Charley, "bosom friend" of the deceased, apparently does his best with his "ingenious train of reasoning" for the unpleasant Mr. Pennifeather, "who would listen to nothing like reason" (M, III, 1044, 1047, 1048). He gives a Mark-Anthony-type speech in his defense and attempts to conceal Mr. Pennifeather's bloodstained knife. But Charley is the guilty party, while the disreputable Mr. Pennifeather is quite innocent. The line between innocence and guilt is deceptive. (It is, then, appropriate that on two occasions in the manuscript Poe inadvertently substitutes the name Goodfellow for Shuttleworthy! [M, III, 1050].) In "The Purloined Letter," the gap is closed completely. Dupin is the criminal. At the same time, the criminal's motivations become increasingly rational, developing from the irrationality of the orangutan, the crime passionel, and greed, to political advancement in "The Purloined Letter." Correspondingly, the ratiocinative display of Dupin or Legrand becomes less impressive but more imaginative. Given that the tales of ratiocination are actually about the artistic process, these developments provide clear illustration that, when the artist creates, his reason and imagination act as one.

IV

Poe elected "The Purloined Letter," which originally appeared in the *Gift for 1845* (available in September, 1844), as "perhaps the best of my tales of ratiocination" (H, I, 258). Today, critical consensus might favor "The Murders in the Rue Morgue," although Howard Haycraft commends "The Purloined Letter" as an example of the balanced and best type of detective story, the other two Dupin tales being too physical or too mental.[10] Certainly, "The Purloined Letter" achieves the best balance between the imaginative and analytical faculties and the most complete identification between Dupin and the criminal: Dupin *is* the Minister D——. Within the story, Poe has demonstrated that the analytic imagination is the surest means to complete understanding, since it involves complete identification and total confusion between the detective and the criminal. Perhaps this was the reason that Poe felt especially satisfied with the tale.

The Minister D——, who has purloined the incriminating letter, is a poet.[11] According to the prefect, this makes him "only one remove from a fool." Dupin admits, "I have been guilty of certain doggerel myself," and agrees with the prefect's judgment (M, III, 979). The narrator, however, denies that the minister is a poet: "There are two brothers, I know; and both have attained reputation in letters. The Minister I believe has written learnedly on the Differential Calculus. He is a mathematician, and no poet." But Dupin corrects him: "I know him well; he is both. As poet *and* mathematician, he would reason well" (M, III, 986). Poe is identifying Dupin with D—— by suggesting that they are brothers.[12] The minister's "frequent

10. *Ibid.*, 15–21.
11. It may be that the incriminating letter is actually a love letter from Dupin to a royal lady, presumably the queen. See Daniel Hoffman, *Poe Poe Poe Poe Poe Poe Poe* (New York: Doubleday, 1972), 134–35.
12. Haycraft suggests that the French brothers Dupin, André Marie Jean Jacques (1783–1865), and François Charles Pierre (1784–1873), are the originals of Dupin

absences from home at night" Dupin explains "as *ruses*, to afford opportunity for thorough search to the police," but this information provides a further point of identification between Dupin and D—— (M, III, 988). Only with "the advent of the true Darkness" did Dupin and his companion sally "forth into the streets" (M, II, 533).

At the tale's conclusion, it becomes even more apparent that Dupin and D—— are one. After Dupin has discovered the letter in the most obvious place, he plays exactly the same trick on D—— that D—— played on the "exalted personage" (M, III, 977). He replaces the valuable letter with a facsimile during a moment of disturbance. At this point, Dupin reveals that, like the minister, he has "political prepossessions." Dupin attributes his interest to an "evil turn" that D—— once did him in Vienna, but this is no more to be taken literally than Le Bon's service to him (M, III, 993). Just as Dupin identifies himself with Madame L'Espanaye in "The Murders in the Rue Morgue," so in "The Purloined Letter" he is to be identified with D——. "The old philosophy of the Bi-Part Soul" leads the narrator of "The Murders in the Rue Morgue" to amuse himself "with the fancy of a double Dupin—the creative and the resolvent" (M, II, 533). In "The Purloined Letter, " the ambidextrous nature of Dupin and the fusion of imagination and reason are given full paradoxical display.

Because Dupin is detective, victim, and criminal in one, there is nothing surprising about his ability to solve the various mysteries. Consequently, Poe admits of his tales of ratiocination that "people think them more ingenious than they are—on account of their method and *air* of method." "The hair-splitting" is "all done for effect," and the reader is made to "confound the ingenuity of the supposititious Dupin with that of the writer of the story" (*Letters*, II, 328). In fact, it is Poe who is detective, victim, and criminal because —except in the case of "Marie Rogêt"—he has created the tangle for Dupin inductively to unravel. It is likely that Poe chose the name

---

and the Minister D—. He also notes the connection between the detective and the criminal in this tale and jests, "Perhaps some scholar of the future will uncover more specific evidence: academic hoods have been awarded for contributions less notable!" See Haycraft, *Murder for Pleasure*, 22–24.

Dupin for its suggestion of duplicity. However this may be, the closing gap between the ratiocinator and the criminal provides some insight into Poe's changing aesthetic theory. Moreover, this movement toward closure may be related to the apparently widening gulf, discussed in Chapter 3, between the ego and the alter ego in the doppelgänger tales written during the same period of time. Such a correlation *might* indicate that the intellectual synthesis expressed in the tales of ratiocination was achieved at the cost of personal schizophrenic breakdown.

10

The Full Design

In *Eureka*, published in 1848, Poe claims to have discovered the secret mechanics of the universe, and many of his critics
believe they have discovered a key to his writings.[1] Actually, the
work is more valuable as revelatory of Poe's state of mind rather than
as a contribution to modern science; and insofar as critics place the
cart before the horse, interpreting the tales and poems in the light of
Poe's cosmology, they obscure his philosophical development. Only
toward the end of his life did Poe seem prepared consciously to reconcile reason and imagination, truth and beauty. He offers *Eureka* as
a "Book of Truths" because of "the Beauty that abounds in its Truth"
and "as a Romance; or, if I be not urging too lofty a claim, as a Poem"
(H, XVI, 183).

In the final pages, this identity of truth and beauty is attributed to
their common dependence upon "consistency" or "symmetry": "It is

1. For example, the approach to Poe in the Introduction and Notes to Richard
Wilbur (ed.), *Poe: Complete Poems* (New York: Dell, 1959), depends upon the cos-
mology in *Eureka*. Geoffrey Rans, *Edgar Allan Poe* (Edinburgh and London: Oliver &
Boyd, 1965), discusses *Eureka* before the poetry and the fiction presumably with the
idea of implying connections he does not quite make. See also Charles O'Donnell,
"From Earth to Ether: Poe's Flight into Space," *PMLA*, LXXVII (1962), 85–91; Joseph J.
Moldenhauer, "Murder as a Fine Art: Basic Connections Between Poe's Aesthetics,
Psychology, and Moral Vision," *PMLA*, LXXXIII (1968), 284–97. The poorest example
of this critical approach is Louis Broussard, *The Measure of Poe* (Norman: University
of Oklahoma Press, 1969). John F. Lynen's chapter, "The Death of the Present: Edgar
Allan Poe," in *The Design of the Present: Essays on Time and Form in American Literature* (New Haven, Conn.: Yale University Press, 1969), 205–71, is the most successful
example.

the poetical essence of the Universe . . . which, in the supremeness of its symmetry, is but the most sublime of poems. Now symmetry and consistency are convertible terms:—thus Poetry and Truth are one. . . . *A perfect consistency . . . can be nothing but an absolute truth*" (H, XVI, 302). The assumption is that, as an explanation of the past, present, and future conditions of the universe, *Eureka* itself displays a perfect consistency and not just Poe's overweening paranoia and megalomania. Poe proposes to explain the ways of God to man in accordance with his formulation of 1836: "To look upward from any existence, material, or immaterial, to its *design*, is, perhaps, the most direct, and the most unerring method of attaining a just notion of the nature of the existence itself" (H, VIII, 281). *Eureka* will provide "the full design" briefly anticipated in "Mesmeric Revelation" (M, III, 1037).

Similarly, Poe's correspondence reflects a haughty confidence in the literal truth of his theory. He wrote George W. Eveleth in February, 1848, apparently without irony: "What I have propounded will (in good time) revolutionize the world of Physical & Metaphysical Science" (*Letters*, II, 362). In a letter to Charles F. Hoffman, he grandly diminished the extent of his debt to the nebular theory of Pierre Laplace: "The ground covered by the great French astronomer compares with that covered by my theory as a bubble compares with the ocean on which it floats" (*Letters*, II, 380). In fact, as science *Eureka* is a hit-and-miss hodgepodge, largely indebted to the work of Pierre Laplace, Isaac Newton, and Wilhelm von Humbolt and accidentally anticipative of the theories of Arthur Stanley Eddington, Albert Einstein, and Emile Meyerson.[2] But *Eureka* is less

2. The following studies are concerned with the "scientific" aspect of *Eureka*: Frederick Drew Bond, "Poe as an Evolutionist," *Popular Science Monthly*, LXXI (1907), 264–74; Margaret Alterton, *Origins of Poe's Critical Theory* (Iowa City: University of Iowa Press, 1925), 112–22, 132–69; George Norstedt, "Poe and Einstein," *Open Court*, XLIV (1930), 173–80; Philip P. Wiener, "Poe's Logic and Metaphysic," *Personalist*, XIV (1933), 268–74; Clayton Hoagland, "The Universe of *Eureka*: A Comparison of the Theories of Eddington and Poe," *Southern Literary Messenger*, n.s., I (1939), 307–13 (for Eddington's comments on *Eureka* see Arthur Hobson Quinn, *Edgar Allan Poe: A Critical Biography* [New York: Appleton-Century-Crofts, 1941], 555–56); "Poe's *Eureka*: The Problem of Mechanism," in Frederick W. Connor, *Cosmic Optimism* (Gainesville: University of Florida Press, 1949), 67–91; Haldeen Braddy, "Poe's Flight from Reality," *Texas Studies in Literature and Language*, I (1959), 394–400.

important as science than as a cosmological structure based on aesthetic principles. As such, it develops Poe's epistemological philosophy and makes strangely compelling reading. If the tales of ratiocination represent a demonstration that reason and imagination work together during the artistic process, an item in "A Chapter of Suggestions," published in the 1845 *Opal*, indicates that, at this point in his career, Poe regarded intuition and imagination as virtually synonymous terms: "That intuitive and seemingly casual perception by which we often attain knowledge, when reason herself falters and abandons the effort, appears to resemble the sudden glancing at a star, by which we see it more clearly than by a direct gaze; or the half-closing the eyes in looking at a plot of grass the more fully to appreciate the intensity of its green" (H, XIV, 189–90). Previously, the half-closed eye was equated only with the imagination as something opposed to reason. But in *Eureka* Poe equivocates the distinction between reason and imagination by using the concept of intuition in a way that either incorporates reason silently or discards it altogether. Poetic truth is the province of this ambiguous intuition.

II

The earlier of Poe's two final metaphysical pieces, "The Power of Words," first published in the New York *Democratic Review* for June, 1845, sets the stage for *Eureka*. It contains the notion of the artist as creator, or even as God, the role that Poe elects for himself in his cosmology. As in the two previous colloquies, the time is post-apocalyptic. Oinos (Greek for One), a survivor from "Shadow—A Parable," is told by Agathos (Greek for Good) that "not even here is knowledge a thing of intuition": Is not "the spiritual vision . . . arrested by the continuous golden walls of the universe?—the walls of the myriads of the shining bodies that mere number has appeared to blend into unity?" (M, III, 1212). Not until *Eureka* does Poe claim access to intuitive knowledge. As they speed through the universe, Agathos explains "secondary creation," the prerogative of man (M, III, 1213). Because any movement sets up an endless radiation or vibration that "must, *in the end*, impress every individual thing that exists *within the universe,*" thus modifying the old and creating something new, and because "a true philosophy has long taught that the source of all motion is thought," Agathos concludes that words effect creation (M, III, 1214, 1215). The fertile but volcanic planet over which they pass is an example. Apparently, the words that Agathos uttered three centuries earlier at the feet of her lover, possibly Oinos, brought this world into existence. If one need only say something to make it so, no wonder Poe had such confidence in the cosmology of *Eureka.* It is a work of "secondary creation." In the "Marginalia," he affirms his "faith in the *power of words*" to the extent of compelling "the Heaven into the Earth" (H, XVI, 89). In *Eureka* he pauses to reflect: "If I venture to displace, by even the billionth part of an inch, the microscopical speck of dust which lies now upon the point of my finger ... I have done a deed which shakes the Moon in her path, which causes the Sun to be no longer the Sun, and which alters forever the destiny of the multitudinous myriads of stars that roll and glow in the majestic presence of their Creator" (H, XVI, 218).

Paradoxically, Poe's awed sense of responsibility for the words he is to use verges on mumbo jumbo: "What terms shall I find sufficiently simple in their sublimity—sufficiently sublime in their simplicity—for the mere enunciation of my theme?" (H, XVI, 185). Definitely not the old terms associated with inductive and deductive proof because—and the statement provides a crucial gloss on all that follows—"there is, in this world at least, *no such thing* as demonstration" (H, XVI, 185). Truth is to be perceived intuitively. The notion of intuition is exemplified in Poe's instruction that the seeker after truth ascend Mount Aetna and, when at the top, spin on his heel in order "to comprehend the panorama in the sublimity of its *oneness.*" If he remains stationary, he is conscious only of "the *extent and diversity* of the scene" (H, XVI, 186). Had Poe forgotten that Aetna is an active volcano? Presumably, his ironic point is that the attainment of the state of oneness involves individual death and universal apocalypse. In connection with a later mountain panorama, he points out: "The extent of such a prospect, on account of the *successiveness* with which its portions necessarily present themselves to view, can be only very feebly and very partially appreciated:—yet the entire panorama would comprehend no more than one 40,000th part of the mere *surface* of the globe" (H, XVI, 282). Man's customary perception is hopelessly straitjacketed. Consequently, "we require something like a mental gyration on the heel" to destroy the deceptive material world by a strategy of fusion: "We need so rapid a revolution of all things about the central point of sight that, while the minutiae vanish altogether, even the more conspicuous objects become blended into one. Among the vanishing minutiae, in a survey of this kind, would be all exclusively terrestrial matters" (H, XVI, 187). Poe assumes that the unity thus revealed constitutes the primal ideal state of the universe. This solipsistic process, which he calls intuition, leads to his general proposition: *"In the Original Unity of the First Thing lies the Secondary Cause of All Things, with the Germ of their Inevitable Annihilation"* (H, XVI, 185–86). A total conflation of ends and means seems basic to Poe's theory.

Further clarification of his notion of intuition is provided by a letter "found corked in a bottle" (H, XVI, 187). Since it is dated "the year *two* thousand eight hundred and forty-eight"—Poe was writing in 1848—and contains the information included in the letter-tale "Mellonta Tauta" set in the same year, it can be assumed that subsequent history has vindicated Poe. (Pundita in "Mellonta Tauta" puts her letter into a bottle and throws it into the sea.) The letter writer, as reproduced in *Eureka*, explains that for a long time *"but two practical roads to Truth"* existed—the deductive or a priori method associated with Aries Tottle (Aristotle) and the inductive or a posteriori method associated with Hog (Bacon) (H, XVI, 188). However, the greatest advances in science are made "by seemingly intuitive *leaps*" (H, XVI, 189). The writer uses the adverb *seemingly* because he is not creating a distinct third category if intuition is a matter of the combination or fusion of reason and imagination, or of imaginative synthesis. While the merely inductive and deductive approaches were prevalent, scientific progress was reduced to a crawl. Some truth inevitably was discovered, but "the repression of imagination was an evil not to be counterbalanced even by *absolute* certainty in the snail processes" (H, XVI, 190).

With some ingenuity, the writer disposes of the "*à priori* path of axioms" by allowing only one axiom to stand: "Ability or inability to conceive . . . is in no case to be received as a criterion of axiomatic truth" (H, XVI, 192). This axiom, of course, provides the basis of Poe's assumptions about human liability to deception. "If ability to conceive be taken as a criterion of Truth, then a truth to David Hume would very seldom be a truth to Joe: and ninety-nine hundredths of what is undeniable in Heaven would be demonstrable falsity upon Earth," a point that recurs in the main body of Eureka (H, XVI, 193, 240–41). All this brings the writer to contrast "those regions of illimitable intuition . . . the majestic highway of the Consistent" (H, XVI, 195). Two examples are offered: the method by which "the cryptographist attains the solution" and the laws of Kepler which he "guessed—that is to say, he imagined" but which, as Poe later points out, were "subsequently demonstrated and accounted for by the patient and mathematical Newton" (H, XVI, 196, 197, 279).

Kepler himself attributed his discoveries to "mere dint of intuition," and the writer will not allow any qualification (H, XVI, 197). With heavy irony he adds: "Alas, poor ignorant old man! Could not any metaphysician have told him that what he called 'intuition' was but the conviction resulting from deductions or inductions of which the processes were so shadowy as to have escaped his consciousness, eluded his reason, or bidden defiance to his capacity of expression?" (H, XVI, 197). Such is not the writer's view. For him, intuition is totally a matter of visionary awareness. Yet, a few pages later without irony, Poe defines intuition not at all in terms of visionary power, although with reference to the previous passage: "We have attained a point where only Intuition can aid us: —but now let me recur to the idea which I have already suggested as that alone which we can properly entertain of intuition. It is but the conviction arising from those inductions or deductions of which the processes are so shadowy as to escape our consciousness, elude our reason, or defy our capacity of expression" (H, XVI, 206). This contradiction is the most illuminating aspect of Eureka, revealing Poe torn between the desire to throw out reason entirely in favor of imagination or to accommodate reason, in disguise, by an ambiguous concept of intuition.

In "Mellonta Tauta" this divided attitude is almost flaunted. On the one hand, Poe is arguing that man lives in an inevitable and total state of time-bound deception. On the other hand, Pundita argues that the highway of intuition can penetrate to the truth. Yet Pundit and Pundita give no evidence themselves of possessing intuition. Thus historical errors and the misnaming of philosophers, although indicative of Poe's often banal humor, also indicate that the knowledge which the people of 2848 possess is generally erroneous. If error is to be attributed to inductive and deductive reasoning, the reader must conclude such to be the basis of their misunderstanding. If intuition is to work consistently, must it, as a form of exalted imagination, be entirely divorced from reason? Such, at least, is the conclusion to be drawn from "Mellonta Tauta" and the introduction to *Eureka*. Yet Poe's argument throughout the main body of *Eureka* is not independent of reason. He seems to accept the involvement of induction, deduction, and intuition, or the fusion of reason and imagination. After all, the initial axiom involved in deductive reasoning is said to be a matter of intuition or imagination.

Indeed, Poe speaks of the introductory letter as a "somewhat impertinent epistle" and refers to "the chimerical, not to say revolutionary, fancies of the writer—whoever he is—fancies so radically at war with the well-considered and well-settled opinions of the age" (H, XVI, 198). Is Poe being ironic? The reader cannot be sure. Similarly, the reader cannot be certain about the identity of the letter writer. Poe does not admit to the authorship of the letter, and consequently, he allows for further ironic license because the reader is not justified in assuming the views expressed by the writer—"whoever he is"—to be Poe's. Because of the uncertainty of the irony, particularly that surrounding the term *intuition*, the apparent contradictions in *Eureka* cannot be pinned down. By means of an ambiguous irony, Poe has resolved aesthetically, if not philosophically, the central paradox of his nature. *Eureka* is a work of complex irony. Insofar as it has value, Poe is the creator of that irony and not the victim of it.

The existence of irony in *Eureka* has been observed but otherwise accounted for by G. R. Thompson, who also points to the existence of irony in the tales but—and the omission is revealing—not in the poetry. In Thompson's view Poe's irony serves not only to burlesque the gothic machinery of the tales, but also to mock what often appears to be a positive belief in a transcendent state of unity. Thus *Eureka* is actually about "nothingness": "It is only in the vision of void that Poe comes close to 'belief.'"[3] Certainly, this reading would be hard to support from the poetry, operating as it does largely beyond the realm of intellectual argument—argument allowing for the demonstration of the kinds of contradictions on which the only "hard" case for irony can be built. All else must depend upon the tricky identification of tone that can never be entirely free from the charge of existing only in the irony-cued mind of the reader. Poe probably couched a visionary philosophy in the trappings of Gothic horror partly because of market considerations. Consequently, there is an element of irony in his tales at the expense of Gothic formulae. There is also a genuine melancholy and horror on Poe's part stemming, from the realistic recognition that he may after all be wrong; the deceptive material world may be either the only reality or at least preferable to any alternative subsequent reality. But this apprehension is secondary to his faith in ideality. The reader's own doubt and apprehension, not Poe's literary accomplishment, make him a writer of horror stories or, as Thompson would have him, a proponent of the nihilist absurd.

The kind of irony in *Eureka* that can be "proven" serves a "protective" function in view of the possible alternatives to the primarily positive position taken. Another sense in which Poe's irony may best be viewed as protective is suggested by *The Narrative of A. Gordon Pym*, wherein language appears to be an important aspect of the fabric of deception in which man is trapped.[4] In the circumstances, Poe could not in good faith write the expository prose of *Eureka* without a sense of irony. Only by an intricate play of irony could he create

3. G. R. Thompson, *Poe's Fiction: Romantic Irony in the Gothic Tales* (Madison: University of Wisconsin Press, 1973), 189. On page 191, Thompson tries to advance his case by, in effect, taking words out of Poe's mouth in failing to complete the quote "*A perfect consistency . . . can be nothing,*" which continues "*but an absolute truth.*" Barton Levi St. Armand does well to emphasize what Poe himself stresses, "that it is the human imagination which is forced to conceive of a void or 'nothingness' as the logical antonym of a principle of Absolute Unity. What the void is from God's perfectly adaptive point of view, we can only guess, or intuit." See St. Armand, " 'Seemingly Intuitive Leaps': Belief and Unbelief in *Eureka*," *American Transcendental Quarterly*, no. 26 (Spring, 1975), 11. This is a *Eureka* symposium issue.

4. See the discussion of *Pym* in Chapter 4, pages 133–34.

the verbal equivalent of that "perfect consistency" which he hopes characterizes the true nature of the universe.

III

Poe opens his main argument by speaking of "two modes of discussion," one of ascent and one of descent (compare the mountain analogy) (H, XVI, 198). The reader is reminded of the two paths referred to in the letter and is led to equate the mode of ascent with induction and the mode of descent with deduction. Poe uses both procedures: "In combining the two modes of discussion to which I have referred, I propose to avail myself of the advantages peculiar to both—and very especially of the *iteration in detail* which will be unavoidable as a consequence of the plan" (H, XVI, 199). A combination of what is best in the two methods would presumably amount to his definition of intuition. The triadic plan of the letter is the key to the triadic structure of the entire work. The discourse breaks respectively into three parts: the past, the present, and the future condition of the universe.

In each, the three methods of understanding are utilized. In dealing with the past, Poe begins with a descent, then balances it with an ascent. From this balance, an imaginative tension emerges that might be called intuition. In discussing the present state of the universe, he begins with the deductive nebular cosmogony of Laplace and afterward goes on inductively to speak of "more definitive conceptions," again enabling a third mode to emerge from the contrast (H, XVI, 277). The same three methods may be discerned in the third part, although they are now interwoven. This thesis-antithesis-synthesis development works not only within each part but overall. Because the first part is concerned with the past, the process of deduction predominates. In the second, since the concern is with the present, the process of induction predominates. And naturally enough, in envisioning the future, imagination or intuition comes to the fore. Only by failing to see this plan can Carol Hopkins Maddison criticize the rhapsodic conclusion as out of place.[5] Admit-

5. Carol Hopkins Maddison, "Poe's *Eureka*," *Texas Studies In Literature and Language*, II (1960), 359. See also the excellent case for unity provided by Edward William Pitcher, "Poe's *Eureka* as a Prose Poem," *American Transcendental Quarterly*, no. 29 (Winter, 1976), 61–71.

tedly, the intentionally repetitive approach almost obscures that plan, but it does provide a tension that, while inhibiting understanding, makes for vitality. Tension, in fact, underlies Poe's conception of human existence and the universe.

In the first part of his discussion, Poe begins with a descent, analogous perhaps to the descent of the universe from a state of unity to a state of multiformity. The conception of the infinity of space is dismissed as "one of those *phrases* by which even profound thinkers ... have occasionally taken pleasure in deceiving *themselves*" (H, XVI, 200). In his own use of the term, Poe indicates that he is referring to "the 'utmost conceivable expanse' of space—a shadowy and fluctuating domain, now shrinking, now swelling, in accordance with the vacillating energies of the imagination" (H, XVI, 204). This is almost to say that man's imagination creates the dimension of space, or that man is God. Toward the conclusion of *Eureka*, Poe uses similar imagery to pose his conception of a pulsating "novel Universe swelling into existence, and then subsiding into nothingness, at every throb of the Heart Divine" (H, XVI, 311). God is designated as spirit, and spirit as apart from matter, in spite of Poe's previous insistence in "Mesmeric Revelation" that the spiritual is matter in an extreme state of rarefaction.[6]

After this definition of terms, Poe comes to "the sole absolute *assumption*" of the work: matter originally existed in a state of simplicity or oneness (H, XVI, 206). Presumably, this conclusion is to be attributed to the operations of intuition. At any rate, in maintaining that "no human conclusion was ever, in fact, more regularly—more rigorously deduced:—but alas! the processes lie out of the human analysis—at all events are beyond the utterance of the human tongue," Poe is defining intuition for the third time (H, XVI, 206). The present condition of the universe results from the diffusion of the "normally One into the abnormal condition of Many" (H, XVI, 207). The diffused atoms are imagined as "heterogeneous, dissimilar, unequal, and inequidistant," and such is the human state

6. *Eureka* is subtitled *An Essay on the Material and Spiritual Universe*; but in the advertisements of Putnam, the publisher, the full title reads *Eureka, A Prose Poem: Or the Physical and Metaphysical Universe*. "This is a significant variation if it is Poe's wording," notes Burton R. Pollin, "Contemporary Reviews of *Eureka*: A Checklist," *American Transcendental Quarterly*, no. 26 (Spring, 1975), 27.

(H, XVI, 208). However, "on withdrawal of the diffusive Volition," a subsidence into one would take place (H, XVI, 210). Consequently, to understand the "completion of the general design," Poe is forced into the further assumption, which he calls "an intuitive conviction," that God has interposed by providing a repulsive tendency (H, XVI, 210, 212). The impulse toward unity is identified as Newtonian gravity and the repulsive influence as electricity. Electricity is characterized by "heterogeneity" in that "only where things differ is electricity apparent" (H, XVI, 212).

Thus far the logic is straightforward. But Poe continues with a series of equations that insidiously and ironically undercut the distinction between electricity and gravity. Initially, to the "strictly spiritual principle" of electricity, Poe attributes the "phaenomena of vitality, consciousness and Thought" (H, XVI, 213). Insofar as thought is a consequence of reason, reason would appear to be responsible for maintaining the state of heterogeneity. If so, the association of reason and spirit is apparently contradictory, unless it is postulated that, as an extension of the argument of "The Power of Words," thought may be creative. Consistent with the equation of thought and spirit, Poe drops the terms gravitation and electricity and states categorically that attraction is the body while repulsion is the soul: "The one is the material; the other the spiritual, principle of the Universe" (H, XVI, 214). By allying the pejorative associations of repulsion with the soul, Poe again inverts expectations, this time traditional Christian values, by making the soul responsible for man's fall from unity to diversity. Poe concludes that "only as attraction and repulsion" is matter "manifested to Mind"—"that attraction and repulsion are matter" (H, XVI, 214). If the mind is to be linked with thought and the soul, then matter is only appreciable in spiritual terms. As with the contrary processes of induction and deduction, Poe's perverse and ironic logic is moving toward an imaginative synthesis or mystical paradox.

At this point, Poe abandons deduction for induction and turns to an examination of "what it was that Newton proved—according to the grossly irrational definitions of proof prescribed by the metaphysical schools" (H, XVI, 215). He points out that Newton's observations demonstrate that each atom is attracted to every other atom in the attempt to return to the primal condition of unity. He then moves to the *modus operandi* of gravity, "an exceedingly simple and perfectly explicable thing . . . when we regard it from the proper point of view" (H, XVI, 224). What this means, in effect, is that Poe's method is now intuitive, or a combination of induction and deduction. As "a connection between these two ideas—unity and diffusion," Poe proposes a third, the idea of irradiation: "Absolute Unity being taken as a centre, then the existing Universe of stars is the result of *irradiation* from that centre" (H, XVI, 225). Since Poe's intuitive perception is largely a matter of analogy, he consequently explains the concept of irradiation (or radiation, his preferred later term in the Notes) by means of a ray of light (H, XVI, 321–35). However, this analogy suggests to Poe an inequability of distribution that is not found in the present condition of the universe. Apparently, a further flight of intuition is called for, but first Poe observes that it is by grappling with such anomalies that truth is revealed. Thus the reader is encouraged, almost obliged, to accept as true Poe's in no way startling proposition of a determinate radiation occurring in concentric rays or for that matter, as the Notes emend, in "one instantaneous flash" (H, XVI, 326).

Clearly, intuition to some extent is a matter of faith. What Poe cannot explain inductively or deductively, he attributes to divine volition: "The Thought of God is to be understood as originating the Diffusion—as proceeding with it—as regulating it—and, finally, as being withdrawn from it upon its completion" (H, XVI, 238). So Poe concludes the first part of his argument gnomically by recalling the affinity of attraction and repulsion: "Thus *The Body and The Soul walk hand in hand*" (H, XVI, 244).

IV

All the information that Poe musters in the second part of his argument derives from observing the present condition of the universe. In rehashing the nebular cosmogony of Laplace, he once again engages in a deductive descent. Painstakingly, he describes the development from agglomeration to solar system, introducing the whirlpool image that figures so prominently in his work: "Now, the condition of this mass implies a rotation about an imaginary axis—a rotation which, commencing with the absolute incipiency of the aggregation, has been ever since acquiring velocity" (H, XVI, 246). He labors the whole business. After explaining in detail the formation of Neptune, is it really necessary that he explain in detail the formation of the other planets, sixteen in all (including the eight asteroids and allowing for the fact that Pluto was, in Poe's time, undiscovered)? Typically, Poe prophesies that the inconsistent revolutions of the satellites of Uranus "will, sooner or later, be found one of the strongest possible corroborations of the general hypothesis" (H, XVI, 252). And again typically, in a footnote, he speaks of the matter as a possible "perspective anomaly arising from the inclination of the axis of the planet" (H, XVI, 253). Meanwhile, the terms *attraction* and *repulsion* have gathered further associations. Attraction is now equated with centripetal force and repulsion with centrifugal force. Because one force cannot exist without the other, Poe repeats that "*the Body and the Soul walk hand in hand*" (H, XVI, 256).

True to his belief that understanding apparent inconsistencies will reveal the truth, Poe examines the nature of some of the nebulae. Although originally thought to be stars in Laplace's process of condensation, upon closer observation, these were identified as star clusters, in no way concordant with Laplace's hypothesis, and therefore, in Dr. Nichol's view, evidence to overthrow the hypothesis. Ever contrary, Poe asserts, "It will be seen that, in my view, a failure to segregate the 'nebulae' would have tended to the refutation, rather than to the confirmation, of the Nebular Hypothesis" (H, XVI, 263). He argues that just as systems of atoms are drawn together to form an assemblage or cluster, so planetary systems are drawn together to form nebulae. At present, the universe is poised "on the awful threshold of *the Future*" when "the increase of in equability" reaches the point of inconsistency attributed to the structure of the house of Usher (H, XVI, 269). Following these "incipient stages" of consolidation, the universe will return to the condition of unity. The largest nebulae will absorb all the others.

Poe then turns to man's own nebula, the Galaxy or Milky Way, to point out that it is flat and circular in shape, although from the perspective of his solar system situated "near the shore of the island," it appears to be shaped like a capital *Y*. Similarly, the universe, which consists of an agglomeration of nebulae, forms "one supreme and Universal *sphere*" surrounded by space and *"to all human perception untenanted"* (H, XVI, 273, 275). But arguing analogically and urging the fondness of the human brain for the *"infinite,"* he points to the possibility of "a *limitless* succession of Universes" and "a class of superior intelligences, to whom the human bias alluded to may wear all the character of monomania"—a mania for oneness (H, XVI, 275–76). Poe is even willing to allow, indirectly, that his intuition of unity may be referable to idiopathic factors. This sentence must be considered a part of the delicate web of irony by which Poe endeavors to maintain his integrity in *Eureka*.

Poe's generally deductive approach toward the present condition of the universe is followed by a concern with "specification" and "more definitive conceptions," or a generally inductive approach (H, XVI, 277). Heavenly bodies it is explained, move in ellipses in accordance with "the three immortal laws *guessed* by the imaginative Kepler" and subsequently ratified by Newton—Poe's key example of the process of intuition, deduction, and induction working as one: "The suggestion of these laws by Kepler, and his proving them *á posteriori* to have an actual existence, led Newton to account for them by the hypothesis of Gravitation, and, finally, to demonstrate them *á priori*, as necessary consequences of the hypothetical principle" (H, XVI, 279). The distinction between intuition and deduction is particularly fine here. Poe's main object, during this ascent, is to convey some impression of the physical dimensions of the universe, to "bring the matter more distinctly before the eye of the mind" by a consideration of ever increasing distances that, in ironically unironic asides, are dismissed as trivial (H, XVI, 283, 284, 285, 289). The expansive effect is dizzying. He concludes that the actual distances are inestimably greater than man's powers of perception, dependent upon the establishment of a measurable parallax, can possibly handle.

Incidentally, various similarities in this section between Poe's description of the awesome magnitude of the universe and Melville's description of the size and nature of the white whale suggest that, in all probability, Melville read *Eureka* before, or while, writing

Moby-Dick. The whale is after all a symbol of the external universe; and a poetically oriented study of God's creation, along the lines of *Eureka*, would undoubtedly have fired Melville's imagination. The following line occurs in *Eureka*: "But if the mere surface of the Earth eludes the grasp of the imagination, what are we to think of its cubical contents?" (H, XVI, 282). A similarly phrased rhetorical question occurs in *Moby-Dick*: "But if I know not even the tail of this whale, how understand his head? Much more, how comprehend his face, when face he has none?" Speaking of the colossal force required to move Jupiter, Poe exclaims, "The thought of such a phaenomenon cannot well be said to *startle* the mind:—it palsies and appals it" (H, XVI, 283). In the chapter entitled "The Whiteness of the Whale," Melville identifies that color as "the intensifying agent in things the most appalling to mankind" and concludes that "the palsied universe lies before us a leper."[7] Patrick Quinn has pointed to similarities between *Arthur Gordon Pym* and *Moby-Dick*.[8] The imaginative reach of *Eureka* may have been an equally potent influence.

V

The remainder of *Eureka* envisages the future condition of the universe. In this part, the line between induction and deduction is less easily drawn because the two processes are now subsumed under the process of intuition. Poe opens with the insight anticipated in "The Colloquy of Monos and Una": "*Space and Duration are one*" (H, XVI, 290). The immensities of mere void or space in the universe are referable to the extreme length of time during which consolidation has been taking place. The intervening space has increased with consolidation. This brings Poe to the subject of divine adaptation, whereby it becomes impossible to distinguish cause from effect, because the one is equally dependent upon the other. Thus—and the point is crucial—the confusion and contradiction in Poe's terminology is ironically defensible in terms of "the complete

7. *The Works of Herman Melville*, Standard Edition (16 vols.; London: Constable, 1922–24), VII 123, 244.
8. Patrick F. Quinn, *The French Face of Edgar Poe* (Carbondale: Southern Illinois University Press, 1957), 205–15.

mutuality of adaptation. . . . In Divine constructions the object is either design or object as we choose to regard it—we may take at any time a cause for an effect, or the converse—so that we can never absolutely decide which is which" (H, XVI, 291–92). The example given was first expressed in the "Marginalia" for November, 1844:

In polar climates, the human frame, to maintain its due caloric, requires, for combustion in the stomach, the most highly ammoniac food, such as train oil. Again:—In polar climates, the sole food afforded man is the oil of abundant seals and whales. Now, whether is oil at hand because imperatively demanded?—or whether is it the only thing demanded because the only thing to be obtained? It is impossible to say. There is an absolute reciprocity of adaptation, for which we seek in vain among the works of man. (H, XVI, 9)

A writer, Poe explains, aims at a similar reciprocity between incidents, or elements, in constructing a plot; but only God's is perfect in this respect: "The Universe is a plot of God" (H, XVI, 292). Nevertheless, the reciprocity of adaptation in *Eureka* is almost perfect.

According to Poe, the symmetrical instinct of humanity, "if the symmetry be but a symmetry of surface," demands "an endless extension of this system of *cycles*. Closing our eyes equally to *deduction* and *induction*, we insist upon imagining a *revolution* of all the orbs of the Galaxy about some gigantic globe which we take to be the central pivot of the whole" and upon all the nebulae revolving around a proportionally larger orb (H, XVI, 293). But a thin dividing line separates an analogical argument, such as Poe says this is, and genuine intuition: "We have reached a point at which the intellect is forced, again, to struggle against its propensity for analogical inference—against its monomaniac grasping at the infinite" (H, XVI, 292). Analogy appeals to the fancy and intuition to the imagination. On this basis, Poe rejects Johann Mädler's hypothesis of a non-luminous "stupendous globe" or "an immaterial centre of gravity" around which the universe revolves (H, XVI, 294, 295). For neither of these, Poe maintains, is there an analogical basis in the universe. This leads Poe to reflect on "how sad a puzzle the *why is it so* must prove to all *á priori* philosophers" (H, XVI, 295). But he will agree with Sir John Herschel in seeing the universe as "in a state of *progressive collapse*" (H, XVI, 297).

To account for the decrease in the orbit of Enck's comet and the apparent decrease in the orbit of the moon (explained by Joseph Lagrange), scientists declared the existence of a retarding ether. As in "Mesmeric Revelation," Poe denies the existence of such an ether while admitting an ether of a different kind associated with the force of repulsion with its "various phaenomena of electricity, heat, light, magnetism; and more—of vitality, consciousness, and thought—in a word, of spirituality" (H, XVI, 305–306). Poe's ether is not material but spiritual. If a material retarding ether were to exist, Poe asserts that "Creation would have affected us as an imperfect *plot* in a romance, where the *dénoûement* is awkwardly brought about by interposed incidents external and foreign to the main subject" (H, XVI, 306).[9] He proposes that, as a reaction to the original radiation, all the bodies of the universe are at present moving inward in generally straight lines. When he speaks of the moment of apocalypse as "a common embrace," one is tempted to see the image in terms of the sexual union of Usher and Madeline (H, XVI, 308). All this comes under the heading of "a not irrational analogy" (H, XVI, 307). The distinction between a surface symmetry and a genuine symmetry and the corresponding distinction between an irrational and a rational analogy must be considered the flimsiest portion of the argument.

To conclude his case, Poe returns to a situation anticipated earlier, namely that "when the irradiation shall have returned into its source—when the reaction shall be completed—the gravitating principle will no longer exist" (H, XVI, 301). As a corollary, matter would also no longer exist since he declared, "in an *á posteriori* consideration," and now repeats, "Matter *exists* only as Attraction and Repulsion" (H, XVI, 309, 310). If the achievement of unity nullifies attraction, it is now clear why Poe considers attraction to be the body and repulsion the soul. Overturning the conventional cause and effect relationship, he states that the ether does not exist for the sake of matter but the reverse. In "Mesmeric Revelation," spirit is un-

9. Although it cannot be proven, Thompson notes that this quotation allows for the ironic possibility that Creation *is* "an imperfect plot in a romance." See Thompson, *Poe's Fiction*, 190. By quoting the passage out of context, Thompson makes this seem Poe's primary intention, something which is unsupported in Poe's own context.

271

particled matter; now Poe defines matter as *"Spirit individualized"* (H, XVI, 309). In the context of his argument, there is no contradiction. It makes no difference whether God is designated to be material or spiritual, since Poe's ironic principle of reciprocity has eradicated any meaningful distinction between the two states and, by implication, any meaningful distinction between man and God. Man is God or God is man. Or, in these concluding words taken from a passage in "The Island of the Fay," "All is Life—Life—Life within Life—the less within the greater, and all within the *Spirit Divine"* (H, XVI, 315).

Earlier in this rapturous epilogue, Poe declares that *"during our Youth"* men are conscious of their divine destiny until "a conventional World-Reason awakens us from the truth of our dream" (H, XVI, 312). If intuition exists, it is in the form of these Wordsworthian memories. The letter introducing *Eureka* opens with a reference to "the night of Time" when Aristotle lived (H, XVI, 188). At the conclusion, the voices of memory refer to "an epoch in the Night of Time" when God created a self-projected universe (H, XVI, 313). In aesthetic terms Aristotle, a man, and God are being equated; and in aesthetic terms, *Eureka* is a spectacular success. Through irony and the principle of perfect reciprocity (an ironic principle itself, in that it allows at any point for an overturning of the argument), Poe creates a vital universe in which deduction, induction, and intuition; past, present, and future; radiation, repulsion, and attraction exist in a web of tensions created by their mutual dependence. In terms of length, the first part of Poe's main argument balances almost exactly the second. Likewise, the balance of centripetal and centrifugal forces maintains the *status quo*. In the much shorter third part, the tension is collapsed; and any basis for distinction is lost. Similarly, it is impossible to distinguish among the possible targets of the irony that pervades *Eureka* and remains its final effect. To the extent that Poe is self-deceived about the powers of his intuition, he is the object of that irony. To the extent that *Eureka* is a work of intuitive truth, the irony may be directed at readers. But to the demonstrable extent that Poe is a conscious artist, *Eureka* is deliberately ironic at the expense of the limitations of language and an untractable reality.

VI

If the conclusions Poe reaches are the product of genuine intuition, by definition they must be true. The sense that much which seems intuitive may be a form of analogic monomania might seem to undercut the validity of much of *Eureka*, were it not that Poe is aware of this possibility. Indeed, he himself raises every logical objection to his own conclusions. Thus although *Eureka* shows evidence of Poe's paranoia, he is artist enough not to be ruled by it. Furthermore, in one sentence an analogy is intimated between the universal situation and Poe's personal situation. Pertaining to the diffused atom's complusion toward unity, he writes: "*This* is their lost parent" (H, XVI, 220). Poe had lost his own parents. Conceivably, the God-projected universe of *Eureka* projects his own alienated condition.

In fact, Poe's feeling of alienation is national as well as personal. America's separation from England and Europe is somewhat analogous to the movement from unity to diffusion in *Eureka*. The work can be read as a vaguely adumbrated historical "allegory." Poe himself spent some of his early years in England and, in terms of original recognition, came home not in America but in France. Certainly, Poe believed that America was characterized by the kind of division and heterogeneity exemplified in his own clique-ridden magazine world. He would have noticed the tendency of periodicals and newspapers—like the New York *Acturus*, the New York *Sun*, the Boston *Galaxy* and the Boston *Universalist*—to look toward astronomy for their titles. Curiously enough, in describing the state of literary America, James Russell Lowell anticipates the terminology of *Eureka*:

> The situation of American literature is anomalous. It has no centre, or, if it have, it is like that of the sphere of Hermes. It is divided into many systems, each revolving round its sun, and often presenting to the rest only the faint glimmer of a milk-and-watery way. Our capital city, unlike London or Paris, is not a great central heart, from which life and vigor radiate to the extremities, but resembles more an isolated umbilicus, stuck down as near as may be to the centre of the land, and seeming rather to tell a legend of former usefulness than to serve any present need. Boston, New York, Philadelphia, each has its literature almost more distinct than those of the different di-

273

alects of Germany; and the Young Queen of the West has also one of her own, of which some articulate rumor barely has reached us dwellers by the Atlantic. (H, I, 367–68)

This appeared in *Graham's Magazine* in February, 1845, and may well have contributed to the subconscious development of *Eureka*. Marshall McLuhan sees Poe as a man cut off from his traditional European origins: "Poe's tones and accents are those of a man conscious of possessing a European and cosmopolite heritage. In America, Poe—the Renaissance man with the Ciceronian ideal— "objectified the pathetic cleavages and pressures of the age in a wholly unprovincial way."[10] With his penchant for relating everything to a consistent whole, Poe could not have failed to see these analogies. Thus, in the "Marginalia" he writes, "The United States' motto, *E Pluribus unum*, may possibly have a sly allusion to Pythagoras' definition of beauty—the reduction of many into one" (H, XVI, 71). The areas of literary satire directed primarily at the Transcendentalists, which may be tricked out of the pun-encrusted and devious text of *Eureka*, should be understood as an aspect of this historical dimension.[11]

In conclusion, a brief comparison between Poe and William Blake (a more rigorous historical allegorist) may clarify the basic cast of Poe's mind. Apparently, D. H. Lawrence is the only critic to see any definite affinity between the two writers. He links Poe with Blake as one of the great "knowers."[12] Like Blake, Poe saw the poet as a prophet. In denying an author the title of poet, Poe points out that "there is nothing of the *vates* about him. He is no poet—and most positively he is no prophet" (H, VIII, 2–3). Both poets saw the human state as one of deception dependent upon the limitations of man's senses. 'With corroding fires" (melting away surfaces), the

10. Marshall McLuhan, "Edgar Poe's Tradition," *Sewanee Review*, LII (1944), 24, 25.

11. See Harriet R. Holman's two articles: "Hog, Bacon, Ram, and Other Savans in *Eureka*: Notes Toward Decoding Poe's Encyclopedic Satire," *Poe Newsletter*, II (1969), 45–55; "Splitting Poe's 'Epicurean Atoms': Further Speculation on the Literary Satire of *Eureka*," *Poe Studies*, V (1972), 33–37. However, the implication that such satire constitutes the central *raison d'être* of *Eureka* does not seem likely.

12. D. H. Lawrence, *Studies in Classic American Literature* (New York: Thomas Seltzer, 1923), 73.

devil in Blake's *The Marriage of Heaven and Hell* writes: "How do you know but ev'ry Bird that cuts the airy way, / Is an immense world of delight, clos'd by your senses five?" (p. 35).[13] Blake maintains that sense ratios determine perception: "If the doors of perception were cleansed everything would appear to man as it is, infinite" (p. 39). In both cases, man's reason is a significant aspect of the fabric of deception and is opposed by the unifying imagination. In *Milton* Blake exhorts man "To cast off Bacon, Locke & Newton from Albion's covering / To take off his filthy garments, & clothe him with imagination." For "the Reasoning Power in Man . . . is a false Body . . . a Selfhood which must be put off & annihilated away" (p. 141). Blake's understanding that reality is a state of perceptual and psychological limitation is clearly expressed in the following lines from *The Everlasting Gospel*:

> This lifes dim Windows of the Soul
> Distorts the Heavens from Pole to Pole,
> And leads you to Believe a Lie
> When you see with not thro the Eye.   (p. 512)

Seeing through the eye can be equated with Poe's half-closed eye of the imagination.

The mythology that culminates in *Eureka* has clear parallels with the mythology, most clearly set forth in *The Four Zoas*, that underlies Blake's entire output. In Blake's system the opposition between reason and imagination is personified as the conflict between Urizen (your reason) and Los. For both Poe and Blake, the Fall is coincident with the Creation and involves the movement from unity to division. Los's emanation, Enitharmon, is the first stage in the descent into multiplicity; the division of the sexes is another. Woman, for Blake, represents the will and man the intellect. Thel is Greek for will, and her fate is a consequence of her weakness in will. There is a similarity here with Poe's Ligeia, who survives by virtue of her willpower. All Poe's women might well be called emanations. Frequently, Blake refers to birth as a division, as in this line: "I was

13. All parenthetical references to Blake may be located in *The Poetry and Prose of William Blake*, ed. David V. Erdman and Harold Bloom (New York: Doubleday, 1965).

divided in darkness & oblivion" (p. 352). Urizen, or Satan, the enchained mind of man divided from its psychic counterparts, works by guile and rejects Luvah, the emotional Zoa, and the other two Zoas who represent instinct and intuition.

Luvah destroys the domination of Urizen, who is ultimately reborn through the realization of the value of a totally integrated experience. Unification takes place in Golganooza, a realm of art where no Zoa is dominant. Like Poe, Blake identifies religion and art and recognizes Jesus Christ as the greatest artist. Both writers place a good deal of weight on "symmetry" and see every pure intellect as a god, in accordance with Neoplatonic philosophy. The forces of attraction and repulsion are two of the contraries in The Marriage of Heaven and Hell, and notions of contraction and expansion occur in The Four Zoas. But the state of dispersion is temporal:

> All Human Forms identified even Tree Metal Earth & Stone. all
> Human Forms identified, living going forth, & returning wearied
> In the Planetary lives of Years Months Days & Hours reposing
> And then Awaking into his Bosom in the Life of Immortality. (p. 256)

Like Poe, Blake comes by his knowledge as a result of intuition: "Knowledge is not by deduction but Immediate by Perception or Sense at once" (p. 653). Given all these similarities—and more might be added[14]—and given that Blake died in 1827, the year in which Poe published his first volume of poems, it would seem (to adopt a line from Milton) like a case of Blake in Poe's left foot. This is not to suggest that Poe was influenced by Blake. There is no hard evidence that Poe had ever heard of the man, let alone read his work. Moreover, the similarities may be explained in terms of common Neoplatonic and Gnostic sources and a common interest in esoteric knowledge. What is suggested is that, in important ways, Poe is an American Blake.

Although a great writer, Poe is not the finest of American writers. But, his sources notwithstanding, he is the most original. At the

14. Among incidental similarities, Blake is especially close to Poe in admitting that a long poem must occasionally lapse into the prosaic and in stating that "Fable or Allegory are a totally distinct and inferior kind of Poetry" (p. 544). Furthermore, both writers make considerable use of the word ratio.

same time, of the classic American writers, he is in many ways the most contemporary. And his work does form an intellectually satisfying and coherent structure. If throughout this study very little emphasis has been put on the horrific aspect of Poe's work, it is because of its negativistic quality from the philosophical viewpoint. The point has been made, but it bears repeating. The horror, where it is not ironically burlesqued, stems from Poe's recognition that he may after all be wrong. His arabesque intimations may themselves be a deception; the deceptive material world may be either the only reality or, at least, preferable to any alternative, nonindividuated subsequent reality. It is a reflection of man's own doubt and apprehension, not of Poe's literary accomplishment, that he is generally regarded as a writer of horror stories. Nevertheless, by the existence of such error is Poe's understanding of man's liability to deception continually vindicated.

Index